Annals of Information Systems

Series Editors
Ramesh Sharda
Oklahoma State University
Stillwater, OK, USA

Stefan Voß
University of Hamburg
Hamburg, Germany

For further volumes:
http://www.springer.com/series/7573

T0142244

Vladan Devedžić · Dragan Gašević
Editors

Web 2.0 & Semantic Web

 Springer

Editors
Vladan Devedžić
University of Belgrade
School of Business Administration
Dept. Information Systems & Technologies
Jove Ilica 154
11000 Belgrade
Serbia
devedzic@fon.rs

Dragan Gašević
Athabasca University
School of Computing
& Information Systems
1 University Drive
Athabasca AB T9S 3A3
Canada
dragang@athabascau.ca

ISSN 1934-3221   e-ISSN 1934-3213
ISBN 978-1-4419-1218-3   e-ISBN 978-1-4419-1219-0
DOI 10.1007/978-1-4419-1219-0
Springer New York Dordrecht Heidelberg London

Library of Congress Control Number: 2009933257

Printed on acid-free paper

Springer is part of Springer Science+Business Media (www.springer.com)

Preface

According to the W3C Semantic Web Activity [1]: *The Semantic Web provides a common framework that allows data to be shared and reused across application, enterprise, and community boundaries.* This statement clearly explains that the Semantic Web is about data sharing. Currently, the Web uses hyperlinks to connect Web pages. The Semantic Web goes beyond that and focuses on *data* and envisions the creation of the *web of data*. On the Semantic Web, anyone can say anything about any resource on the Web. This is fully based on the concept of semantic annotations, where each resource on the Web can have an assigned meaning. This is done through the use of ontologies as a formal and explicit representation of domain concepts and their relationships [2]. Ontologies are formally based on description logics. This enables agents and applications to reason over the data when searching the Web, which has not previously been possible.

Web 2.0 has gradually evolved from letting the Web users play a more active role. Unlike the initial version of the Web, where the users mainly "consumed" content, users are now offered easy-to-use services for content production and publication. Mashups, blogs, wikis, feeds, interface remixes, and social networking/tagging systems are examples of these well-known services. The success and wide adoption of Web 2.0 was in its reliance on social interactions as an inevitable characteristic of the use and life of the Web. In particular, Web 2.0 focuses on creating knowledge through collaboration and the social interactions of individuals (e.g., wikis). These systems use terms (*tags*) to reflect personal assertions about resources, recommend content to the other members in the community, as well as to build a shared community vocabulary (*folksonomy*).

Both Web 2.0 and the Semantic Web obviously offer many benefits, but at the same time exhibit some deficiencies. On the one hand, the Semantic Web requires very expensive knowledge acquisition procedures in order to make use of its full power. Examples are expert involvement in ontology development and advanced semantic annotation techniques. The recent research on ontologies suggests that ontologies are not just about symbols representing knowledge, but also about the social interactions of the ontology users [3]. This notion has considerable influence on the adoption of Semantic Web technologies, as the construction, use, and evolution of ontologies and semantic annotation are difficult tasks [4–6]. On the other hand, Web 2.0 technologies in general, and collaborative tagging in particular, suffer from the problems of ambiguity in their tags' meanings and the lack of semantics (e.g., synonyms), the lack of coherent categorization schemata, and the needed time and size of the community in which they will be used [7]. Intuitively, this can be addressed by ontologies, clearly explaining why the Semantic Web and Web 2.0 are complementary approaches often referred to as the Social Semantic Web or Web 3.0 [8].

Special Issue Theme

This special issue covers both perspectives of – Web 2.0 and the Semantic Web. In addition to the focus on either of these two technologies, the special issue also covers the "third" approach as well – what *other* technologies contribute to both the Semantic Web and Web 2.0? We are witnessing flourishing of service-oriented architectures, model-driven engineering, and Web-mining technologies, to name but a few, that might have a considerable impact on both Semantic Web and Web 2.0. The special issue tries to answer the following questions. Can these other technologies bridge the controversies between the Semantic Web and Web 2.0, or do they only widen the gap and drive the two approaches further away from each other? Alternatively, can *other* technologies take on the role of matching up with the semantic demands of Web 2.0 applications? Can other technologies help users effectively create, maintain, map between, and use RDF/OWL content, in order to further support Web 2.0 participatory ecosystems of content that is supplied and maintained by their users?

Selected Papers

This special issue brings together eight peer-reviewed papers that represent the current state of the research in the areas of Web 2.0 and the Semantic Web. We grouped the papers into four general sections. The first section covers the topics of collaborative tagging, integration of folksonomies, ontology-based disambiguation of collaborative tags, and novel interaction interfaces for semantically enabled knowledge sharing and grouping. The second section investigates the use of adaptivity and personalization of user interfaces in Web 2.0 and Semantic Web applications. The third section is also related to user interfaces, but from the perspective of traceability and synchronization of two aspects of knowledge representation, one is suitable for machine reasoning and another one is suitable for human use. The final section looks at possible benefits of the combined use of Semantic Web technologies with the techniques of the data mining and model-driven software engineering disciplines in the domains of e-learning and digital libraries.

Tagging and Semantics

The first section of the special issue is dedicated to the topics of collaborative tagging, integration of collaborative tags, and semantic enrichment of collaborative tags. The paper "A system for integration and leveraging of collaborative tags" by Milan Stanković and Jelena Jovanović looks into the problems of integration of collaborative tags created at different locations. Due to the collaborative nature of tagging systems such as del.icio.us, Flickr, and CiteULike, users can easily share content and knowledge. However, once the users move from one collaborative tagging system to another one, the tags are typically encapsulated inside their original systems, while some of those (CiteULike) even do not provide any APIs to access them. To address this problem, Stanković and Jovanović developed the TagFusion system. TagFusion implements different strategies for integration of collaborative tagging systems, such as harvesting tags from all systems a user is subscribed to, and their integration into the tag cloud of the application at hand. TagFusion also supports more advanced usage scenarios where it is possible to automatically tag some content by using the collaborative tags created elsewhere. An important feature of TagFusion is that it distinguishes between human- and machine-created annotations. This can be leveraged in ranking of the discovered resources by giving the higher priority to those resources whose annotator was human.

As the authors of TagFusion state, TagFusion makes one step further toward the idea of the Semantic Web. However, given that different tagging systems are produced by different communities and that they are specific to different contexts, there is a need to consider the integration of collaborative tags by investigating their semantics. This is the problem that Fabian Abel, Nicola Henze, Daniel Krause, and Matthias Kriesell address in their paper entitled "Semantic enhancement of social tagging systems." This paper proposes the GroupMe! system, which combines Web 2.0 and Semantic Web technologies. From the Web 2.0 side, it leverages intuitive user interfaces that allow users to create groups of resources (Web pages, videos, images). Creation of groups, addition of resources to the groups, and any other operation related to the groups are all saved as RDF triples compliant to a set of ontologies that GroupMe! uses. Such an RDF approach to capture group annotations leverages semantic technologies for integration and sharing of groups among the users through the use of Semantic Web benefits. In particular, this eliminates the problems of ambiguity and improves the ranking of the discovered resources.

Adaptability and User Interfaces

Collaborative tagging leverages the idea of collaboration of a number of users on the Web in order to produce shared knowledge (e.g., folksonomies). The key aspect for the success of collaborative technologies, in particular, and Web 2.0 in general, is in the advanced user interfaces that allow users to easily interact with each other and with the content. While collaboration is widely supported, the main challenge is how to develop techniques for personalization of both Web 2.0 and Semantic Web systems. In her paper "Adaptation and recommendation techniques to improve the quality of annotations and the relevance of resources in Web 2.0 and Semantic Web-based applications," Ilaria Torre recognizes that (semantic) annotation is the major factor for the success of both Web 2.0 and Semantic Web. Therefore, she investigates how different adaptation and recommendation techniques can improve the quality of semantic annotation. Starting from an analysis of weaknesses of the Web 2.0 and Semantic Web approaches, Torre comes up with a set of criteria for improvement of the quality of semantic annotation.

As already mentioned, the success of Web 2.0 is often attributed to the use of advanced user interfaces that provide rich user experience. However, the major challenge is to provide rich-user experience on the Semantic Web. Kay-Uwe Schmidt, Roland Stühmer, Jörg Dörflinger, Tirdad Rahmani, Susan Thomas, and Ljiljana Stojanovic in their paper "Adaptive reactive rich Internet applications" analyze the problem of adaptivity of applications that provide rich user experience. The key challenge is to recognize the current context in which the user is working. To address this challenge, Schmidt and his colleagues propose the concept of Adaptive Reactive Rich Internet Applications. The key idea of the concept is its distinction between offline/design-time and online/run-time levels. At design-time, ontologies are used both to annotate Web applications and conceptually mine Web usage. To enable adaptation, Schmidt et al. propose a lightweight rule language based on the paradigm of reaction rules (event–condition–action). These rules are used on the client-side of Web applications and are triggered as a result of semantically enabled data mining. At run-time, the proposed architecture creates user models on the client-side of Web applications and leverages the created user models as the input of the event processing and rule engine, which is also placed on the client-side of the applications.

Knowledge Representation and User Interfaces

Adaptivity is certainly important for personalization of user interfaces, but an equally important challenge is that of traceability between the machine-processable and human-readable representation of knowledge. Danica Damljanović and Kalina Bontcheva in their paper "Towards enhanced usability of natural language interfaces to knowledge bases" investigate the problem of using natural language as an interface to knowledge bases. Considering this in terms of the Semantic Web, natural language is used as the input representation of user queries. Such queries are automatically translated into formal queries and executed against an ontology and ontology-based repository. Damljanović and Bontcheva survey a number of different systems as per a set of usability criteria, which they also identify in the paper. Based on the conclusions of the survey, they propose a set of recommendations for improving usability of natural language interfaces to ontologies from the perspective of end users. In this analysis, they included the following aspects: vocabulary restriction, feedback, guided interfaces, personalized vocabulary, and disambiguation strategies.

Usability is a key aspect for the successful document authoring and management. Many different domains have various standards for document and content management (e.g., IEEE Learning Object Metadata for e-learning) along with the accompanying content management tools. However, current practice indicates that very few content authors use these tools in spite of their very advanced features and compliance to standards. The problem is in the usability and habituality of the tools. Namely, content authors stick to the content authoring tools they are familiar with (e.g., Office tools). Similarly, semantic technologies offer many advanced services for document management, but they are typically not well connected with the user-readable representations of documents. Saša Nešić addresses this problem in his paper entitled "Semantic document model to enhance data and knowledge interoperability." This paper presents the Semantic Document Model (formalized in the OWL language), which allows for transforming current documents into so-called semantic documents. Semantic documents are uniquely identified and semantically annotated composite resources, which can be instantiated into human-readable and machine-processable forms. On top of this model, Nešić developed the Semantic Document Management System for managing semantic documents. This system is integrated into Microsoft Office in order for users to be able to make use of semantically enabled services and benefit from the enhancements of the well-known and proven user interfaces for document authoring and management.

Data Mining, Software Engineering, and Semantic Web

Web 2.0 and Semantic Web are not isolated technologies, but they very much make use of the other complementary technologies. In this special issue, we selected two such papers. The first paper authored by Ana Kovačević is entitled "Ontology-based data mining in digital libraries." Data mining is a well-established data management discipline whose major goal is to discover relevant knowledge from (semi-)structured sources of data. As such, it has a very complementary objective to the one of the Semantic Web. In her paper, Kovačević demonstrates how ontologies and data mining techiques complement each other in the domain of digital libaries. Kovačević investigates the problem of the diversity of journal abbreviated names listed in the Journal Citation Reports. The paper illustrates the use of data mining to generate light-weight ontologies of the journal names. The automatically generated ontologies are used in the clustering task of data mining, and the obtained results outperform the results of the clustering task without the use of ontologies.

Current research on the relations between software engineering and the Semantic Web technologies has demonstrated many beneficial synergies [9]. The work of Sonja Radenković, Nenad Krdžavac, and Vladan Devedžić presented in the paper "An assessment system on the Semantic Web" builds on the successful results in integration between model-driven software engineering and ontology languages [10]. This paper illustrates the use of description logics, underlying formalism of ontology languages, to assess automatically students' assignments where assignments include open-ended questions. The authors make use of the description logic reasoner LoRD, which is fully implemented by using model-driven engineering principles and which is built on top of the recently adopted standard Ontology Definition Metamodel at the Object Management Group. Likewise, the use of model transformations allows the authors to transform the questions and answers represented in the IMS Question and Test Interoperability specification into OWL-based ontology assertions. Once the questions and answers are translated to OWL, ontology reasoning services are used to analyze students' answers.

Summary

As with virtually everything else, one can always find evangelists, devotees, and fans of specific Web technologies. Web 2.0/Social Web and the Semantic Web are no exception to this rule. Still, as Tom Gruber stresses, it is a "popular misconception that the two worlds are alternative, opposing ideologies about how the Web ought to be. Folksonomy vs. ontology. Practical vs. formalistic. Humans vs. machines. This is nonsense, and it is time to embrace a unified view" [2]. Since both Web 2.0 and the Semantic Web have advantages and deficiencies, why not take the best of both worlds and make a synergy of both technologies for the benefit of all users?

In addition, why not identify and tackle problems that neither of the two technologies addresses properly, and make the synergy open for "third-party add-ons"? Note that both Social and Semantic Web lack a more sound software engineering foundation, and both would benefit from deploying advanced, personalized, and multimodal user interfaces for knowledge and data acquisition and sharing. More automation is certainly welcome in the area of semantic annotation, where social tagging and folksonomies represent at best the first step on the ladder. After all, dialog-based human–computer interaction and natural language interfaces are both very social and very semantic-rich, so they can be investigated as a natural extension to the synergy of Semantic and Social Web. Last but not the least, there are still very few applications that really reason over the Web of data. This creates a great challenge for future exploration and integration of the Social Semantic Web with more advanced technologies.

Acknowledgments

This special issue would not have been possible without the significant contributions of many individuals and organizations. Prof. Stefan Voß, the editor of Annals of Information Systems, provided us with invaluable assistance and guidance.

We are also grateful to the reviewers for their dedication in reviewing the papers and providing the authors with substantial feedback. Here we provide the full list of the reviewers:

- Giuseppe Carenini, University of British Columbia, Canada
- Alexandra Cristea, University of Warwick, UK
- Darina Dicheva, Winston-Salem State University, USA
- Juan-Manuel Dodero, University of Cádiz, Spain
- Jon Dron, Athabasca University, Canada
- Adrian Giurca, Brandenburg University of Technology at Cottbus, Germany
- Jelena Jovanović, University of Belgrade, Serbia
- Miloš Kravčík, Open University of The Netherlands, The Netherlands
- Oscar Lin, Athabasca University, Canada
- Sergey Lukichev, Brandenburg University of Technology at Cottbus, Germany
- Alexander Mikroyannidis, University of Leeds, UK
- Michael Minock, University of Umeå, Sweden
- Sasa Nešić, University of Lugano, Switzerland
- Adrian Paschke, Free University Berlin, Germany
- Fernando Sanchez-Figueroa, University of Extremadura, Spain
- Richard Schwerdtfeger, IBM, USA
- Sofia Stamou, University of Patras, Greece
- Heiner Stuckenschmidt, University of Mannheim, Germany
- Carlo Torniai, University of Southern California, USA
- Dunwei Wen, Athabasca University, Canada

We also thank the authors for their efforts in writing and then revising their papers, and we thank Springer for publishing the papers and for a great collaboration throughout the all stages of the work on this special issue.

Belgrade, Serbia   *Vladan Devedžić*
Athabasca, AB, Canada   *Dragan Gašević*

References

1. SW Activity. Semantic Web Activity Statement, W3C [Online], 2008. Available: http://www.w3.org/2001/sw/Activity [Accessed: 2008, December 23].
2. Gruber, T. Collective Knowledge Systems: Where the Social Web Meets the Semantic Web, *Journal of Web Semantics*, 2008, 6(1), 4–13.
3. Mika, P. Ontologies Are Us: A Unified Model of Social Networks and Semantics, *Journal of Web Semantics*, 2007, 5(1), 5–15.
4. Alani, H., Kalfoglou, Y., O'Hara, K., Shadbolt, N. Towards a Killer App for the Semantic Web. In *Proceedings of the 4th International Semantic Web Conference*, 2005, pp. 829–843.
5. Greenberg, J., Robertson, W.D. Semantic Web Construction: An Inquiry of Authors' Views on Collaborative Metadata Generation. In *Proceedings of International Conference on DC Metadata for e-Communities*, 2002, pp. 45–52.

6. Maedche, A., Staab, S. Ontology Learning. In Staab, S., Studer, R. (Eds.) *Handbook on Ontologies, International Handbooks on Information Systems*. Springer, Berlin, 2004, pp. 173–190.
7. Mikroyannidis, A. Toward a Social Semantic Web, *Computer*, 2007, 40(11), 113–115.
8. Hendler, J. Dark Side of the Semantic Web, *IEEE Intelligent Systems*, 2007, 2(1), 2–4.
9. Gašević, D., Kaviani, N., Milanović, M. Ontologies and Software Engineering. In Staab, S., Studer, R. (Eds.) *Handbook on Ontologies*. Springer, Berlin, 2009, 811 p.
10. Gašević, D., Djurić, D, Devedžić, V. *Model Driven Engineering and Ontology Development, 2nd edition*. Springer, Berlin, 2009, 378 p.

Contents

Section 4: Data Mining, Software Engineering, and Semantic Web

Contributors

Fabian Abel IVS, Semantic Web Group, Leibniz University Hannover, Appelstr. 4, Hannover, Germany, abel@kbs.uni-hannover.de

Kalina Bontcheva University of Sheffield, Department of Computer Science, Regent Court, 211 Portobello Street, Sheffield, UK, K.Bontcheva@dcs.shef.ac.uk

Danica Damljanovic Department of Computer Science, University of Sheffield, Regent Court, 211 Portobello Street, Sheffield, UK, D.Damljanovic@dcs.shef.ac.uk

Vladan Devedžic FON, School of Business Administration, University of Belgrade, Serbia, devedzic@etf.rs

Jörg Dörflinger SAP Research CEC Karlsruhe, Vincenz-Prießnitz-Straße 1, Karlsruhe, joerg.doerflinger@sap.com

Dragan Gašević School of Computing & Information Systems, Athabasca University, Athabasca AB T9S 3A3, Canada, dragang@athabascau

Nicola Henze IVS, Semantic Web Group, Leibniz University Hannover, Appelstr. 4, Hannover, Germany, henze@kbs.uni-hannover.de

Jelena Jovanović FON, School of Business Administration, University of Belgrade, Jove Ilića 154, Belgrade, Serbia, jeljov@gmail.com

Ana Kovacevic Faculty of Security Studies, University of Belgrade, Gospodara Vučića 50, Beograd, Srbija, fikana1@gmail.com

Daniel Krause IVS, Semantic Web Group, Leibniz University Hannover, Appelstr. 4, Hannover, Germany, krause@kbs.uni-hannover.de

Nenad Krdžavac FON, School of Business Administration, University of Belgrade, Serbia, nenadkr@tesla.rcub.bg.ac.yu

Matthias Kriesell Department of Mathematics, University of Hamburg, Bundesstraße 55, Hamburg, Germany, kriesell@math.uni-hamburg.de

Saša Nešić Faculty of Informatics, University of Lugano, Via G. Buffi 13, Lugano, Switzerland, sasa.nesic@lu.unisi.ch

Sonja Radenkovic FON, School of Business Administration, University
of Belgrade, Serbia, sonjam@fon.rs

Tirdad Rahmani SAP Research CEC Karlsruhe, Vincenz-Prießnitz-Straße 1,
Karlsruhe, tirdad.rahmani@sap.com

Kay-Uwe Schmidt SAP Research CEC Karlsruhe, Vincenz-Prießnitz-Straße 1,
Karlsruhe, kay-uwe.schmidt@sap.com

Milan Stanković FON, School of Business Administration, University
of Belgrade, Jove Ilića 154, Belgrade, Serbia, milstan@gmail.com

Ljiljana Stojanovic FZI Forschungszentrum Informatik, Haid-und-Neu-Straße
10-14, Karlsruhe, ljiljana.stojanovic@fzi.de

Roland Stühmer SAP Research CEC Karlsruhe, Vincenz-Prießnitz-Straße 1,
Karlsruhe, roland.stuehmer@sap.com

Susan Marie Thomas SAP Research CEC Karlsruhe, Vincenz-Prießnitz-Straße 1,
Karlsruhe, susan.marie.thomas@sap.com

Ilaria Torre Department of Computer Sciences, University of Torino, Corso
Svizzera 185, Torino, Italy, ilaria.torre@di.unito.it

Section 1: Tagging and Semantics

Chapter 1
TagFusion: A System for Integration and Leveraging of Collaborative Tags

Milan Stanković and Jelena Jovanović

1.1 Introduction

In recent years the way users perceive the Web has changed significantly. From the passive source of information and services, the Web has become, in the eyes of users, a platform for collaboration, a place where their contribution counts. This shift is primarily influenced by the appearance of new kinds of Web sites focusing on socialization, openness, and collaboration that stimulate each individual to participate in enriching the Web content and in the growth of the Web itself. Web sites such as del.icio.us, Flickr, and Facebook belong to this new trend commonly called Social Web (or Web 2.0 in some sources).

The Social Web has offered many new opportunities to Web users, like the ability to easily publish content (using blogs and wikis), share photos and comment on other peoples' photos (using Flickr), or share bookmarks (using del.icio.us). These changes and improvements that the Social Web has brought to Web users should be considered in the context of the original purpose of the Web. In his book *Weaving the Web* [1], Tim Berners-Lee has written: "The web is more a social creation than a technical one. I designed it for a social effect — to help people work together — and not as a technical toy. The ultimate goal of the Web is to support and improve our web-like existence in the world." In this context it is easy to perceive Social Web as a technologically advanced approach to the basic goals of the original Web.

Social Web applications allow users to contribute content to the Web more easily, to publish content even without the knowledge of the underlying technologies (e.g., HTML), to publish opinions without much effort (just by clicking on thumbs up or thumbs down buttons), etc. However, the easiness of contribution and collaboration

Milan Stanković and Jelena Jovanović
FON, School of Business Administration, University of Belgrade, P.O. Box 52, Jove Ilića 154, 11000 Belgrade, Serbia, e-mail: {milstan,jelena}@gmail.com

V. Devedžić and D. Gašević (eds.), *Web 2.0 & Semantic Web*, Annals of Information Systems 6, DOI 10.1007/978-1-4419-1219-0_1,
© Springer Science+Business Media, LLC 2010

is not the only significant change that Social Web has brought. The model of use of the early Web where users browsed the content in order to find what they were looking for is getting compromised by the ever larger and increasing quantity of available content. The awareness of the necessity to easily access the right content without browsing is increasing, and it is there where content metadata begins to matter. The ability of information to be easily found is gaining more and more importance on the Web where content is being more and more rapidly added, and that ability is closely related to formally expressed semantics.

To provide advanced services, such as personalization and better use of the available content, machines need formal semantics. To make the Web a place of semantically enriched content relying on ontologies became the mission of a promised Semantic Web. The Semantic Web vision inspired the efforts of research circles to develop and standardize formats for representing semantically rich metadata. Such richly represented metadata would give machines knowledge about content, which would raise their possibilities beyond simple manipulation of data and bring them closer to the possibility to process the content in a more human-like manner. In addition, the idea of semantically rich metadata gave wings to the dream about intelligent software agents capable of performing many actions that are done today by humans [2].

Meanwhile many Social Web sites turned to less precise, but easier to collect form of metadata – tags. Without taking rich knowledge representations much into account, those Web sites have in a short period of time collected huge repositories of tags describing Web resources.

Despite the obvious differences between the formal approach of the Semantic Web and a more pragmatic approach of Social Web, which may lead us to think of them as of opposed directions of tracing the advancement of the current Web, the full potential of the Web may actually arise from merging these two approaches.

To bring tags closer to the needed level of interoperability outlined by the Semantic Web technologies, many approaches have been suggested to enhance their semantic richness [3, 4]. Apart from that, for bringing tagging metadata to its full potential, it is necessary to overcome the current lack of cooperation between tag repositories and find a way to make machines partners in annotation process.

In this paper we address the latter issue, namely the problem of cooperation between repositories of tags as well as the problem of aggregating human annotations with those provided by machines. In Sect. 1.2 we explain basic facts regarding tags and folksonomies. In Sect. 1.3 we go further into analysis of the problem of cooperation between tagging systems and propose a way how this problem could be addressed. We also present a concrete system called TagFusion that implements the proposed approach. Special attention has been given to the possible ways to attract users to use the system, thus making it a valuable metadata repository. In Sect. 1.4 we give an overview of related work and finally give conclusions in Sect. 1.5.

1.2 Background

In this section we explain the concepts of tags and folksonomies, focusing on their advantages and disadvantages, in order to give a solid ground for understanding currently existing problems in the field that we address in this article.

1.2.1 Tagging

Tagging gained significant popularity in Social Web sites, as a way to describe resources (e.g., Web pages, photos, blog articles, etc.) for classification and search. In the tagging process users assign freely chosen keywords to Web resources they wish to describe. This activity is usually incorporated as an optional part of the service offered by a Web site (e.g., on Flickr where adding tags to uploaded photos is optional), but there are also Web sites that relate tagging more closely to their primary service (e.g., del.icio.us where tagging is used to classify bookmarks).

Considerable differences between collaborative tags and taxonomies or folder structures (sometimes used for organizing bookmarks) represent the source of both the popularity of tagging and the drawbacks it brings. Taxonomies are hierarchical and exclusive, thus an object can belong to only one unambiguous category which is in turn within a more general one. Folder trees function similarly. For example, consider a hypothetical user who wants to save an audio file in his music collection. Let it be the recording of Montserrat Caballe performing Puccini's Madam Butterfly. Our user could save this file in the folder c:/music/classical/Puccini or c:/music/classical/Caballe. The reason for this dilemma is obvious: it is often hard for users to assign an asset to one single category. The existence of these two folders would in fact make further searches for this file more difficult by forcing the user to search both locations. On the other hand, tags are neither exclusive nor hierarchical, so if our user could classify the file just by assigning tags he could easily choose tags like classical, Puccini, Caballe, thus making it easy to later search for this file. Apart from the obvious advantage, the chosen set of tags does not give any information to specify that music composed by Puccini and performed by Caballe belongs to classical music genre. When tagging is used, all keywords are considered as equal, regardless of their possible hierarchical or any other semantic relations.

For better understanding of the nature of tags and possibilities for their application, we will look at their main advantages and disadvantages. On the advantages side, we can point out the following:

- Simplicity and low entry barriers: Tagging requires no special skill, and a good will can make any user a successful tagger. No knowledge of predefined vocabularies is required, which makes tagging a very easy and straightforward process for which anyone is eligible.
- Quick adaptation to new terms: Since no predefined vocabularies are used, new terms that appear more and more frequently in IT and other fast developing

domains are easy to emerge and become popular for annotating related resources. Some authors [5] make the analogy with "desire lines," foot-worn paths that sometimes appear in a landscape over time.

- A means for organization of resources: As described in the example with Montserrat Caballe recording, tags provide a way to organize and classify resources, which can be considered superior to traditional classification systems in some aspects.

Apart from the promising list of advantages, there are many limitations and drawbacks that prevent tags from being the right form of metadata for some applications.

- Ambiguity: In tagging systems vocabulary is uncontrolled and there is no way to make sure which tag corresponds to which concept. The word "apple" is the most used and now famous example, since it relates to a fruit, computer hardware manufacturer, and the daughter of Gwyneth Paltrow (who was born at the same time when tagging hype began and – thanks to this coincidence – gained her popularity in research circles).
- Synonyms: Different words or word forms (e.g., plurals) can be used to describe the same concept, and tagging systems provide no means to store the information that two tags relate to the same concept.
- Multiple words and spaces: In some systems (e.g., del.icio.us) users provide tags separated by spaces, and the only way to represent a concept usually described by two or more words is to concatenate them in some way. Different users use different strategies for concatenation (e.g., likeThis, likethis, like-this), and the system ends up with different representations used as a reference to the same concept.
- Basic level problem [6]: When users classify a resource, related terms used for describing it vary from very general to specific. For example, while some passionate drivers could tag photography with the word Audi, for others it would be just a car.
- Lack of semantics: Tags provide limited information about the context in which they are related to the resource being tagged. For example, if a Web page is tagged with the tags "music" and "Madonna" we could not know whether it relates to a page containing some reviews of Madonna's music or it actually contains audio or video samples.

These drawbacks inspire the efforts of scientific community to find solutions that would bridge the gap between the needed level of semantic richness and the level offered by tags [7, 8].

Apart from these inherent disadvantages of tags, there are also considerable problems regarding popular systems for collaborative tagging that should be mentioned.

Tagging systems do not cooperate. For the last couple of years, since tagging systems came in use, many of them (most notably del.icio.us, Flickr, and Technorati) have collected a significant base of annotations, but there is very little effort made to integrate those annotation bases and benefit from quantity of metadata, which hopefully can be used to generate more accurate annotations [9]. Some of the systems do not provide any possibility to retrieve metadata they have gathered, while others provide some application interfaces (APIs), but neither makes effort to collaborate, nor to facilitate interoperability of the collected tagging data. Some important interoperability issues are discussed in [10].

The other significant problem is that no system can work with both human annotations and automatic annotations provided by, for example, keyword extraction services or autonomous agents. Even systems that do provide interfaces for possible involvement of such artificial users (with del.icio.us API this is theoretically possible) are not able to distinguish automatic annotations from those collected by humans; instead they mix these two types of annotations, thus making them less usable.

1.2.2 Folksonomies

In collaborative tagging systems, benefits of tags as a means of classification are combined with social effects. When multiple users tag a resource with the same tag, we could say that it gains more relevance in the eyes of others. Apart from the quantity of annotations, the confidence in the user who has annotated a resource with a certain tag also plays a significant role in evaluating tag relevance. Consequently, collaborative systems are bringing tagging to the level of an advanced classification scheme. This result of collaborative tagging is generally referred to as folksonomy.

Even though a folksonomy is often (mistakenly) equated with a set of tags created by a certain user community, it actually consists of three sets of entities [11]:

- Users – actors who assign tags to Web resources in collaborative tagging systems
- Tags – keywords assigned by users to resources in order to describe them
- Resources – digital objects being tagged by users (e.g., Web pages, photos, blog articles)

Since in this manuscript we consider folksonomies in a broader context than the one implied by isolated tagging systems, it is necessary also to take into account the origin of tags (i.e., the source system they originate from) as a component that determines the tagging context. Perceived in this way, namely as a combination of the aforementioned components and the source system, tagging context plays the essential role in creating the possibility for improving the semantic richness of tags.

1.2.3 Problem Description

We have already indicated the lack of cooperation between existing collaborative tagging systems as one of the major obstacles for making better usage of available tagging metadata. Many systems like del.icio.us, Flickr, CiteULike,[1] and Technorati

---

[1] http://www.citeulike.org/

continuously increase the quantity of human generated annotations in the form of tags, but unfortunately those annotations remain encapsulated in individual systems and rarely become used externally (Fig. 1.1). Many systems (e.g., CiteULike) do not even provide a public API that would enable other applications to use the collected tagging metadata. Other systems (e.g., Technorati) provide limited APIs that make it hard or even impossible to connect tags with other elements that form the tagging context (i.e., users, resources, and sources of origin). Those systems that do provide a usable API (like del.icio.us and Flickr) make no effort to integrate with or even make use of other available APIs.

Since the integration of tags from various systems opens possibilities for enhanced usage of tagging metadata, we have set as our goal to develop an approach for integration of tags from different tagging systems. The TagFusion system that implements this approach is presented in the next section. To make our approach widely adopted by today's tagging systems, we have formulated differ-ent strategies for attracting these systems and making them adopt this approach and actually begin to integrate (see Sect. 1.3.3).

Fig. 1.1 Current state of cooperation between collaborative tagging services

The other problem we aim to address relates to the fact that currently popular tagging systems support only contributions of humans and make limited or no effort to integrate automatic annotators (e.g., Yahoo Term Extraction Service[2]) or open the possibility for the potential involvement of intelligent agents capable of annotation.

We argue for the involvement of autonomous annotators in the collaborative annotation process as a step toward the realization of the Semantic Web vision, which predicts a Web with machine-readable content, capable of supporting the involvement of intelligent agents. Berners-Lee et al. [2] consider the Semantic Web as "an extension of the current one [Web], in which information is given well-defined

---

[2] http://developer.yahoo.com/search/content/V1/termExtraction.html

meaning, better enabling computers and people to work in cooperation." This ability of computers to work in collaboration with people is often viewed as a crucial step forward in the advancement of the Web. Therefore, currently available systems and systems in development should follow this idea as much as possible, within the possibilities of available technologies. When applied to tagging the idea could be realized by integrating human annotations with annotations provided by autonomous entities capable of keyword extraction and tagging. Those automatically generated annotations could be especially helpful in the case of resources for which human annotations do not exist. Therefore, we are determined to enable the involvement of artificial entities in the process of integrating metadata from various systems and consider the model of their involvement that would be most flexible and most useful.

1.3 Integrating Metadata from Collaborative Tagging Systems

We have already identified the need for exchange and integration of (meta)data among collaborative tagging systems. In this section we present our approach for achieving that goal.

We base our approach on building a system that captures, integrates, and provides access to the tagging context data from various Web sites and applications. This system, dubbed TagFusion, is based on a common repository of tagging context data and an extensible set of services leveraging the tagging data to provide different kinds of functionalities. These services are organized in a layered architecture that we present in Sect. 1.3.1.

Since the usefulness of the TagFusion system is highly correlated to the quantity of annotations it possesses, it was of critical importance for us to consider its usability aspects and potential modalities of use. We discuss these issues in Sect. 1.3.2.

Before we go into specifics of the system, it is necessary to define its target users. Since we want to integrate annotating efforts of both humans and autonomous annotators (e.g., intelligent agents) our target users are all applications that enable annotation of digital resources regardless of the nature of entities that perform the annotation activity. We refer to those applications as user systems. This implies that humans are not meant to use our system directly, but through Social Web sites, Web applications, etc. (all being considered user systems in our terminology).

1.3.1 The Architecture of the TagFusion System

Having defined our target users as a higher level abstraction, which includes in fact many different categories of users, we had to model a very flexible system that could support such heterogeneity of needs it has to satisfy. A common approach to this engineering problem is to introduce architectural levels providing different services (Fig. 1.2), where higher level services rely on more basic level services.

The basic level service, called TagFusion Core Service, represents the core component of this multilevel architecture. Its role is to provide support for common data manipulation operations over the repository of tagging context data. In particular, it allows for storage and retrieval of tags, together with information about the resources that were annotated with those tags, the users who used those tags for annotation, as well as the information about the source system(s) from which tags originate. Special attention has been paid on methods for annotation retrieval, with intention to enable queries based on different criteria (e.g., user, resource, tag, or their combinations). The narrow scope of functionalities of this core service is a payoff for our design decision to make the service highly flexible. More details about this service and its design and implementation are given in the subsection that follows.

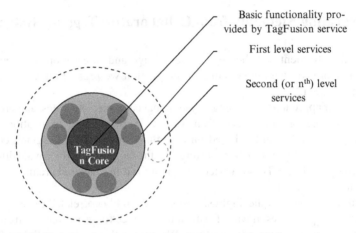

Basic functionality provided by TagFusion service

First level services

Second (or nth) level services

Fig. 1.2 The TagFusion system composed of services arranged in levels

Higher levels of the system architecture consist of services responsible for providing advanced functionalities to end users or other services, thus contributing to the overall functionalities of the system. In general, there may be three kinds of the higher level services: (1) services that create new annotations in the system, (2) services that process existing annotations in order to provide a new functionality, and (3) those that do both. Examples of functionalities that could be provided by these services include the following:

- Filtering annotations by different criteria: For example, retrieving annotations for a certain resource, filtering annotations based on the given/approved trust mechanism, or merging tags that could be considered having the same semantics in a given context (inferred by a set of heuristics).
- Ranking tags related to a resource by different criteria: Quantitative criteria (e.g., number of times the tag appears in annotations for a certain resource) are the most obvious way to perform the ranking, but other methods, possibly relaying

on user's connections, and other information that can be inferred about user's interests, offer more promising results.

- Importing annotations from other systems, etc.

In each case functionalities provided by higher level services are meant to motivate user systems to aggregate the critical mass of annotations that would transform the TagFusion system into a highly useful repository of tagging metadata for all user systems.

Having introduced the concept of higher level services, we want to point out that those services can also be considered user systems from the perspective of the basic TagFusion Core Service. In other words, user systems are not only the aforementioned agents and Social Web sites, but also other services that use the Tag-Fusion Core Service. With this abstract approach to defining user systems, we achieve the ability to model chains of services relying on one another in order to provide diversity of functionalities for different needs of various end user sites or applications.

It is also necessary to notice that the system makes a difference between annotations created by humans and automatically created ones by storing the data about author's (human or machine) nature. In this way higher level services can treat those annotations differently if needed.

1.3.1.1 TagFusion Core Implementation Details

The TagFusion Core is very flexibly implemented allowing for future changes of its building blocks without affecting the interface (implemented as a Web Service). The flexibility is achieved by introducing three-layer architecture (Interface–Application Logics–Data Storage). In the current implementation a relational database is used as data storage, but due to its flexible design, based on DAO design pattern,[3] it can be easily reconfigured to support other ways to persist data (e.g., XML files). Flexibility in the design of Application Logics layer is introduced by using various Design patterns (e.g., Bridge, Template Method, etc.) [12].

To give an idea on how the data about resources, tags, and users is persisted in the system we give a simplified UML diagram of the domain model. As it is shown in Fig. 1.3, the *Annotation* class is used to bind the *Resource* being tagged, the list of Tags assigned to the resource, and the User who performed the tagging. It is important to observe the property *isHuman* in the class *User*, which is used to realize the earlier emphasized idea of allowing the artificial entities to participate in the annotation process.

The system is implemented using Java technology. The Web Service technology was used to provide interfaces to other user systems and thus allow for the interoperability with first or *n*th level services built in other platforms.

---

[3] http://java.sun.com/blueprints/corej2eepatterns/Patterns/DataAccessObject.html

1.3.2 Modalities of Use and Attracting Users

Defining a flexible and extensible architecture was a necessary precondition for making TagFusion a usable system. Another issue that we had to address is how to attract user systems (i.e., their developers) to actually use TagFusion and accumulate the critical mass of annotations. For this reason, we have developed some basic modalities of use, which consist of the potential user systems, a scenario of use, and most importantly the motivation for use. In what follows we present each of these modalities in turn.

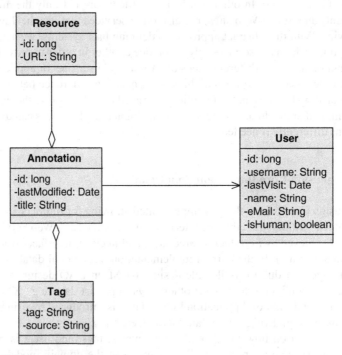

Fig. 1.3 UML diagram of domain classes

1.3.2.1 Web Sites Send Metadata to the TagFusion System

The first scenario assumes that (Social) Web sites send tagging metadata related to their content to the TagFusion system, motivated by the need/desire to promote their content to potentially interested parties. This modality of use is inspired by a very similar approach already applied by the Ping the Semantic Web[4] service, which receives notifications from various Social Web sites (most notably blogging sites) about new RDF metadata that they generate. The purpose of this service is to

---

[4] http://www.pingthesemanticweb.com/

propagate those notifications to other interested parties that can make use of newly available RDF content. As a result, Web sites that use this service to announce new content usually achieve better visibility by search engines.

Similar to this approach, Social Web sites that collect tagging metadata about their content would have a clear interest to export that metadata to the TagFusion system, thus advertising their content and making it more visible for potential users. For example, a blogging site can share tagging metadata related to its posts and articles and subsequently profit from better visibility of its content.

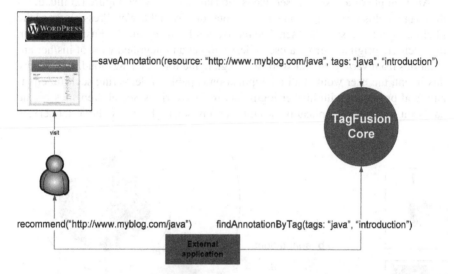

Fig. 1.4 Blog sends metadata to the TagFusion system

Figure 1.4 illustrates this scenario: a blog site discussing different issues of Java programming (ranging from introductory articles to highly sophisticated ones) regularly sends its tagging metadata to the TagFusion system. An external application conducting the search (e.g., on behalf of a student learning to program in Java) for content annotated with certain tags – let us say the tags "java" and "introduction" – can consult the TagFusion system and retrieve all the resources tagged with the provided set of tags. The answer received from the TagFusion system will contain, among other resources, articles originating from our example blog site. The application is then able to recommend these articles to the user who can then visit the blog and read them. The circle of interest clearly provides enough motivation for Web sites to share tagging metadata related to their content, as well as for applications to use the common repository of tagging metadata.

1.3.2.2 Harvesting Data from Social Web Sites

Some Social Web sites provide interfaces (APIs) for other applications to retrieve their accumulated metadata and reuse it. Unfortunately, the number of sites that provide usable interfaces is not significant yet. However, those few Web sites that do not neglect the importance of cooperation represent examples of the practice that is slowly but steadily emerging and is expected to be followed by most Web sites in the near future. On this emerging trend we build our second modality of TagFusion usage that relies on metadata augmented in large collaborative tagging systems. With regard to our multilevel architecture, we rely on the first level services to harvest annotations from available sources and import them into the TagFusion system.

An example of a first level service is the Harvester service. Figure 1.5 illustrates the usage of this service for collecting annotations from the WordPress blog and the Flickr account of a specific user. The motivation for using the TagFusion system in this scenario originates from a user's desire to get an integrated view of his/her annotations from various Social Web sites, e.g., in the form of a tag cloud. Inspired by this intent, the user would call an application capable of delivering such functionality and provide it with his/her login data for the various Social Web sites he/she has been using. The application would then invoke TagFusion's Harvester service

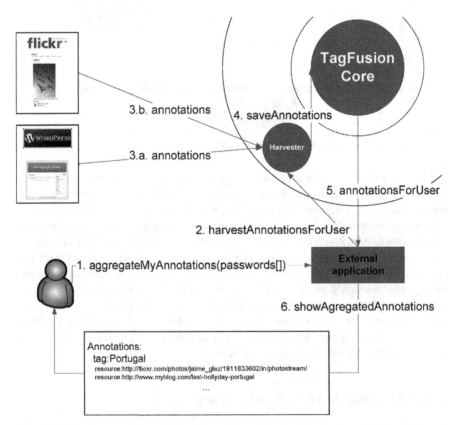

Fig. 1.5 Harvesting annotations from collaborative tagging sites (the numbers indicate the flow of interaction)

to harvest the user's annotations from those Web sites. The Harvester service stores the acquired annotations into the system's repository. The application then leverages the TagFusion Core Service to retrieve all the annotations for the specified user.

TagFusion's upper level services in fact provide motivation for other parties to use the system and increase the amount of collected annotations, thus making it a valuable resource for many applications and Web sites. This circle of interest promises to ensure good prospects for our system to continuously attract new users and increase the amount of the available metadata, thus making it a prominent base for building advanced services on top of it. Those advanced services would be able to address the problem of semantic richness of tags as well as other problems identified in Sect. 1.2.1.

1.3.3 Leveraging Automatic Annotators

We have already mentioned the possibility of integrating metadata generated by automatic annotators and keyword extractors in the TagFusion system. In addition, TagFusion can benefit the prominent field of concept extraction. The research efforts that have been undertaken in this field, such as those presented in [13] and [14] aim at automatic generation of metadata whose semantic richness goes beyond simple keywords and tags, thus bringing the idea of the Semantic Web closer to its realization. We believe that by integrating tagging metadata from different systems and making that data accessible through a variety of services, TagFusion offers a highly beneficial service for systems that aim to generate semantically rich annotations. Besides, TagFusion itself can benefit from contributions of those advanced systems, as well.

1.3.4 Example of Use

To illustrate the usefulness of this approach and to show the benefits of the proposed multilevel architecture we have built two first level services to complement the basic TagFusion Core service. One of these two services is the Harvester service, already mentioned in previous sections. Its purpose is to collect annotations made by a user in different collaborative tagging systems. In this example we import annotations only from del.icio.us since this Social Web site has one of the best APIs for retrieving tags and it will be enough to illustrate the concept of harvesting. We also use the Yahoo Term Extraction service to obtain machine-generated annotations and merge them with human annotations.

The other first level service that we have built is the TagFilter service that takes annotations from the basic service and produces an ordered list of tags for a certain resource. When performing the ordering, the service gives priority to those tags that were more frequently associated with a resource and also gives higher importance to human annotations, considering automatic ones less accurate [15]. The design of this service allows for the use of various filtering algorithms, but in order to keep the example simple and illustrative, we have chosen the simplest one.

Table 1.1 Human tags imported from del.icio.us and tags provided by Yahoo Term Extraction service

Tags imported from del.icio.us	Tags provided by Yahoo Term Extraction service	
Blogging	blogdigger	pubsub
blog	ivillage	contact
metadata	bloglines	sulekha
semanticWeb	meetup	feedster
web2.0	edgeio	movable type
RDF	blogads	netvibes
	xanga	blogging
	5ive	verisign
	newsgator	openbc
	wordpress	attensa

In this example we first invoke the Harvester service to import all bookmarks and their associated tags from the first author's del.icio.us account. The service saves these as human annotations since they originate from an end-user system. Then we call the automatic annotator to generate annotations for the resources harvested from del.icio.us. After this is finished, we have actually merged annotations from two independent systems in our annotation base. To show the effect of this integration we will focus on one specific resource annotated both in del.icio.us and by the automatic annotator, the Web page http://structuredblogging.org/. Annotations imported from del.icio.us and obtained from Yahoo Term Extraction service that refer to this resource are shown in Table 1.1. Since only the tag blogging appears in both annotation sets, one would expect this tag to appear first in the ordered list of tags generated by the TagFilter service. In fact, the service did give the highest priority to the tag blogging, followed by other human-provided tags, and putting other machine-generated tags to the end of the list.

By merging annotations from two independent systems of totally different nature, namely an end-user system and an automatic annotator, we enriched our annotation base while preserving contexts in which tags appear in those independent systems. As such, our enriched database, containing several annotations for the same resource, served as a ground for deriving additional information about tag relevancy. The algorithm used to process tags and derive new information was purely based on tag frequency and origin. Similarly, other first level services could be built to implement more complex algorithms, maybe involving some trust mechanisms, for making use of available annotation contexts and generating semantically more valuable metadata. One possible scenario involving the use of such services is presented in the next section.

1.3.5 Advanced Scenario of Use

In this section we present an advanced scenario of use that we are currently beginning to implement. The motivation for building services involved in this scenario comes from the fact that bringing highly relevant Web content to users is still an unsolved issue. Despite the existence of many link-sharing services (e.g., Digg, Del.icio.us, etc.) and many services where information on users' social interactions is collected, to our knowledge, there is still no really useful service that would make use of all that information in selecting relevant content for a user. We argue that semantics of social interactions that can be extracted from social networks could help recommend highly relevant content to the user, by looking at his/her friends' annotations. We also favor the use of trust mechanisms to discern the social interactions that could be relevant for recommending content.

Figure 1.6 shows the structure of services used in this scenario as well as the flow of interactions between them. Actions are identified by numbers on the arrow lines and will be further referred to by using those numbers. First, a user application invokes the Recommender Service (1). By user application we mean any Web application that aims at bringing relevant content to its users (e.g., an RSS aggregator). That would be an application that works with end users and rely on services such as ours to provide the core functionality. Recommender Service acts as a front end service in this scenario, being able to return relevant recommendation links for a particular user.

By the sequence of connected service calls (omitted in the picture for the purpose of clarity) different harvester services are called (2a, 2b, and 2c) to import information on user's social interactions from social networks and other similar sites into the Social Interactions Base service. Most social networks (like Facebook and LiknedIn) provide usable APIs or even plug-ins for extracting the semantics of a user's contacts. However, for extracting information about a user's friends in his/her network, some workaround is often needed (as in the case of Del.icio.us).

After being integrated in the Social Interactions Base service, information about a user's contacts can easily be used by other services in the system, namely by the Trust Service (3). The Trust Service takes into account the user's social connections on various social services and tries to determine the user's most relevant contacts, where relevancy depends on the applied trust metrics. Even though trust is a relatively new topic on the Web research agenda, with many unresolved issues, we expect that the results of the TrustLet[5] project, which provides analysis of different trust metrics, could be of great use for building the Trust Service. This service also takes into account the similarity of tags used and the resources being tagged by the user and each particular contact (4) in order to give higher priority to contacts with similar interests. As a result, it returns a list of users whose annotations could be the most relevant to the user in question.

---

[5] http://www.trustlet.org/wiki/Main_Page

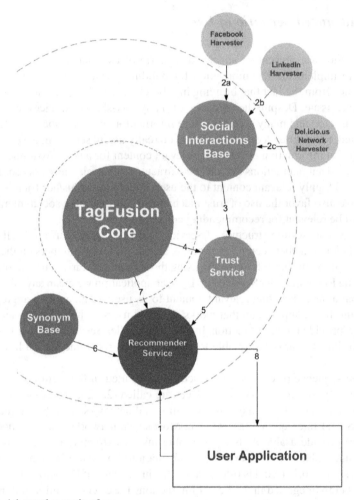

Fig. 1.6 Advanced scenario of use

Having obtained that filtered list of the user's contacts (5), the Recommender Service can now consult the annotations base (7) from the TagFusion Core service. It can even increase the possibility of finding relevant new content by relying on the Synonym Base service (that we plan to create using the Wordnet[6] dataset) to provide information on synonyms among the words used for tags (6). As the final result the Recommender Service returns a list of possibly highly relevant links found in the annotations of the user's contacts (8).

---

[6] http://wordnet.princeton.edu/

1.4 Related Work

In this section we describe a few prominent systems that approach similar problems in different contexts. We believe that much can be learned from comparing ideas of TagFusion project with those projects, as well as from their practical experiences.

1.4.1 RSS

Initially conceived as a format for publishing frequently updated content in a standardized way, RSS has become a ubiquitous format, largely used by news services and blogs. Apart from the core functionality, RSS allows publishers to assign tags to published content. This favorable property could easily be used for sharing the tagging context metadata since it allows one to connect the resource URL, tags, and the information about the user by publishing it within an RSS feed. However, in practice tags are rarely used in RSS feeds. This state of practice combined with the existence of various RSS standards stands in the way of RSS to reach its full potential in tagging context metadata exchange.

Recently a promising service, Yahoo! Pipes,[7] emerged as an easy to use platform for manipulating RSS feeds. It allows users to create their derivate RSS feeds based on different operations (e.g., merging, filtering, etc.) over existing RSS feeds. However, integrating feeds with this service requires direct involvement of a user in the choice of feeds, and the functionality is limited to the sources chosen in the time of pipe creation. Those limits significantly affect the usefulness of the system for the purpose of integrating tags, compared to the TagFusion System that supports adding new tag sources in runtime without users or user systems having to worry about specifying tag sources.

1.4.2 SIOC

SIOC (Semantically Interlinked Online Communities) is a project that addresses a problem of data exchange and integration in the domain of online communities [16]. The work focuses on community Web sites that are widely used to support collaboration among people such as exchange of ideas, decision making, and other tasks related to group activities. SIOC creators noticed that those online communities do not cooperate in order to integrate conversations into a unique discourse: while people use several online communities to discuss the same subject, their conversations remain unlinked. SIOC aims at making the information available on the Internet more valuable by inferring links between the various online communities

---

[7] http://pipes.yahoo.com

and types of information and eventually fusing the dispersed information related to the same topic/user.

SIOC uses Semantic Web technology to approach the goal of interlinking online communities. SIOC ontology is used to unify the representation of data from different online communities. In addition, much effort has been made by the SIOC project members to create plug-ins for most popular online community applications, thus enabling to spread the idea of integration.

The idea of interlinking online communities as currently unconnected islands is very similar to the idea of integrating tags from independent collaborative tagging systems. Plug-ins built by SIOC developers to spread its usage correspond to the first level services that we have been developing for retrieving data from external systems and importing it into TagFusion.

1.4.3 Twine

Twine[8] is an innovative Web application aimed at enabling people to organize and share knowledge and information. It is often described as knowledge networking site where users are encouraged to connect with other people, but its main focus is not on socializing but on sharing and organizing information. Twine uses Semantic Web technologies to enable sophisticated services. It has the ambition to be a tool that would rule out all others, by integrating facilities currently available in different tools and combining that with social aspects similar to current Social Web applications.

Twine relies on user-provided content and bookmarks, allowing various ways to classify and organize the collected knowledge. Tags are one of the means of classification, and automated content annotation is integrated with human-provided tags. Like TagFusion, Twine also makes difference between human tags and tags automatically generated by the employed algorithms. While Twine also relies on user submissions like TagFusion, it seems to be a much more ambitious project that targets much more potential uses than annotation. Twine is also meant for direct use of end users, while TagFusion is more an infrastructure facility.

1.4.4 OpenTagging Platform

The OpenTagging[9] Platform is a very recent project started at DERI Institute, Galway, Ireland, to meet the challenge of integrating tags from heterogeneous sources. The project aims to make tagging data open, more universal, and apply it across different social tagging sites. To allow users and developers to leverage

---

[8] http://www.twine.com

[9] http://opentagging.org/

the social capabilities underlying tagging data, the platform consists of open data models (based on ontologies), export and sharing methods, and a platform for reuse and exchange of tagging data across multiple communities and multiple delivery platforms (i.e., Web-based systems, desktop, and mobile applications). The brief description of the platform given at this phase does not provide enough details to compare the flexibility of architecture with the approach applied in TagFusion, but the general idea seems to be very promising.

1.5 Conclusions and Future Work

In this paper we identified the problem of integrating metadata from independent collaborative tagging systems, as well as the unused possibilities for integration of human annotations with annotations provided by automatic services or autonomous software entities. We offered an approach to meeting these challenges by building a common repository for tagging metadata that integrates currently unlinked annotations from various systems. This approach promotes a flexible and extensible multilayer architecture of services that rely on one another in order to provide different functionalities and satisfy different needs of different types of users.

Special effort has been made to develop various modalities of use of the system and consider motivation for its use in order to assure the ability of the system to attract users and collect the critical amount of metadata. As such, we expect the system to become a useful repository and possibly a base for building more sophisticated services on top of it. Those services could possibly address the problem of semantic gap and meet the challenges imposed by disadvantages of tags as a form of metadata.

Besides those basic modalities of use, presented in this chapter, further modalities could be developed in the future, especially those influenced by the appearance of new kinds of Social Web sites with innovative purposes.

Future work will focus on building more first level services that could further explore the possibilities to use the accumulated metadata in different ways. One of the possible directions could be the involvement of some trust mechanisms relying on users' connections, as it is exemplified in the Sect. 1.3.5. The results of FOAFRealm project [17] could also show to be helpful for representing and making use of users' connections.

Another direction of future work is the development of a first level service to deal with tag ambiguity. We plan to experiment with the DBPedia[10] dataset and the recently released UMBEL[11] ontology, to uniquely identify concepts that hide behind

---

[10] DBPedia is a project aimed at extracting structured information from Wikipedia and allowing access to it via SPARQL endpoint. More information can be found at the project's Web site http://wiki.dbpedia.org/

[11] UMBEL (Upper Mapping and Binding Exchange Layer) is a lightweight upper-level ontology based on OpenCyc – an open source version of the world's largest knowledge base. For more information interested readers are advised to visit the project's Web site at http://www.umbel.org/

simple textual tags. The process of creating tag-concept mappings could rely on previously built functionalities. For example, the TagFusion Core service is planned to be used as a source for information on tag co-occurrence that could help position a user in a cluster defining his/her primary interests. Such information would 'represent the ground for introducing advanced heuristics in tag-concept mapping.

We also plan to create an interface that would enable SPARQL[12] queries over the annotations collected in TagFusion Core service. For this purpose we expect that the results of research presented in [18] and [19] could be highly useful.

References

1. Berners-Lee, T. Weaving the Web: The Original Design and Ultimate Destiny of the World Wide Web. Collins (2000)
2. Berners-Lee, T., Handler, J., Lassila, O. The Semantic Web. Scientific American (May 2001)
3. Mika, P. Ontologies Are Us: A Unified Model of Social Networks and Semantics, ISWC 2005, pp. 522–536 (2005)
4. Au Yeung, C. M., Gibbins, N., Shadbolt, N. Understanding the Semantics of Ambiguous Tags in Folksonomies, International Workshop on Emergent Semantics and Ontology Evolution held at ISWC2007 (2007)
5. Merholz, P. Metadata for the Masses. October 19 (2004). http://www.adaptivepath.com/ publications/essays/archives/000361.php
6. Golder, S., Huberman, B. A. The Structure of Collaborative Tagging Systems (2005)
7. Van Damme, C., Hepp, M., Siorpaes, K. FolksOntology: An Integrated Approach for Turning Folksonomies into Ontologies, Proceedings of the Workshop Bridging the Gap Between Semantic Web and Web 2.0, pp. 57–70 (2007)
8. Specia, L., Motta, E. Integrating Folksonomies with the Semantic Web, In Proceedings of the European Semantic Web Conference (ESWC 2007), Innsbruck, Austria: Springer (2007)
9. Golder, S. A., Huberman, B. A. Usage Patterns of Collaborative Tagging Systems, Journal of Information Science, Vol. 32, No. 2, pp. 198–208 (2006)
10. Tonkin, E. Folksonomies: The Fall and Rise of Plain-Text Tagging, Ariadne Issue 47, April 2006. http://www.ariadne.ac.uk/issue47/tonkin/
11. Vander Wal, T. Folksonomy (2004). http://vanderwal.net/folksonomy.html
12. Gamma, E., Helm, R., Johnson, R., Vlissides, J. Design Patterns: Elements of Reusable Object-Oriented Software. Addison-Wesley Longman (1995)
13. Cimiano, P., Ladwig, G., Staab, S. Gimme' the Context: Context-Driven Automatic Semantic Annotation with c-pankow. In Proceedings of 14th WWW, ACM (2005)
14. Liu, B., Chin, C. W., Ng, H. T. Mining Topic-Specific Concepts and Definitions on the Web. In Proceedings of the Twelfth International World Wide Web Conference (WWW'03), Budapest, Hungary (2003)
15. Al-Khalifa, H. S., Davis, H. C. Folksonomies Versus Automatic Keyword Extraction: An Empirical Study. In: IADIS Web Applications and Research 2006 (2006)
16. Breslin, J. G., Harth, A., Bojars, U., Decker, S. Towards Semantically-Interlinked Online Communities, Proceedings of the 2nd European Semantic Web Conference (ESWC '05), LNCS, Vol. 3532, pp. 500–514, Heraklion, Greece (2005)
17. Kruk, S. R. FOAF-Realm – Control Your Friends' Access to Resources. In FOAF Workshop Proceedings (2004). http://www.w3.org/2001/sw/Europe/events/foaf-galway/papers/fp/ foaf_realm/

---

[12] http://www.w3.org/TR/rdf-sparql-query/

18. Gruber, T. Ontology of Folksonomy: A Mash-up of Apples and Oranges, International Journal on Semantic Web & Information Systems, 3(2), (2007)
19. Kim, H. L., Breslin, J. G., Yang, S. K., Kim, H. G. Social Semantic Cloud of Tag: Semantic Model for Social Tagging, In Proceedings of the 2nd KES International Symposium on Agent and Multi-Agent Systems: Technologies and Applications, Incheon, Korea (2008)

Chapter 2
Semantic Enhancement of Social Tagging Systems

Fabian Abel, Nicola Henze, Daniel Krause, and Matthias Kriesell

2.1 Introduction

Recent trends in the World Wide Web have shown an impressive growth of Web 2.0 systems, which are characterized by easy-to-use, interactive, and participatory usage scenarios. Users in Web 2.0 applications are more than ever active in the Web content lifecycle: They contribute with their opinion by annotating content (the so-called *tagging*); they add and annotate content (e.g., by using public, shared applications for their bookmarks, pictures, videos, etc.); they rate content or create content with sorts of online diaries (so-called *blogs*).

This new interactivity is possible by applications that are easy-to-use: users can use these applications right from the start; no remarkable training is required. Among the benefits for the users are of course, the gained interactivity and active participation and the possibility to profit from the commonly created knowledge: to search for content that has been annotated by other users with relevant tags, to explore new content by following *often used trails*, by digging into content that certain user groups assume relevant, and so forth. The collaboratively created, shared knowledge of a plethora of users provides interesting new means to detect, select, and recommend relevant knowledge items to Web users.

The Web 2.0 focusses especially on the usage dimension in the Web. Other dimensions such as the enhancement of the semantics dimension do improve accessibility and provide means to reason about Web content. Here, Web resources are embedded in a (machine understandable) context, where knowledge 04 bases

Fabian Abel, Nicola Henze, and Daniel Krause
IVS – Semantic Web Group, Leibniz University Hannover, Appelstr. 4, D-30167 Hannover, Germany, e-mail: {abel,henze,krause}@kbs.uni-hannover.de

Matthias Kriesell
Department of Mathematics, University of Hamburg, Bundesstraße 55 D-20146 Hamburg, Germany, e-mail: kriesell@math.uni-hamburg.de

V. Devedžić and D. Gašević (eds.), *Web 2.0 & Semantic Web*, Annals of Information Systems 6, DOI 10.1007/978-1-4419-1219-0_2,
© Springer Science+Business Media, LLC 2010

(so-called *ontologies*) provide pointers and references to both the content as well the context of Web resources and reveal important information.

Combining Web 2.0 ideas with semantic technologies gives benefits to both approaches. Semantic technologies supplement the *intercreativity* in Web 2.0 with expressive formats and languages to better employ and use created content and information. On the other hand, the Web 2.0 approach of easy participation provides possibilities to create valuable semantic metadata and, the Semantic Web still lacks sufficient (valuable) metadata.

In this article, we propose a novel way to combine semantic technologies and Web 2.0 paradigms. With the GroupMe! system [1], we have realized an appealing Web 2.0 application that enables users to easily construct groups of Web content that they consider interesting for some topic. GroupMe! users can group arbitrary Web resources such as videos, news feeds, images, etc. Within a GroupMe! group these resources are visualized according to their media type – e.g., videos can directly be played within a group, news feeds list their latest items, etc. – so that the content of groups is easy to grasp. GroupMe!'s tagging functionality allows users to annotate resources as well as groups. Hence, whenever resources are annotated, this is done in the context of a group.

The immediate benefit of the GroupMe! approach is that we are now able to see Web resources in a context, namely the group context: Web resources that were previously not related at all now have in common that they belong to some group which defines a common context. Together with tagging, we can even further specify this relation between the members of a group: The group's tags are likely to be relevant for the members of the group, and vice versa. Our belief in this relevance can be specified by giving the relation between a member of a group and the group's tags an appropriate weight. Thus, we capture the *semantics* of user interactions (creating a group, moving a Web resource into a group, resizing a Web resource, tagging it or the group, etc.) and produce – without additional overhead – valuable semantic metadata. Furthermore, groups of content provide us with a database of *hand-picked resources* for certain topics, which are specified by the group and its tags. Presumably, these resources are of high relevance for the topic – in comparison to search results lists – as a subject is screening the search results and decides which to add to the group, and which not.

In this article, we describe the GroupMe! system and investigate how to make use of this database of hand-picked resources and how to exploit the grouping structure on resources in order to improve the quality of ranking strategies in folksonomies. We benchmark our investigation against a popular ranking strategy in folksonomies, the FolkRank algorithm [2]. It turns out that the grouping structure significantly improves the quality of ranking.

The article is organized as follows: In the next section we introduce the GroupMe! system and architecture and present analysis describing the usage of the system. The captured semantic information is formally modeled in the GroupMe! folksonomy, which will be described and discussed in Sect. 2.3. Sect. 2.4 introduces and discusses ranking strategies in folksonomies, which are evaluated subsequently.

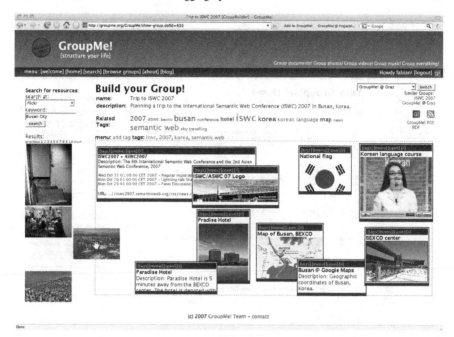

Fig. 2.1 Screenshot of GroupMe! application: A user drags a photo from the left-hand side Flickr search bar into the GroupMe! group on the right-hand side

In Sect. 2.5 we compare our approach to related work in the Semantic Web and Web 2.0. We conclude with an outlook on current and future work.

2.2 GroupMe! System

GroupMe![1] is a new kind of resource sharing system. It extends the idea of social bookmarking systems with the ability to create groups of multimedia Web resources. Therefore, it provides an enjoyable interface, which enables the creation of groups via *drag & drop* operations. Resources within GroupMe! groups are visualized according to their media type so that users can grasp content without visiting each resource separately. GroupMe! groups form new sources of information as they bundle content, which is, according to the group creator, relevant for the topic of a group. GroupMe! groups are not only accessible for humans, but also for machines, because GroupMe! captures user interactions as RDF, i.e., whenever a user adds a resource to a group, annotates a resource/group, etc. GroupMe! produces RDF (see Sect. 2.2.1).

Figure 2.1 shows a screenshot of the GroupMe! system. It illustrates a scenario, in which someone utilizes the GroupMe! system in order to plan a trip to the *ISWC*

---

[1] http://groupme.org

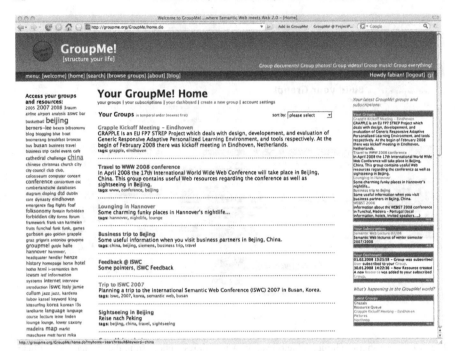

Fig. 2.2 Screenshot of the personal GroupMe! page. It lists the groups a user has created, groups she has subscribed to, events that recently occurred in groups of interest (*dashboard*), etc. Via a personal tag cloud (see left hand) the user can navigate to groups and resources she has annotated

2007 conference in Busan, Korea. Therefore, the user builds a GroupMe! group, which he names "Trip to ISWC 2007," containing resources that are relevant for the trip. Building such a group is simple and can be done in two ways:

Browser Button.　While browsing the web users can click on the GroupMe! browser button (*bookmarklet*) to add resources, they are interested in, to a group. When clicking the button users are directed to an input form where they can select the group(s) and specify tags they want to assign to the resource.

Group Builder.　GroupMe! integrates different services such as Google or Flickr that enable users to discover and search for resources they may want to add to their groups. Figure 2.1 demonstrates how a user drags an image gathered from Flickr into his group. Drag & drop operations also allow to arrange resources within a group, i.e., to position and resize resources.

An important feature of the GroupMe! system is its visualization of groups. Resources are visualized according to their media type, e.g., pictures are displayed as thumbnails; videos and audio recordings can be played directly within the group, and RSS feeds are previewed by displaying recent headlines. Hence, content of GroupMe! groups can be grasped immediately. For example in Fig. 2.1, the Korean language video lecture can be watched instantly, the latest news about the conference is listed within the group, and photos of a hotel and the conference venue are displayed. Altogether the arranged group in Fig. 2.1 appears like a *collage of information artifacts* about *ISWC 2007 trip* and gives an overview of the resources' content.

GroupMe! groups are interpreted as regular Web resources and can also be arranged within groups. This enables users to build hierarchies of Web resources and to make use of the information hiding principle – detailed information can be encapsulated into groups. Users who just want to get a rough overview about a topic do not need to visit those groups that contain detailed information.

GroupMe! groups are dynamic collections, which may change over time. Other users who also plan to attend the ISWC are enabled to subscribe to the group and will be notified at their *personal GroupMe! page* (see Fig. 2.2) whenever the group is modified, e.g., a new resource is added or removed, new tags have been assigned, etc. Users can also utilize their favored news reader to be up-to-date about changes within the group as each GroupMe! group provides an RSS feed. Thus, GroupMe! can be considered as a lightweight blogging tool where creation of blog entries is done via simple mouse operations instead of writing text. Information content is captured also by the group context, e.g., by adding the Web site "powerset.com" to a group "Promising Web 2.0 companies" the user denotes what he thinks about the corresponding company.

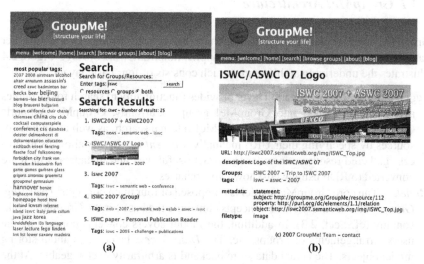

Fig. 2.3 (a) Search result list when searching for tag "iswc", and (b) visualization of a single resource within the GroupMe! system

To ease future retrieval GroupMe! allows to tag both resources and groups. The personal GroupMe! page lists tags that a user has assigned to resources/groups he is interested in: the *user tag cloud*. By clicking on a tag *t* within the user tag cloud he receives all resources/groups he has annotated with *t*. Tag clouds are furthermore computed and displayed for each GroupMe! group (see Fig. 2.1). Such group-specific tag clouds help users to get an overview about the topic of a group. Another advantage of group-specific tag clouds is that they enable users to explore the GroupMe! corpus. Clicking on a tag *t* of a *group tag cloud* invokes a GroupMe! search operation, which results in a list of related resources and groups (see Fig. 2.3.a) – not only those resources that are directly tagged with *t*, as described in Sect. 2.4. Starting from a search result list, the user can navigate to other resources and groups (see Fig. 2.3.b). In general, all entities in GroupMe! – users, tags, resources, and groups – are clickable and resolvable, which results in an advanced browsing experience, e.g., each group points to similar groups (see top right in Fig. 2.1), or Resources refer to groups they are contained in.

Another important feature of GroupMe! is that content of groups is not only accessible and understandable for humans, but for machines, too. GroupMe! is therewith an RDF generator as it extracts RDF (meta)data about resources and captures each user interaction as RDF. RDF created in GroupMe! is made available to other Web applications and can be accessed via RSS and RDF feeds or RESTful [3] API. Hence, other applications can benefit from the feature of grouping and enriching resources with machine understandable semantics. The RDF generation functionality is described in more detail in the next section.

2.2.1 GroupMe! Architecture

GroupMe! is a modular Web application that adheres to the Model-View-Controller pattern. It is implemented using the J2EE application framework *Spring*.[2] Figure 2.4 illustrates the underlying architecture, which consists of four basic layers:

Aggregation.   The aggregation layer provides functionality to search for resources a user wants to add into GroupMe! groups. Currently, GroupMe! supports Google, Flickr, and of course a GroupMe!-internal search, as well as adding resources by specifying their URL manually. *Content Extractors* allow us to process gathered resources in order to extract useful data and metadata, which are converted to RDF using well-known vocabularies.

Model.   The core GroupMe! model is composed of four main concepts: *User, Tag, Group*, and *Resource.* These concepts constitute the base for the GroupMe! folksonomy (cf. Sect. 2.3). In addition, the model covers concepts concerning the users' arrangements of groups, etc. The *Data Access* layer cares about storing model objects. The actual data store backend is arbitrarily exchangeable. At the moment we are using a MySQL database.

Application logic.   The logic layer provides various controllers for modifying the model, exporting RDF, etc. The internal GroupMe! search functionality, which is implemented according to the strategy pattern in order to switch between different search and ranking strategies, is made available via a RESTful API. It enables third parties to benefit from the improved search capabilities (cf. Sect. 2.4.3), and to retrieve RDF descriptions about resources – even such resources that were

---

[2] http://springframework.org

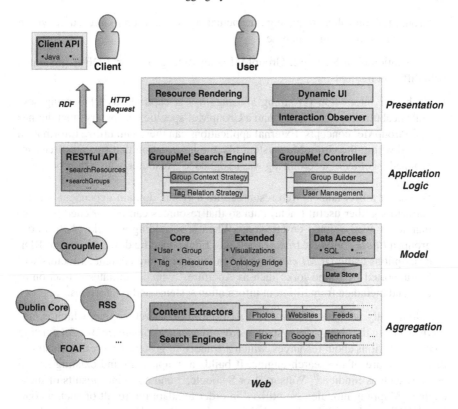

Fig. 2.4 Technical overview of the GroupMe! application

not equipped with RDF descriptions before they were integrated into GroupMe!. To simplify usage of exported RDF data, we further provide a lightweight Java *Client API*, which transforms RDF into GroupMe! model objects.

Presentation. The GUI of the GroupMe! application is based on AJAX principles. Therefore, we applied Ajax and JavaScript frameworks like script.aculo.us,[3] DWR,[4] or Prototype.[5] Such frameworks already provide functionality to drag & drop elements, resize elements, etc. Visualization of groups and resources is highly modular and extensible. Switching between components that render a specific resource or type of resource can be done dynamically, e.g., visualization of group elements is adapted to their media type (see Fig. 2.1). In the future, visualizations of resources and groups should be adaptable by the users (see also Sect. 2.6).

When creating or modifying groups, each user interaction (e.g., moving and resizing resources) is monitored and immediately communicated to the responsible

---

[3] http://script.aculo.us

[4] http://getahead.org/dwr

[5] http://prototypejs.org

GroupMe! controller so that e.g., the actual size or position of a resource within a group is stored in the database.

As mentioned in Sect. 2.2, GroupMe! is an RDF generator. RDF is generated with different methods.

1. Each user interaction (grouping and tagging) is captured as RDF using several vocabularies, e.g., *FOAF*[6] and a GroupMe!-specific vocabulary[7] that defines new GroupMe! concepts. External applications can therewith utilize information gained within the GroupMe! system like the information that two resources are grouped together or a certain tag was assigned to a resource within the context of a group.
2. Whenever a user adds a Web resource into a group, domain-dependent content extractors gather useful (meta) data so that resources can be enriched with semantically well defined descriptions. When, e.g., adding a Flickr photo into a group, a *Photo content extractor* translates Flickr-specific descriptions into RDF descriptions using *DCMI element set*.[8] In the near future content extractors will be supported by frameworks such as Aperture,[9] which facilitates extraction of data and metadata from different information systems and file formats.

Additionally we have implemented a (Meta) RDF search engine, which is currently added to the GroupMe! system in order to *query the Semantic Web* for existing RDF descriptions about resources, which are added to groups. Figure 2.5 illustrates the architecture of the search engine. It builds a wrapper around existing search engines such as Sindice,[10] Watson,[11] or Swoogle,[12] and combines results of those engines. Mapping modules are utilized in order to adapt the result of such a combined RDF search result into a vocabulary that is understood by the requesting client, whereas the client's vocabulary capabilities are given as list of namespaces the client is aware of. At the moment we provide a module to translate from FOAF to Dublin Core vocabulary, and vice versa, e.g., we map (#bob, foaf:knows, #mary) to (#bob, dc:relation, #mary) and deliver both statements to the client.

To let other applications benefit from the semantics captured and gathered by the GroupMe! system, RDF descriptions of groups and resources are made available as feeds. An RDF description of group consists of, on one hand, RDF statements that describe the group itself and, on the other, statements, which describe the resources that are contained in the group. Figure 2.6 lists RDF produced by the current version of the GroupMe! system and represents parts of the RDF description of the group demonstrated in Fig. 2.1. The group is basically described with a name (dc:title), description (dc:description), and a list of contained resources

---

[6] http://xmlns.com/foaf/spec/

[7] http://groupme.org/rdf/groupme.owl

[8] http://dublincore.org/documents/dces/

[9] http://aperture.sourceforge.net

[10] http://sindice.com

[11] http://watson.kmi.open.ac.uk

[12] http://swoogle.umbc.edu

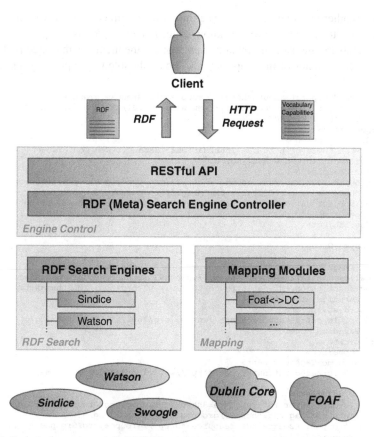

Fig. 2.5 Technical overview of the RDF (Meta) Search Engine

(groupme:resource). The extract of the group's RDF description specifies two resources, an image (foaf:Image), which represents a photo of a hotel in Busan, and a Web site (foaf:Document), which represents a certain Google map[13]. Via the concept *TagAssignment* it is stated which tags are assigned to groups/resources, e.g.,the tag with id 90 was assigned to the photo within the *ISWC group* by user 3 on November 10, 2007. The photo also provides a simplified version of the formal tag assignment description by utilizing the attribute dc:subject. The Google map resource is even equipped with longitude (wsg84:long) and latitude information (wsg84:lat), whereby the location of Busan is specified precisely.

The RDF description displayed in Fig. 2.6 illustrates the main characteristics of the GroupMe! approach. By grouping resources, which were (possibly) not related

---

[13] http://maps.google.com

with each other beforehand, they are set into a well-defined context, which enables applications to deduce additional knowledge. For example, as the photo and the Google map are thematically related to each other, the metadata that specify the geographic coordinates of the map may also be applicable to the photo of the hotel.

```
...
<groupme:Group rdf:about="http://groupme.org/GroupMe/group/630">
  <dc:title rdf:datatype="http://www.w3.org/2001/XMLSchema#string">
    Trip to ISWC 2007
  </dc:title>
  <dc:description >
    Planning a trip to the International Semantic Web Conference
    (ISWC) 2007 in Busan, Korea.
  </dc:description>
  <groupme:resource rdf:resource="http://groupme.org/GroupMe/resource/634"/>
  <groupme:resource rdf:resource="http://groupme.org/GroupMe/resource/653"/>
  <dc:subject rdf:datatype="http://www.w3.org/2001/XMLSchema#string">
    Semantic Web
  </dc:subject>
  ...
</groupme:Group>

<foaf:Image rdf:about="http://groupme.org/GroupMe/resource/653">
  <owl:sameAs rdf:resource="http://iswc2007.semanticweb.org/paradise.jpg"/>
  <dc:description rdf:datatype="http://www.w3.org/2001/XMLSchema#string">
    Paradise hotel in Busan
  </dc:description>
  <dc:title rdf:datatype="http://www.w3.org/2001/XMLSchema#string">
    Paradise Hotel
  </dc:title>
  <groupme:tas>
    <groupme:TagAssignment>
      <dc:created rdf:datatype="http://www.w3.org/2001/XMLSchema#date">
        2007-10-30
      </dc:created>
      <groupme:user rdf:resource="http://groupme.org/GroupMe/user/3"/>
      <groupme:tag tag="http://groupme.org/GroupMe/tag/90>
      <groupme:resource rdf:resource="http://groupme.org/GroupMe/
      resource/653"/>
      <groupme:group rdf:resource="http://groupme.org/GroupMe/group/630"/>
    </groupme:TagAssignment>
  </groupme:tas>
  <dc:subject rdf:datatype="http://www.w3.org/2001/XMLSchema#string">
    ISWC
  </dc:subject>
    ...
</foaf:Image>

<foaf:Document rdf:about="http://groupme.org/GroupMe/resource/634">
  <owl:sameAs rdf:resource="http://maps.google.de/maps?amp;q=Busan+Korea"/>
  <dc:description rdf:datatype="http://www.w3.org/2001/XMLSchema#string">
    Geographic coordinates of Busan, Korea.
  </dc:description>
  <dc:title rdf:datatype="http://www.w3.org/2001/XMLSchema#string">
    Busan @ Google Maps
  </dc:title>
  <wsg84:lat rdf:datatype="http://www.w3.org/2001/XMLSchema#double>
    52.393442
  </wsg84:lat>
  <wsg84:long rdf:datatype="http://www.w3.org/2001/XMLSchema#double>
    9.8061
  </wsg84:long>
  ...
</foaf:Document>
...
```

Fig. 2.6 Extract of RDF description of the group displayed in Fig. 2.1

An application that searches for photos according to a location specified via geographic coordinates is now able to retrieve photos by locations even if these photos are not directly annotated with geographic coordinates.

2.2.2 Evaluation of the GroupMe! System

In the previous section, we introduced the GroupMe! system and the concept of building groups of resources. To outline the benefit of our system, we evaluated how users interact with the GroupMe! system; in particular, we focused on usage and tagging characteristics, and investigated the effects of the structure given by the groups to search and retrieve resources. The data underlying the analysis was collected during the first six months after the system's launch on July 14, 2007. During the observed period, GroupMe! had a total of 1351 resources of which 1078 were normal resources and 273 (20.2%) were groups. Altogether, 1758 tag assignments were monitored, with 1.3 tags per resource in average. The overall evolution of resources and groups is given in Figure 2.7.

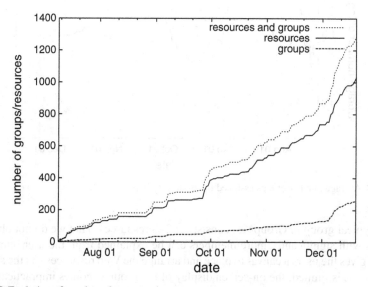

Fig. 2.7 Evolution of number of resources/groups

According to the *tagging system design taxonomy* proposed in [4], GroupMe! is a free-for-all tagging system, which allows users to annotate multimedia content for future retrieval. Hence, GroupMe! allows for broad folksonomies as every user is allowed to tag every resource or group without any restriction. Tagging a resource r is done when users are situated in the view of a certain group g. Thereby, users are only able to see those tags that have been assigned to r within the context of the group g (same holds for group g). Explicit tag suggestions are not provided by the GroupMe! system. However, the tag cloud of a group and the resource's visualization, which is adapted to the media type of the resource, help the users to reflect on appropriate tags for the resource.

Interestingly, groups were tagged more intensively than ordinary resources: In average, 1.98 tags were assigned to groups, whereas only 1.13 tags were attached to other resources. Thus, groups were tagged 1.75 times more often than traditional resources. This effect was present over time, as depicted in Figure 2.8. Furthermore, at the end of the observed period only 36.98% of the groups were not annotated with any tag in contrast to 52.41% of the resources. These initial observations give support for the hypothesis that users adopt the group idea to organize Web resources, and that they also invest time in the group construction process.

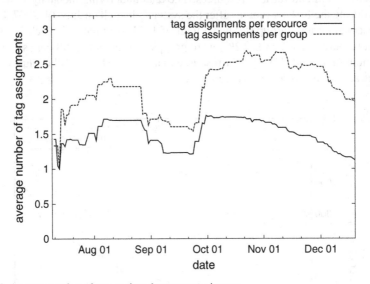

Fig. 2.8 Average number of tags assigned to resources/groups

A typical group in GroupMe! consists of 2–8 resources. That we do not observe groups with significantly more members can be explained from the user interface, which gives the users a canvas to place and arrange the Web resources. As the size of this canvas is limited, the on-screen display of the group becomes impractical with too many Web resources. Users collect resources with different media types in their group, as can be seen in Table 2.1. Most popular among the media types are images, followed by videos and RSS feeds. Web sites, academic papers, presentation slides, etc. are denoted as *other Web resources* and are not mentioned separately, because to users they appear as simple bookmarks, i.e., their visualization is not yet adapted to their media type particularly. The possibility to include groups into a group was only seldomly used; we explain this by the small number of available groups during the observation period.

Table 2.1 Percentage of resources' media types that are part of GroupMe! groups

Type of resource	AVG occurrences (%)
Images	39.77
Videos	5.66
Rss feeds	3.0
Groups	3.33
Other Web resources	48.22

2.2.2.1 Results

The evaluation of the GroupMe! system shows that users appreciate the grouping facility to organize Web resources they are interested in. Furthermore, we have shown that users benefit from the media independence of GroupMe!, as a rich mixture of media types is used in the GroupMe! system. Groups can be seen as *hand-picked* collections of Web content for a certain topic or domain. As such, they are also valuable results to perform search queries, which we investigate in the following sections.

2.3 GroupMe! Folksonomy

To develop FolkRank-based group-aware ranking strategies we have to embed the group context introduced by the GroupMe! approach into the formal folksonomy model. The term *folksonomy*, introduced by Thomas Vander Wal in 2004 [5], defines a taxonomy, which evolves over time when users (the *folks*) annotate resources with freely chosen keywords. Folksonomies can be divided into *broad* folksonomies, which allow different users to assign the same tag to the same resource, and *narrow* folksonomies, in which the same tag can be assigned to a resource only once [6]. Formal models of a folksonomy are, e.g., presented in [7] or [8]. They are based on bindings between users, tags, and resources. According to [9] a folksonomy is defined as follows:

Definition 1. A *folksonomy* is a quadruple $\mathbb{F} := (U, T, R, Y)$, where:

- U, T, R are finite sets of instances of *users*, *tags*, and *resources*, respectively.
- Y defines a relation, the *tag assignment*, between these sets, that is, $Y \subseteq U \times T \times R$.

In [10], tag assignments are furthermore attributed with a timestamp and Hotho et al. also embed relations between tags into the formal folksonomy model [9]. To simplify the formalization we do not include these features. GroupMe! introduces groups as a new dimension in folksonomies.

Definition 2. A *group* is a finite set of resources.

A group is a resource as well. Groups can be tagged or arranged in groups, which effects hierarchies among resources. In general, tagging of resources within the GroupMe! system is done in context of a group. Figure 2.9 presents a basic GroupMe! tagging scenario, in which users u_1 and u_2 have grouped resources r_{1-3} into g_1 and g_2, and have tagged both resources and groups with keywords t_{1-3}. The tag assignment tas_2 (u_1, t_2, r_2, g_1) in Fig. 2.9 describes that user u_1 has annotated resource r_2 in context of group g_1 with tag t_2. The group context of tags helps to detect ambiguous tags. For example, r_2 has also been tagged with t_2 in context of group g_2, which indicates that the meaning of t_2 is probably the same in both groups.

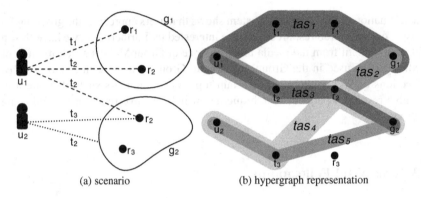

(a) scenario   (b) hypergraph representation

Fig. 2.9 (a) Scenario in which two users assign tags to resources in context of different groups and (b) the corresponding representation as a hypergraph

Assume that there is a group, which does not contain any of the resources of g_1, and t_2 would be the only tag that occurs in both groups, then the meaning of t_2 is possibly ambiguous. If users assign tags to a group, which is itself not contained in a group, then the group context information is not available ($\rightarrow$ $(u_2, t_2, g_2, \varepsilon)$) and within the hypergraph representation the tag assignment can be interpreted as an edge containing only three vertices ($\rightarrow$ tas_5). Overall, a GroupMe! folksonomy is formally characterized via Definition 3 (cf. [1]).

Definition 3. A GroupMe! folksonomy is a 5-tuple $\mathbb{F} := (U, T, \check{R}, G, \check{Y})$, where:

- U, T, R, G are finite sets that contain instances of users, tags, resources, and groups, respectively.
- $\check{R} = R \cup G$ is the union of the set of resources and the set of groups.
- $\check{Y}$ defines a *GroupMe! tag assignment*: $\check{Y} \subseteq U \times T \times \check{R} \times (G \cup \{\varepsilon\})$, where ε is a reserved symbol for the *empty group context*, i.e., a group that is not contained in another group when it gets tagged by a user.

In comparison to traditional folksonomies (see Definition 1), in which relations between tags mainly rely on their co-occurrences (i.e., two tags are assigned to the same resource), a GroupMe! folksonomy gains new relations between tags:

1. A relation between tags assigned from (possibly) different users to different resources, where the resources are contained in the same group.

2. A relation between tags assigned to a group g and tags assigned to resources that are contained in g.

Relations between resources become more explicit in GroupMe! folksonomies, than in traditional folksonomies. The latter allow to derive such relations if, e.g., the same tag was assigned to different resources, or if the same user has annotated different resources. In the GroupMe! system users create groups with respect to a specific topic. All resources that are arranged together in a certain GroupMe! group are related to the group's topic and are also related to each other.

The relationship between a group and the resources contained in the group can be interpreted as a *part-of-relation*. In case of constructing hierarchies among groups (groups that contain groups) further types of relations are implicated, e.g., tags that are assigned in superior might be understood as broader concepts (cf. *skos:broader* – SKOS [11]), or resources in inferior groups may be more specific than those of superior groups.

In the following section we present ranking algorithms, which exploit some of these new relations.

2.4 Ranking Strategies

In this section we present GroupMe! ranking strategies. All strategies are based on the FolkRank algorithm [2] and differ in the way GroupMe! tag assignments (which form a *4-uniform hypergraph*, cf. Definition 3) are exploited in the graph construction process. Figure 2.9 shows a tagging scenario and the hypergraph formed by the tag assignments of the scenario. The challenge of adapting the FolkRank algorithm to GroupMe! folksonomies is to identify semantically appropriate strategies for constructing a graph (*folksonomy graph*), whose adjacency matrix serves as input for the PageRank-based FolkRank algorithm.

2.4.1 FolkRank Algorithm

The core idea of the FolkRank algorithm is to transform the hypergraph formed by the traditional tag assignments (see Definition 1) into an undirected, weighted tripartite graph $\mathbb{G}_F = (V_F, E_F)$, which serves as input for an adaption of PageRank [12]. At this, the set of nodes is $V_F = U \cup T \cup R$ and the set of edges is given via $E_F = \{\{u,t\},\{t,r\},\{u,r\}|(u,t,r) \in Y\}\}$ (cf. Definition 1). The weight w of each edge is determined according to its frequency within the set of tag assignments, i.e., $w(u,t) = |\{r \in R : (u,t,r) \in Y\}|$ is the number of resources the user u tagged with keyword t. Accordingly, $w(t,r)$ counts the number of users who annotated resource r with tag t, and $w(u,r)$ determines the number of tags a user u assigned to a resource r. With $\mathbb{G}_F$ represented by the real matrix A, which is obtained from the adjacency matrix by normalizing each row to have 1-norm equal to 1, and starting with any vector $\vec{w}$ of nonnegative reals, adapted PageRank iterates as follows:

$$\vec{w} \leftarrow dA\vec{w} + (1-d)\vec{p}. \tag{2.1}$$

Adapted PageRank utilizes vector $\vec{p}$ as a preference vector, fulfilling the condition $||\vec{w}||_1 = ||\vec{p}||_1$. Its influence can be adjusted by $d \in [0,1]$. Based on this, FolkRank is defined as follows [2]:

Definition 4. The *FolkRank algorithm* computes a topic-specific ranking in folksonomies by executing the following steps:

1. $\vec{p}$ specifies the preference in a topic (e.g., preference for a given tag).
2. $\vec{w}_0$ is the result of applying the adapted PageRank with $d = 1$.
3. $\vec{w}_1$ is the result of applying the adapted PageRank with some $d < 1$.
4. $\vec{w} = \vec{w}_1 - \vec{w}_0$ is the final weight vector. $\vec{w}[x]$ denotes the *FolkRank* of $x \in V$.

2.4.2 Group-Aware Ranking Strategies

To adapt the FolkRank algorithm to GroupMe! folksonomies we confine ourself on adapting the process of constructing the folksonomy graph $\mathbb{G}_\mathbb{F}$ from the hypergraph formed by the GroupMe! tag assignments. Therefore, we introduce three main strategies:

A. *Traditional Tag Assignments.* This approach reduces GroupMe! tag assignments to traditional tag assignments, as illustrated in Figure 2.10. Groups are just taken into account as resources that might or might not be tagged. Building the tripartite graph $\mathbb{G}_\mathbb{A} = (V_\mathbb{A}, E_\mathbb{A})$ is done analogously to FolkRank. The set of nodes and edges is given as follows: $V_\mathbb{A} = U \cup T \cup \check{R}$ and $E_\mathbb{A} = \{\{u,t\}, \{t,r\}, \{u,r\} | u \in U, t \in T, r \in \check{R}, g \in G \cup \{\varepsilon\}, (u,t,r,g) \in \check{Y}\}$. Computing the weight of each edge also corresponds to the FolkRank approach, e.g.: $w(u,t) = |\{(u,t,r,g) \in \check{Y} : r \in \check{R}, g \in G \cup \{\varepsilon\}\}|$ is the number of resources the user u tagged with keyword t in any group g. This strategy corresponds to the *normal FolkRank* algorithm. It just requires the preprocessing step, in which the GroupMe! folksonomy is transformed into a traditional folksonomy. The motivation of this strategy is to have a

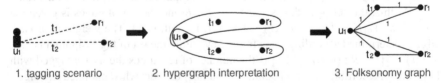

1. tagging scenario   2. hypergraph interpretation   3. Folksonomy graph

Fig. 2.10 Graph construction in traditional folksonomies. The tagging scenario represents an extract of the scenario illustrated in Fig. 2.9. The group context is ignored

benchmark strategy, which we use in order to analyze if the new group structure in folksonomies has an impact on the quality of the FolkRank algorithm.

B. *Groups as Tags.* GroupMe! users create groups about a certain topic. In general they only arrange those resources together in a group which are related to the group's topic. Resources within a same group are thus closely related to each other. The strategy "Groups as Tags" tries to emphasize this relation and creates artificial tags $t_g \in T_G$, $T_G \cap T = \emptyset$, for each group g and assigns such tags to all resources contained in g, whereby the user who added a resource to the group is declared as the *tagger*. The set of nodes is extended by T_G: $V_\mathbb{B} = V_\mathbb{A} \cup T_G$.

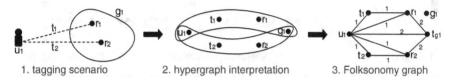

| 1. tagging scenario | 2. hypergraph interpretation | 3. Folksonomy graph |

Fig. 2.11 Graph construction when interpreting groups as tags. Again, the tagging scenario represents an extract of the scenario illustrated in Fig. 2.9

The edges added to $V_\mathbb{F}$ by the strategy are $E_\mathbb{B} = E_\mathbb{A} \cup \{\{u,t_g\},\{t_g,r\},\{u,r\}|u \in U, t_g \in T_G, r \in \check{R}, u$ has added r to group $g\}$. We use a constant value w_c to weight these edges because a resource is usually added only once to a certain group. Hence, counting, e.g., the number of users who added a resource to a specific group would not make sense.[14] A hypergraph, which functions as database for this graph construction strategy, is depicted in Fig. 2.11. Here, for the group g_1, which is treated as normal resource, a new artificial tag t_{g_1} is introduced and assigned to those resources that are member of the corresponding group.

C. *Group Context-based Tags.* The actual meaning of (possibly ambiguous) tags is hard to infer in traditional folksonomies, i.e., it is difficult to detect that a tag has ambiguous meaning, because the context of tags is only established via the users and the resources. In order to detect fuzzy usage of a tag t other tags of the users, who assigned t to a resource, and other tags, which have been assigned to resources that are tagged with t, can be utilized. The group context provides more explicit alternatives to overcome this problem. If users assign a certain tag to resources in different groups then the meaning of the tag may differ. As denoted at the end of Sect. 2.3, we can compute the degree of overlap between groups, i.e., a tag t that occurs in two groups, which do not have any other common tags and do not contain same resources, has in all probability a (slightly) different meaning depending on the group.

This strategy embeds the group context directly into the tags and replaces every tag t with a tag t_{tg}, which indicates that tag t was used in group g. It then transforms all GroupMe! tag assignments into normal tag assignment triples. For example, the GroupMe! tag assignment (u_1,t_2,r_2,g_1), presented in Fig. 2.12, is interpreted as (u_1,t_{2g_1},r_2) $(= tas_1)$, and (u_1,t_2,r_2, g_2) is converted

---

[14] Instead we select, e.g., $w_c(t_g,r) \approx max(|\{u \in U : (u,t,r,g) \in \check{Y}\}|)$ as we believe that grouping a resource is in general more valuable than tagging it.

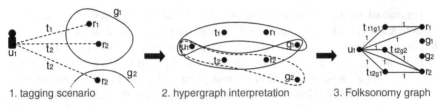

Fig. 2.12 Graph construction process when applying strategy "Group Context-based Tags" by example of an extract of the scenario illustrated in Fig. 2.9

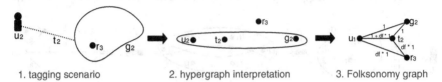

Fig. 2.13 Scenario illustrating that *group tags* are propagated attenuated by the dampen factor df

into $(u_2, t_{t_2 g_2}, r_2)$ (= tas_2). The construction of $\mathbb{G}_C$ is done as in the normal FolkRank algorithm, described in Sect. 2.4.1. Detecting equality of tags is the only exception, e.g., given tas_1 and tas_2 from above, the weight $w(u_1, t_{t_2 g_1})$ is not only determined by tas_1 but also partially by tas_2, although the tag $t_{t_2 g_1}$ in tas_1 is not exactly equal to $t_{t_2 g_2}$ in tas_2. We compute the similarity between two tags $t_{t_x g_y}$ and $t_{t_v g_w}$ and therewith the influence of a tag assignment to a weight as follows:

$\wedge$	$t_x = t_v$	$t_x \neq t_v$
$g_y = g_w$	1.0	0.2
$g_y \neq g_w$	0.4	0

Hence, based on tas_1 and tas_2 it is $w(u_1, t_{t_2 g_1}) = 1.4$.

In addition to the three strategies that can be applied to generate the folksonomy graph $\mathbb{G}$, which serves as input for the FolkRank algorithm, we present two further strategies to exploit a GroupMe! folksonomy. They can be applied as extensions to the strategies above. The motivation of both strategies is that a tag t, which was assigned to resource r or group g in certain context, is to some extent relevant to resources and groups that occur in the same context. Hence, the core idea of both strategies is to propagate tags assigned to one resource/group to other resources or groups. Such techniques synthetically increase the amount of input data and do not require to change the strategies described above substantially.

Propagation of Group Tags.   GroupMe! users tag groups about 1.75 times more often than common resources [13] (see Sect. 2.2.2). By propagating tags, which have been assigned to a group (*group tags*), to the group's resources we try to counteract this situation. For example in Fig. 2.9, tag t_2, which is assigned to group g_2, can be propagated to all resources contained in g_2. An obvious benefit of this procedure is that untagged resources like r_3 obtain tag assignments (here: (u_2, t_2, r_3, g_2)). To adjust the influence of inherited tag assignments, we weight these assignments by a dampen factor $df \in [0, 1]$. Figure 2.13 demonstrates how the folksonomy graph is constructed when group tags are propagated.

Propagation of All Tags. In the same way tags can be propagated among resources that are contained in the same group. This strategy induces propagation of (1) group tags to resources within the group, (2) resource tags of one resource to other resources within a group, and (3) resource tags to the group itself. Note that only tag assignments that have been carried out within the context of the corresponding group are considered for propagation.

2.4.3 Evaluation

Different extensions of the FolkRank algorithm have been developed and were described in the last section. To decide whether the additional information in the GroupMe! system (*the group context*), can help to improve the search performance, we have to evaluate if any of the group-aware ranking strategies, which adapt FolkRank by exploiting the group context can outperform the classical FolkRank algorithm.

2.4.3.1 Metrics

The adapted FolkRank algorithms described in Sect. 2.4.2 compute rankings for all entities of a folksonomy (users, tags, resources, and groups). In the evaluation we concentrate on ranking of resources and groups as search for resources is the most common use case of ranking in folksonomy systems. To measure the quality of our ranking strategies we used the *OSim* and *KSim* metrics as proposed in [14]. $OSim(\tau_1, \tau_2)$ enables us to determine the overlap between the top k resources of two rankings, τ_1 and τ_2.

$$OSim(\tau_1, \tau_2) = \frac{|R_1 \cap R_2|}{k}, \qquad (2.2)$$

where $R_1, R_2 \subset \check{R}$ are the sets of resources that are contained in the top k of ranking τ_1 and τ_2 respectively, and $|R_1| = |R_2| = k$.

$KSim(\tau_1, \tau_2)$, which is based on Kendall's τ distance measure, indicates the degree of pairwise distinct resources, r_u and r_v, within the top k that have the same relative order in both rankings.

$$KSim(\tau_1, \tau_2) = \frac{|\{(u, v) : \tau_1, \tau_2 \text{ agree on order of } (u, v), u \neq v\}|}{|U| \cdot (|U| - 1)}. \qquad (2.3)$$

U is the union of resources of both top k rankings. τ_1' corresponds to ranking τ_1 extended with resources R_1' that are contained in the top k of τ_2 and not contained in τ_1. We do not make any statements about the order of resources $r \in R_1'$ within ranking τ_1'.t τ_2' is constructed correspondingly.

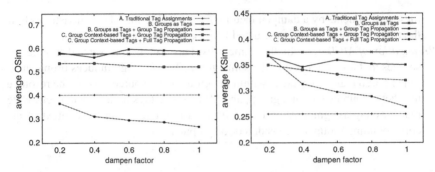

Fig. 2.14 Average OSim and KSim (with respect to 10 different top 20 ranking comparisons) for varying dampen factors, which control the influence of propagated tags, and different ranking strategies

Together, *OSim* and *KSim* are suited to measure the quality of a ranking with respect to an optimal (possibly hand-selected) ranking. Our evaluations are based on 50 hand-selected rankings: Given 10 keywords, which were out of T, and the entire GroupMe! data set, 5 experts independently created rankings for each of the keywords, which represented from their perspective the most precise top 20 rankings. By building for each keyword the average of these rankings, we gained ten optimal rankings. Among the ten keywords, there were frequently used tags as well as seldomly used ones.

2.4.3.2 Measurements and Discussion

Table 2.2 Overview of OSim and KSim for different ranking strategies ordered by OSim, where the dampen factor for propagating tags is 0.2. A denotes the *"Traditional Tag Assignments"* strategy, B is the *"Groups as Tags"* strategy, and C is the *"Group Context-Based Tags"*

	Strategy	OSim	KSim
(i)	C + Full Tag Propagation	0.610	0.369
(ii)	B + Group Tag Propagation	0.585	0.368
(iii)	B	0.580	0.375
(iv)	C + Group Tag Propagation	0.540	0.351
(v)	B + Full Tag Propagation	0.465	0.273
(vi)	A	0.405	0.255
(vii)	C	0.390	0.257
(viii)	A + Group Tag Propagation	0.360	0.237
(ix)	A + Full Tag Propagation	0.345	0.247

Table 2.2 gives an overview on the measured results for each ranking strategy introduced in Sect. 2.4.2 with respect to OSim and KSim metrics. The strategies are ordered according to their OSim performance, whereas both OSim and KSim values

are averaged out of ten test series (for the ten different keywords and corresponding hand-selected rankings). In terms of the OSim, "C – Group Context-Based Tags" can be identified as best strategy: It computes rankings, which contain 61% of the resources that also occur in the corresponding hand-selected top 20 ranking lists. Group tag propagation does not influence the approach "B – Groups as Tags" strongly as strategies (ii) and (iii) have nearly the same OSim values. This can be explained with the functionality of "B": For each group, "B" introduces artificial

Table 2.3 Top 10 rankings computed by different ranking strategies (and by hand, respectively) for the term *"socialpagerank"*.

Rank	Hand-selected	A. Traditional TAS	B. Groups as Tags	C + Full Tag Propagation
1.	Optimizing Web search using social annotations	Optimizing Web search using social annotations	Optimizing Web search using social annotations	Yahoo! research
2.	Exploring social annotations for the sem. . .	The Semantic Web: Will It All End In Tiers?	HITS	Optimizing web search using social annotations
3.	Personalized PageRank	New *Semantic* Web!	Webpage Ranking *(group)*	Ontologies are us
4.	SimRank	The Semantic Web: An Introduction	SimRank	Bibsonomy
5.	PageRank	The Semantic Web: Scientific American	PageRank	HITS
6.	FolkRank	LEGOLAND	Topic-sensitive PageRank	SimRank
7.	Ontologies are us	eschbach *(group)*	Personalized PageRank	PageRank
8.	Topic-sensitive PageRank	Andreas Eschbach Wikipedia	Yahoo! research	Topic-sensitive PageRank
9.	Bibsonomy	Andreas Eschbach Homepage	FRank	Personalized PageRank
10.	FRank	Andreas Eschbach: Der Nobelpreis	Ontologies are us	FolkRank

tags and assigns those tags to the group's members. Considering the graph structure, this almost conforms to propagating the tags of a group to its members.

Strategy (vi) does not exploit the group structure as it reduces GroupMe! tag assignments to traditional tag assignments (see Sect. 2.4.1) and can therewith be interpreted as the traditional FolkRank algorithm. The extensions of FolkRank, (viii) and (ix), which rudimentary exploit the group structure, do not improve the overlapping similarity of 0.405 but rather degrade the quality of FolkRank. We assume that the approach of propagating tags without modeling the group dimension within the graph, which serves as input for the ranking algorithm, primarily increases the recall but has a negative effect on the precision.

Regarding the KSim, strategy (iii), which treats groups as tags, performs best, followed by strategies (i), (ii), and (iv). The quality of the strategies (i)–(iv) is, in view of KSim, more than 30% better than the quality of strategies (v)–(ix).

Figure 2.14 gives an idea about how the ranking strategies behave when varying the dampen factor for tag propagation. Naturally, the dampen factor does not effect strategies "A – Traditional Tag Assignments" and "B – Groups as Tags" because both strategies do not make use of tag propagation. When varying the dampen factor, the OSim value is comparatively constant as well as for the strategies that base on propagation of group tags. The OSim and KSim of strategy "C + Full Tag Propagation" continuously degrades when the dampen factor increases. Gazing at the idea of "Full Tag Propagation" illustrates this behavior: Assume there is a resource r in a group g, which contains 20 other resources, and r is the only resource, which is tagged with t. Then, propagation of t to g and all resources of g with a dampen factor of 1.0 would conceal the prominent role of resource r in terms of tag t. Hence, ranking the resources of g in an adequate order gets difficult (see KSim value), and the increased recall complicates the process of identifying resources to put into the top k of the ranking for tag t.

Table 2.3 outlines example rankings computed for the tag *"socialpagerank"* by different ranking strategies. Furthermore, it lists the corresponding hand-selected ranking, which is based on votings of five experts. Within the GroupMe! data set the resource *"Optimizing web search using social annotations,"* a paper which proposes the SocialPageRank algorithm, was the only resource tagged with the keyword "socialpagerank." This resource was ranked at first place in the hand-selected ranking, and almost every ranking strategy conforms to this decision. Starting from the second position the ranking of strategy "A," which represents the traditional FolkRank algorithm, gets imprecise. As strategy "A – Traditional Tag Assignments" does not exploit the group structure, the only solution to discover other relevant resources rests upon the users, who annotated the resource, and other tags that have been assigned to the resource. The group-based ranking strategies, on the other hand, are able to detect adequate resources via the group containing the resource. In the given example, this group is *"Webpage Ranking"* and strategy "B – Groups as Tags" is the only strategy that lists the group also within the top ten.

2.4.3.3 Results

The goal of our investigation was to identify whether grouping of resources in folksonomies has an impact on the quality of search strategies in social networks. To give proof on our hypothesis that grouping improves the quality of search, it is necessary to compare the search strategies that explore the grouping context to those search strategies which do not. As benchmark, we have chosen the FolkRank algorithm and have developed search algorithms that extend FolkRank to exploit the group context as described in Sect. 2.4.1. All algorithms, FolkRank as well as the group-aware extensions, were tested under the same conditions, i.e., the same set of data, hardware, etc.

We tested our hypothesis with a one-tailed t-test. The null hypothesis H_0 is that some group-aware FolkRank extension is as good as a the normal FolkRank without group- awareness, and tested it with a significance level of $\alpha = 0.05$. Tests were performed for the two measures OSim and KSim (see Sect. 2.4.3):

OSim. With respect to OSim, the strategy "B – Groups as Tags" is significantly better than normal FolkRank.

Furthermore, FolkRank did not improve if we applied any of the tag-propagation strategies described in Sect. 2.4.2, and, indeed, the strategy "B – Groups as Tags" was significantly better than normal FolkRank with or without tag propagation. The variations of "B – Groups as Tags" to reflect tag propagation were, one compared to the other, not significantly different, but only the propagation of group tags showed significant improvement in comparison to FolkRank (with or without tag propagation).

Also the strategy "C – Group Context-based Tags," where full propagation of tags was performed (damping factor 0.2), was significantly better than the normal FolkRank regardless of whether any propagation of tags was performed in the latter. From our test data, we hypothesize that strategy "C" benefits from the propagation of tags while "B" does not. Our actual data did not give statistically significant results on this, and we will investigate the impact on tag propagation in our future work.

KSim. With respect to KSim, the strategy "B – Groups as Tags" is significantly better than normal FolkRank, whether or not the latter uses any tag propagation strategy.

Also the strategy "C – Group Context-Based Tags," where group tags are propagated (damping factor 0.2) is significantly better than normal FolkRank, whether or not the latter uses any tag propagation strategy.

OSim and KSim. Only the strategy "B – Groups as Tags" (without tag propagation or with group tag propagation, damping factor 0.2) was significantly better with respect to both measures, OSim and KSim, than normal FolkRank (whether or not the latter uses any tag propagation strategy).

Our evaluation indicated that the grouping of resources significantly improves the quality of search in folksonomies. The grouping activity itself brings many advantages for users: they can organize resources of interest, they can overlook and inspect a group's content, they can share groups with fellow users, and can explore the information in a folksonomy in novel ways, e.g., by requesting new, artificial groups that collect contents of all groups for the same topic, that collect the most popular groups or resource, etc. Furthermore, the drag & drop metaphor realized in the GroupMe! system makes the grouping activity intuitive for users, and from our experience with running GroupMe! we have seen that users like grouping [13]. Thus, while grouping is an easy and well-received feature for folksonomies, this activity provides, on the technical side, valuable information to detect relevant resources, and to improve the quality of search, and seems to be a very promising approach to improve current folksonomy systems.

2.5 Related Work

With the advent of Web 2.0 and its new design patterns, which are proposed in [15], social tagging systems like del.icio.us,[15] Flickr,[16] or Last.fm[17] became quite successful. In [4], the authors developed a *tagging system design taxonomy*, which allows to characterize such tagging systems regarding different dimensions. Table 2.4 summarizes characteristics of GroupMe! according to the this design taxonomy and compares them with three related tagging systems: (1) BibSonomy [9] is a social

Table 2.4 GroupMe! tagging design in comparison to other social tagging systems. And user incentives for tagging

Dimension/system	GroupMe!	BibSonomy	del.icio.us	Flickr
Tagging rights	Free-for-all	Free-for-all	Free-for-all	Permission-based
Tagging support	Blind/viewable	Suggested	Suggested	viewable
Aggregation model	Bag	Bag	Bag	Set
Object type	Multimedia	Textual	Textual	Images
Source of material	Global	Global	Global	User-contributed
Social connectivity	Links	Links, Groups	Links	Links
Resource connectivity	Groups	None	None	Groups
User incentives	future retrieval contribution sharing attract attention self presentation	future retrieval contribution sharing	future retrieval contribution sharing attract attention	future retrieval contribution sharing attract attention self presentation

bookmarking and publication sharing platform, (2) del.icio.us is currently the most used social bookmarking platform, and (3) Flickr is a platform, which enables users to upload and share photos. GroupMe! system characteristics and differences to the three other systems are described as follows.

Tagging rights. GroupMe! allows every user to tag everything (*free-for-all*) as this enables us to gather more tags about a resource and also a higher variety of keywords than in constrainted systems such as Flickr, which restricts tagging, e.g., to the resource owner, or her friends.

Tagging support. In the GroupMe! system users always annotate resources within the context of a group. During the tagging process they are not supported with tag suggestions. However, users have the ability to gaze at tags that have already been assigned to resources in context of the actual group. Tags that have been assigned in context of other groups are not visible to the user when tagging as those tags are possibly not adequate to the actual group context. Regarding tagging support GroupMe! allows for both, *blind* and *viewable* tagging. BibSonomy, del.icio.us, and other systems provide tag suggestions to the users, which makes tagging easier for users, but limits, in our opinion, the variety of tags that are assigned to resources.

---

[15] http://del.icio.us

[16] http://flickr.com

[17] http://last.fm

Aggregation model.   In comparison to Flickr, which does not allow for duplicated tags (*set*), GroupMe! allows different users to assign the same tag to a certain resource (*bag*). The aggregation model has a strong impact on the structure of the evolving folksonomy [5], which is, in simple terms, a collection of tag assignments. In [6], Vander Wal differentiates between *narrow* folksonomies, which evolve in tagging systems such as Flickr, and *broad* folksonomies, which arise in systems such as del.icio.us or GroupMe!. Moreover, the structure of a folksonomy influences the choice of appropriate search and ranking strategies. In this article we presented ranking strategies that are optimized for broad folksonomies.

Object type.   GroupMe! is the only system listed in Table 2.4 that supports tagging of resources displayed in a multimedia fashion. Although systems such as del.icio.us enable users to bookmark and tag arbitrary Web resources, they just visualize resources in a textual way. Hence, while tagging, e.g., a video in del.icio.us, users are not able to watch the video they tag within the del.icio.us system, but have to visit the corresponding Web site. *CombinFormation* [16] – a system which also allows (re)organizing Web content – provides similar functionality regarding visualization of resources, however, neither provides tagging functionality nor makes use of the new structures to provide enhanced search and browsing functionalities.

Source of material.   Resources that can be annotated and grouped in GroupMe! are globally distributed over the Web and referenced by their URL. This enables GroupMe! to handle often-changing resources such as RSS feeds appropriately: Whenever a group is accessed, the most recent versions of the contained resources are displayed. From the perspective of *source of material* GroupMe! rather adheres to the idea of social bookmarking than to systems such as Flickr or YouTube, which enable users to upload and publish own content.

Social connectivity.   All systems listed in Table 2.4 allow users to be linked together. GroupMe! does not provide integrated features, but utilizes users' FOAF descriptions in order to identify links between users.

Resource connectivity.   Independent of the users' tags, a few resource sharing systems provide other features to connect resources. There are some systems that allow users to organize themselves into groups and that provide functionality to retrieve resources, which are related to these groups – e.g., BibSonomy or Connotea.[18] Furthermore, del.icio.us allows users to connect tags by building so-called *tag bundles*. However, to the best of our knowledge, Flickr and GroupMe! are at the moment the only notable tagging systems that enable users to assign resources to groups explicitly. GroupMe! groups differ from Flickr groups in two relevant aspects: (1) Flickr groups are simple sets of images unlike GroupMe! groups, which capture arbitrary Web resources of interest and can be fashioned by the users (resources can be resized and arranged), and (2) GroupMe! supports, in contrast to Flickr, tagging of groups.

---

[18] http://www.connotea.org

User incentives.   GroupMe! users have several motivations to annotate resource ranging from simplification of future retrieval to self-presentation (e.g., some users tag resources with *holiday* in order to express which locations they have visited).

Folksonomies represent the database of tagging systems. They evolve, according to [17], like *desire lines* over time. Visualizing such temporal formation is discussed in [18] and demonstrated with *Yahoo! TagLines*.[19] A basic formal folksonomy model is presented in [7, 8, 19]. In [10], Wu et al. extend this model with a time dimension. The GroupMe! folksonomy extends the folksonomy model defined in [9] by adding a group context to tag assignments (see Sect. 2.3). Therewith, new relations between resources, groups, and tags emerge that can be exploited by search and ranking algorithms as we show in this article. Search and ranking algorithms that operate on traditional folksonomies have already been successfully applied in order to improve Web search. In [20], the authors introduce *SocialSimRank*, which adapts *SimRank* [21] and computes similarity between tags and resources, respectively. Furthermore, Bao et al. presented the *SocialPageRank* algorithm, which ranks Web resources according to how popular they are annotated. *FolkRank* [2] is another folksonomy-based search algorithm, which adapts the well-known *PageRank* [12] algorithm and involves user preferences. In this article we described how FolkRank can be applied to GroupMe! folksonomies in order to improve the quality of rankings.

Learning relations between tags is another challenge in social tagging systems that can be utilized to improve retrieval of resources additionally. Hotho et al. presented an approach to mine association rules in folksonomies that point to *subtag–supertag* relations [22]. The GroupMe! folksonomy model provides a foundation to deduce such relations more precisely, e.g., by analyzing tags that have been assigned to a group and tags assigned to the group members. In [23], the authors investigated how to learn more concrete semantics from folksonomies. In particular, they presented an approach to distinguish between *event tags* and *place tags*. Such approaches for learning semantics can also be applied to GroupMe!.

In addition to analysis of emerging semantics, GroupMe! also focuses on explicit combination of Web 2.0 and Semantic Web technologies. Instead of proposing that the Semantic Web, as envisioned by Berners-Lee et al. in [24] and specified by the W3C Semantic Web Activity,[20], is *dead* as provocatively stated by Naaman during a panel discussion at WWW '07 [25]) we follow [26] and believe that bringing both technologies together will originate the future Web. Therefore, the GroupMe! system is implemented as an RDF aggregator and generator, and provides, in addition to RDF and RSS feeds, RESTful interfaces and corresponding client APIs to access these RDF data. In this way, GroupMe! conforms to the *Linked Data* principles outlined in [27]. Most of the other systems such as *CiteULike*[21] or *BibSonomy* just offer RSS export, or deliver data via APIs using application-specific vocabularies to

---

[19] http://research.yahoo.com/taglines

[20] http://www.w3.org/2001/sw/

[21] http://www.citeulike.org

describe data. For example, Flickr provides interfaces to access their data corpus, which return XML- or JSON-formatted data using a Flickr-specific vocabulary instead of referring to well-defined ontologies such as *Friend-of-a-friend* vocabulary [28], e.g., they use "photo" instead of "foaf:Image".

Semantic Wikis [29] and Semantic Blogs [30] prevent lack of semantically well-defined content as they oblige users to link content with ontology concepts. With GroupMe! we do not want to burden the user with knowledge engineering tasks and thus do not foresee such functionality at the moment, but rather plan to make use of ontology learning strategies as proposed in [31]. In [10], Wu et al. present a probabilistic approach to derive semantics from tags assignments, i.e., they determine the conditional probability that a tag refers to a concept (*conceptual space*), where the user, who utilized a tag, represents the pre-condition.

Tagging systems furthermore provide a convenient base for user modeling and personalization functionalities by utilizing tag-based user profiles. In [32], the authors propose an algorithm to learn such user profiles and in [33] they show how to adapt tag-based user profiles over time. The benefit of tag-based user profiles is demonstrated by Firan et al. in [34], where they show that tag-based profiles outperform track-based profiles in order to recommend music tracks to a user. Similar strategies can be exploited by the GroupMe! system in order to recommend content within the GroupMe! system. In this article we present ranking strategies, which can be applied in order to personalize content.

2.6 Conclusions and Future Work

We presented GroupMe!, a social bookmarking and tagging system combining Semantic Web and Web 2.0 techniques. We outlined the innovative character of GroupMe!, characterized by a novel drag & drop based user interface, support for arbitrary multimedia resources, and the feature of grouping resources. We have shown how Web 2.0 systems such as GroupMe! can utilize different data sources (by means of RDF Metadata extractors or RDF search engines) to enrich the resources of the system's data corpus with additional RDF descriptions. We also described our API, which enables other applications to make use of the GroupMe! data. Regarding system usage, our evaluations approved that users appreciate both, the grouping functionality and the comfortable integration of multimedia resources.

We extended the classical folksonomy, containing *users*, *resources*, and *tags* by the *group* context. Based on this extended folksonomy, we proposed different strategies as to how the folksonomy ranking algorithm FolkRank can be extended to take the group context into account in order to improve the search performance in group-aware folksonomies. Our evaluations have shown that the ranking algorithms taking the group context into account perform significantly better than the classical FolkRank algorithm.

In the future, we plan to exploit the group structure of the GroupMe! system in different directions: First, we want to simplify the creation process of a group.

Therefore, we engage link prediction algorithms and recommender systems to automatically group resources that are relevant to a user and are related to a specific topic according to their former group membership. Afterwards users can extend and/or modify this group, which can be interpreted as feedback regarding the quality of the recommendations.

Second, the visualization capabilities of GroupMe! will be extended. We consider on one hand *zoomable interfaces*[22] where a large content can be visualized in different degrees of detail. On a global view, clusters of groups with similar topics can be displayed, enabling users to zoom into a more detailed level visualizing groups. When a user zooms into the group the contained resources and groups become visible. Such a zoomable interface enables users to see the content of the whole GroupMe! system at a glance while the content of any resource is accessible in a few zoom operations. On the other hand, we investigate automatic arrangement techniques for groups. For example, algorithms can be implemented that take usage statistics into account to emphasize important resources in a group by resizing them or rearranging them.

The third direction of extending the GroupMe! system aims on embedding the GroupMe! system into the Web 2.0 sphere. While first steps have already been taken by automatically searching and extracting RDF metadata for GroupMe! resources and providing an API that gives the GroupMe! data back to the Web 2.0 community, we think of techniques that actively push data into the Web 2.0 sphere. Therefore, we plan to improve the integration of services such as del.icio.us, Flickr, CiteULike, or Bibsonomy. For example, when annotating Web resources within the GroupMe! system, we want to give users, who have a del.icio.us account, the opportunity to decide whether their tag assignments should also be propagated to del.icio.us, and vice versa. To set a good role model, we currently extend the GroupMe! system with additional semantically described interfaces, which allow for both, querying and adding/updating GroupMe! data. The RDF (Meta) search engine, described in Sect. 2.2.1, is, for instance, accessible as Semantic Web Service by making use of OWL-S and REST principles.

Enhancing Web 2.0 systems with Semantic Web technologies is, in our opinion, an adequate strategy to realize the visions associated with the Semantic Web, e.g., most Web 2.0 systems make their services available via API so that describing these interfaces semantically would be feasible. GroupMe! demonstrates the benefits of combining Web 2.0 and Semantic Web technologies. GroupMe! brings Web 2.0 and Semantic Web technologies together and reveals the benefits of combining both techniques. It aggregates semantic descriptions about resources, captures the semantics of user interactions, and illustrates how semantic relations between resources, gained by the group context, improve search and ranking strategies.

Acknowledgements We thank Nicole Ullmann, Mischa Frank, Daniel Plappert, Patrick Siehndel, and Zhivko Asenov for their contribution and engagement in realizing the GroupMe! system.

---

[22] http://www.zoomorama.com

References

1. Abel, F., Frank, M., Henze, N., Krause, D., Plappert, D., Siehndel, P.: GroupMe! – Where Semantic Web meets Web 2.0. In: Int. Semantic Web Conference (ISWC 2007) (November 2007)
2. Hotho, A., Jäschke, R., Schmitz, C., Stumme, G.: FolkRank: A ranking algorithm for folksonomies. In: Proc. of Workshop on Information Retrieval 2006 of the Special Interest Group Information Retrieval (FGIR 2006), Hildesheim, Germany (October 2006)
3. Fielding, R.T., Taylor, R.N.: Principled design of the modern web architecture. In: Proc. of the 22nd Int. Conf. on Software Engineering (ICSE '00), New York, NY, USA, ACM Press (2000) 407–416
4. Marlow, C., Naaman, M., Boyd, D., Davis, M.: HT06, tagging paper, taxonomy, flickr, academic article, to read. In: Proc. of the 17th Conf. on Hypertext and Hypermedia (HYPERTEXT '06), New York, NY, USA, ACM Press (2006) 31–40
5. Vander Wal, T.: Folksonomy. http://vanderwal.net/folksonomy.html (July 2007)
6. Vander Wal, T.: Explaining and showing broad and narrow folksonomies. http://www.personalinfocloud.com/2005/02/explaining_and_.html (February 2005)
7. Halpin, H., Robu, V., Shepherd, H.: The complex dynamics of collaborative tagging. In: Proc. of 16th Int. World Wide Web Conference (WWW '07), New York, NY, USA, ACM Press (2007) 211–220
8. Mika, P.: Ontologies are us: A unified model of social networks and semantics. In: Proc. Int. Semantic Web Conference (ISWC 2005). (November 2005) 522–536
9. Hotho, A., Jäschke, R., Schmitz, C., Stumme, G.: BibSonomy: A social bookmark and publication sharing system. In : de Moor, A., Polovina, S., Delugach, H., eds.: Proc. First Conceptual Structures Tool Interoperability Workshop, Aalborg (2006) 87–102
10. Wu, X., Zhang, L., Yu, Y.: Exploring social annotations for the Semantic Web. In: Proc. of 15th Int. World Wide Web Conference (WWW '06), New York, NY, USA, ACM Press (2006) 417–426
11. Brickley, D., Miles, A.: SKOS Core Vocabulary Specification. W3C working draft, W3C (November 2005) http://www.w3.org/TR/swbp-skos-core-spec
12. Page, L., Brin, S., Motwani, R., Winograd, T.: The PageRank citation ranking: Bringing Order to the Web. Technical report, Stanford Digital Library Technologies Project (1998)
13. Abel, F., Henze, N., Krause, D.: A Novel Approach to Social Tagging: GroupMe! In: 4th Int. Conf. on Web Information Systems and Technologies (WEBIST). (May 2008)
14. Haveliwala, T.H.: Topic-sensitive PageRank: A context-sensitive ranking algorithm for Web search. IEEE Transactions on Knowledge and Data Engineering 15(4) (2003) 784–796
15. O'Reily, T.: What is web 2.0? – design patterns and business models for the next generation of software (September 2005)
16. Kerne, A., Koh, E., Dworaczyk, B., Mistrot, J.M., Choi, H., Smith, S.M., Graeber, R., Caruso, D., Webb, A., Hill, R., Albea, J.: combinFormation: A mixed-initiative system for representing collections as compositions of image and text surrogates. In: Proc. of the ACM/IEEE Joint Conference on Digital Libraries (JCDL 2006), Chapel Hill, NC, USA, ACM Press (June 2006) 11–20
17. Merholz, P.: Metadata for the masses. Adaptive Path (October 2004)
18. Dubinko, M., Kumar, R., Magnani, J., Novak, J., Raghavan, P., Tomkins, A.: Visualizing tags over time. In: Proc. of 15th Int. World Wide Web Conference (WWW '06), New York, NY, USA, ACM Press (2006) 193–202
19. Marlow, C., Naaman, M., Boyd, D., Davis, M.: Position Paper, Tagging, Taxonomy, Flickr, Article, ToRead. In: Collaborative Web Tagging Workshop at WWW '06. (May 2006)
20. Bao, S., Xue, G., Wu, X., Yu, Y., Fei, B., Su, Z.: Optimizing Web search using social annotations. In: Proc. of 16th Int. World Wide Web Conference (WWW '07), New York, NY, USA, ACM Press (2007) 501–510
21. Jeh, G., Widom, J.: SimRank: A measure of structural-context similarity. In: Proc. of Int. Conf. on Knowledge Discovery and Data Mining (SIGKDD), Edmonton, Alberta, Canada, ACM Press (July 2002)

22. Hotho, A., Jäschke, R., Schmitz, C., Stumme, G.: Emergent Semantics in BibSonomy. In Hochberger, C., Liskowsky, R., eds.: Informatik 2006: Informatik für Menschen. Volume 94(2) of LNI., Bonn, GI (October 2006)
23. Rattenbury, T., Good, N., Naaman, M.: Towards automatic extraction of event and place semantics from flickr tags. In: Proc. of the 30th Int. ACM SIGIR Conf. on Information Retrieval (SIRIR '07), New York, NY, USA, ACM Press (2007) 103–110
24. Berners-Lee, T., Hendler, J., Lassila, O.: The Semantic Web. Scientific American **284**(5) (2001) 34–43
25. Naaman, M.: The Semantic Web is dead. In: Panel Discussion: The Role of Multimedia Metadata Standards in a (Semantic) Web 3.0, 16th Int. World Wide Web Conference (WWW '07). (May 2007)
26. Ankolekar, A., Krötzsch, M., Tran, T., Vrandecic, D.: The two cultures: Mashing up Web 2.0 and the Semantic Web. In: Proc. of 16th Int. World Wide Web Conference (WWW '07), New York, NY, USA, ACM Press (2007) 825–834
27. Berners-Lee, T.: Linked Data – design issues. Technical report, W3C (May 2007) http://www.w3.org/DesignIssues/LinkedData.html
28. Brickley, D., Miller, L.: FOAF Vocabulary Specification 0.91. Namespace document, FOAF Project (November 2007) http://xmlns.com/foaf/0.1/
29. Oren, E., Völkel, M., Breslin, J.G., Decker, S.: Semantic Wikis for personal knowledge management. In: Bressan, S., Küng, J., Wagner, R., eds.: Proc. of the 17th Int. Conf. on Database and Expert Systems Applications (DEXA 2006). Volume 4080 of LNCS., Kraków, Poland, Springer (September 2006) 509–518
30. Cayzer, S.: Semantic blogging and decentralized knowledge management. Commun. ACM **47**(12) (December 2004) 47–52
31. Cimiano, P., Pivk, A., Schmidt-Thieme, L., Staab, S.: Learning taxonomic relations from heterogeneous sources of evidence. In: Ontology Learning from Text: Methods, Evaluation and Applications. Frontiers in AI. IOS Press (2005) 59–73
32. Michlmayr, E., Cayzer, S.: Learning user profiles from tagging data and leveraging them for personal(ized) information access. In: Proc. of the Workshop on Tagging and Metadata for Social Information Organization, 16th Int. World Wide Web Conference (WWW '07). (May 2007)
33. Michlmayr, E., Cayzer, S., Shabajee, P.: Add-A-Tag: Learning Adaptive user profiles from bookmark collections. In: Proc. of the 1st Int. Conf. on Weblogs and Social Media (ICWSM '06). (March 2007)
34. Firan, C.S., Nejdl, W., Paiu, R.: The benefit of using tag-based profiles. In: Proc. of the 2007 Latin American Web Conference (LA-WEB 2007), Washington, DC, USA, IEEE Computer Society (2007) 32–41

Section 2: Adaptability and User Interfaces

Chapter 3
Adaptation and Recommendation Techniques to Improve the Quality of Annotations and the Relevance of Resources in Web 2.0 and Semantic Web-Based Applications

Ilaria Torre

3.1 Introduction

Web 2.0 and Semantic Web technologies are variously considered to be alternative, complementary, or partially overlapping [28,37,53,55]. However, it seems that there is a general convergence in stating that the Web 2.0 and the Semantic Web (SW, in the following), in different ways, *make the Web more semantic*, but have also *peculiarities* that make them useful in *different contexts*. The Web 2.0[1] provides tools for sharing metadata-enriched data and mainly focuses on collaboration, participation, and social networks. The SW[2] provides tools for sharing metadata-enriched data as well, but it specifically focuses on data exchange and integration, interoperability, and reasoning. Considering the area of intersection between them, that is annotating and sharing resources, in the first case, shared data are enriched with informal metadata, typically related to *folksonomies* [28, 37, 39, 66], while, in the second case, data are enriched with formally defined metadata linked to shared *ontologies* [2, 9, 11, 53].

Given this common feature, an interesting question regarding the possibility to combine Web 2.0 and SW technologies in order to improve the quality of metadata-enriched data. The ideal objective would be to minimize their weaknesses and take the greatest possible advantage of both. The main advantages of the Web 2.0 concern the distributed annotation of resources and their multifaceted representation, while

Ilaria Torre
Department of Computer Sciences, University of Torino, Corso Svizzera 185, 10149 Torino, Italy.
e-mail: ilaria.torre@di.unito.it

[1] Tim O'Reilly, an Open Source movement supporter and father of the O'Reilly Media company, first used the term Web 2.0 in 2004. Then he defined this paradigm more precisely in the famous paper "What Is Web 2.0. Design Patterns and Business Model for the Next generation of Software" [44].

[2] The vision of the SW was first sketched by the W3C director, Tim Berners-Lee, in 1998 [9,10,12].

V. Devedžić and D. Gašević (eds.), *Web 2.0 & Semantic Web*, Annals of Information Systems 6, DOI 10.1007/978-1-4419-1219-0_3,
© Springer Science+Business Media, LLC 2010

the main advantages of the SW concern the unambiguous classification of resources using flexible and standard languages for knowledge modeling.

Several works deal with the issue of integrating these two approaches. Gruber [30], for example, analyzes the contribution of SW technologies applied to resources in the Social Web. Mika [40] takes into account the social context in defining and representing ontologies. Specia and Motta [59] try the approach of ontology learning from folksonomies, and so on.

In this paper we analyze this issue from a specific point of view, which is the contribution of recommendation and adaptation techniques to it. The Web 2.0 and the SW slightly include the idea of personalization in their core principles already. In Web 2.0, annotating resources is, in many cases [38,40], a way to improve content organization and retrieval on the basis of the user personal classification criteria and a way for browsing contents following personal tag-based navigation paths. The social aspect of Web 2.0 systems is often a side effect of actions carried out from people to satisfy personal needs [38]. Tagging systems can even be considered as specific kinds of recommenders. A social bookmarking system, for example, can be seen as a recommender in which the selection and suggestion of URLs is not carried out by the system, but by the users: the users select the resources to bookmark and to tag while the popularity of bookmarks (given by the number of users who saved the same bookmark) and tags (given by the occurrence of tags) works as a recommender for other users. The SW is connected to the idea of personalization too. The vision of a Web where contents are machine-processable, easily integrated, and easy to retrieve, at the right time and in the right way [53], clearly demonstrates a connection with the principles of adaptation and personalization.

The idea in this paper is that strengthening this intrinsic "vocation" for personalization can be good for both the Web 2.0 and the SW and also for their integration. More in detail, the idea is that deploying specific *adaptation and recommendation techniques* can *improve* the *quality of annotations* and the *relevance of annotated resources in Web 2.0 and SW-based applications*. Several works in the literature try to combine these methodologies. By analyzing some of these works, we want to investigate the added value that may come from recommendation techniques to the aforementioned issues. Clearly, it is not a one-way relationship: beyond all doubt, contributions are provided by Web 2.0 and SW technologies to adaptive systems too, as we showed in [64]. However, in this paper, we try to highlight the specific contributions from recommendation technologies to "semantic" technologies. To this aim, we will only take into account systems where the component in charge of the personalization is an added one and not a basic one.

The paper is structured as follows: Section 3.2 sketches the adaptation and recommendation techniques that will be considered in the analysis; Section 3.3 discusses the contribution of recommendation techniques to improve the annotations' quality in Web 2.0 (Sect. 3.3.1), Semantic Web (Sect. 3.3.2), and mixed approaches (Sect. 3.3.3). Section 3.4 discusses the contribution of adaptation and recommendation techniques to improve the relevance of retrieved resources in Web 2.0 (Sect. 3.4.1), Semantic Web (Sect. 3.4.2), and mixed approaches (Sect. 3.4.3). Finally Sect. 3.5 concludes the paper.

3.2 Adaptation and Recommendation Techniques

Adapting and personalizing resources to users' needs and preferences is becoming a common approach in Web sites but also in many other common-use applications. On the Web, consider, for example, that almost all vertical or horizontal portals[3] allow users to customize the layout of pages, personalize the pieces of information to see, and be alerted about interesting news to receive. Moreover, consider the diffusion of recommender systems, which provide personalized suggestion about items to see, to buy, to download, etc. and also the growing availability of personal guides and assistants that help users in tasks of configuration, shopping, and so on. Outside the Web, the possibility to personalize applications is growing in importance as well. Consider, for example, customizable services for handheld devices, Electronic Programming Guides for television, personalized ovens, and washing machines where personalization is carried out on the basis of the user preferences, etc.

From a technical point of view, *adaptation* and *personalization techniques* are used by adaptive systems to dynamically modify the contents to be presented to the users, the layout, and structure of navigation in order to fit the preferences, interests, and needs of the current user, stored in a user model [15]. To achieve this goal, adaptive systems employ different techniques "which can be characterized by a specific kind of knowledge representation and by a specific adaptation algorithm" [15]. Several models exist to define components and tasks of adaptive hypermedia systems, such as the Munich Reference Model [34], AHAM [22], and LAOS [21], a derivation from AHAM. All of them base the adaptation process upon a user model (which can be complemented by a context model). This user model (or user profile) is usually learned by the system by observing the user behavior (what she reads, bookmarks, prints, shops, etc.) and combining these data with other data it collects from the user herself or from other systems. Then, personalization algorithms use this model to personalize the interaction in different ways, for example, filtering the results of a query according to the user interests, tailoring the information's level of detail on the basis of the user knowledge, modifying the layout of a page on the basis of the current device and context, etc. Many adaptation techniques borrow algorithms and concepts from AI and machine learning. A comprehensive presentation of methods and techniques for user modeling and adaptation can be found in [17].

Recommendation techniques can be considered either as a set of techniques included into adaptation techniques or as a set of techniques that intersect adaptation techniques. According to the first point of view, they are a specific kind of adaptation techniques concerning the adaptation of contents to different users. Typically they produce the adaptive sorting of content items on the basis of their relevance to the user. Considering the second point of view, recommendation techniques are

---

[3] A vertical portal is a Web site focused on a relatively narrow range of goods and services, whereas a horizontal portal is a Web site that serves as an entry point to a range of content across several verticals such as news, e-mail, weather, travel, etc.

all the approaches that provide suggestions, taking or not taking into account a user model. A simple example is provided by link sorting based on resources' popularity.

In our analysis, we will take into account systems that use recommendations according to both the points of view, even if we are more interested in showing the contribution of the first one. Depending on the approach they follow, these techniques are typically defined as content-based, collaboration-based, or hybrid. Basically, the former are techniques to recommend an item by comparing the description of the item with a profile of the user's interests [45], and the latter are techniques to recommend an item by calculating similarities between users, without analyzing the items' content [52]. Items to recommend can be of different type. Typically, they can be *resource items*, such as movies, news articles, etc., or *tags*, that is terms suggested to annotate resources. Section 3.4 will deal with the former type of items, while Sect. 3.3 will deal with the latter.

Considering content-based recommendation, items are usually described by a set of features, which can be obtained in different ways. For example, they can be features mapped on a taxonomy at the design time, or features extracted by analyzing the content of the item. In this second case, a common formula to represent textual items is TF*IDF (Term Frequency Inverse Document Frequency) [49]. It represents textual items as vectors of terms and weights them by calculating their frequency in the current document and, basically, the inverse of their frequency in the corpus of documents. The vector space model can be used to represent the user profile as well, and thus similarity measures between vectors can be used, such as the Cosine Similarity. Collaborative filtering, on the contrary, infers the user interest for items on the basis of what similar users are interested in. Often, it is based on users' rating of items. Other times, users' interest in items is inferred by observing their behavior, such as by analyzing the items they purchase.

The next sections will describe how recommendation techniques, including but not limited to the ones we mentioned above as examples, have been exploited, and sometimes readapted, to improve (1) the *quality of annotations* (Sect. 3.3) and subsequently (2) the *relevance of annotation-enriched resources to users* in Web 2.0, Semantic Web, and mixed approaches (Sect. 3.4).

3.3 Annotations' Quality

Considering the issue of improving the quality of annotations, our work started from analyzing advantages and weaknesses of both the Web 2.0 and the SW. Macgregor and McCulloch [37] provide a useful review about that, reporting different researchers' theories. It emerged that plus points can often be considered as drawbacks and vice versa. Just some examples: Shirky [55] states that multifaceted annotations, in Web 2.0 tagging systems, allow to achieve true and more complete representation of knowledge than in taxonomies. However, multifaceted annotations are not expressive enough to represent the kind of relationships between tags and resources. On the contrary, relations between concepts in SW taxonomies are not ambiguous, but have the drawback that they may not represent the mental model of end users.

Mathes [39] and Quintarelli [47] discuss the availability of many entry points in the Web 2.0, showing their advantage in terms of improved chances of search and serendipity. However, this feature can also be considered a cause of entropy, considering, in addition, the frequent number of erroneous tags, compound words, and the problem of polysemy (in Flickr, 40% of tags are erroneous, 28% in del.icio.us [31]). Nevertheless, despite these problems, as illustrated by Golder and Huberman, it is possible that a stable tagging pattern emerges from the chaos of tags applied to resources [28]. Considering the SW, the emphasized possibility to exchange and integrate data is limited by the problem of ontology alignment and matching. Another problem is related to the well-known usability–reusability tradeoff [13], which says that, if concepts are very abstract and general, they will be hardly used in real contexts while, if they are very specific, the reusability is limited. A further ambivalent issue is the subjectivity of the designer: pros and cons of a single point of view (the point of view of the designer) are complementary to pros and cons of many points of view in Web 2.0 systems. Probably, the unique nondisputed issue is that the precision and "unambiguity" offered by the SW has the heavy drawback of cost and difficulty of development.

To analyze how recommendation techniques can improve the quality of annotations, we elaborated a list of criteria, based upon the analysis of advantages and weaknesses mentioned above. Especially, we considered weaknesses, taking them into account as *criteria to improve annotations* in the two approaches.

Given our perspective of analysis, these criteria to improve Web 2.0 and Semantic Web annotations do not address all the weaknesses, but only the weaknesses that can be faced by exploiting recommendation techniques.

The decision to provide a single list of criteria, instead of different lists for Web 2.0 and SW-based applications, comes from the considerations above about advantages and weaknesses, which, as seen, are often complementary in the two approaches. However, since recommendation techniques (see Sect. 3.2) concern techniques that are especially useful when many different users interact with the application, the set of criteria we considered necessarily fits better collaboration-based approaches to annotation building than designer-based ones. That is, it fits (1) Web-2.0 approaches, (2) SW approaches that use collaborative building of ontologies, and (3) mixed approaches, the ultimate objective of our analysis.

The list of criteria we identified to improve annotations is reported in Table 3.1. The first column defines each criterion,[4] while the second column describes the possible contribution of recommendation techniques to address the issues in column 1. More specifically, column 2 contains examples of techniques to satisfy the criteria in column 1, and these criteria are as follows:

(a) Community agreement on annotations: stable patterns of tags
(b) Minimized ambiguity and polysemy: terms with different meanings
(c) Multifaceted annotations: several tags for each resource so as to cover all its facets

---

[4] Notice that Xu et al. in [68] provide a partially similar list of criteria, which however just regards Web 2.0 annotations.

(d) Time-variable annotations: annotations that change, following the dynamics of items' meaning
(e) Facility to recover annotated resources
(f) High coverage of annotated items, in order to avoid sparsity of annotations
(g) Minimized noise, spam, and errors

As it can be seen, some criteria seem to be partially conflicting. This is a direct consequence of the fact that some features can be advantages or weaknesses in different domains and in applications with different objectives. Thus, for example, criterion (a), regarding the objective of achieving, as much as possible, an agreement on annotations among the community's members, seems to contrast criterion (c), regarding the objective of annotating resources from different points of view (facets). In fact, the first criterion aims to achieve a *convergent folksonomy*, or a *relaxed taxonomy*, where each resource is annotated with a limited number of annotations, while the second aims to achieve a whole description of each resource, and consequently, each resource is annotated with many different tags. So, in the first case, the objective is to produce a sort of taxonomy (resources are instances of few classes and synonyms are reduced as much as possible), with the characteristic that the classification is agreed by most of the community's members (differently from taxonomies/ontologies).

Table 3.1 Criteria to improve the quality of annotations by exploiting recommendation techniques

Criteria to improve the quality of annotations	Examples of recommendation techniques to satisfy the criteria in column 1
(a) Community agreement on annotations	Recommendation of popular tags to annotate similar resources, improved by recommending popular synonyms and considering the user's tags preferences
(b) Minimized ambiguity and polysemy	Recommendation of synonyms that do not have other meanings in different context; linking of tags to structured knowledge
(c) *Multifaceted* annotations	Recommendation of variously related tags, aimed to describe resources in the most comprehensive way. The recommended tag can be extracted with document analysis, tags of similar documents, etc.
(d) Time-variable annotations	Recommendation of recent tags in unstable domains, subject to frequent changes. It can be improved by considering the user reputation.
(e) Facility to recover annotated resources	Recommendation of tags the user already used to tag similar pages. The basic idea is to support the user in classifying resources according to her preferences and her organization model.
(f) High coverage of annotated items	Recommendation of tags in order to minimize the effort of annotation, thus allowing more resources to be annotated by many users
(g) Minimized noise, spam, and errors	Recommendation of tags in order to (1) reduce errors, uniform acronyms, and compound words, (2) increase the popularity of good tags with respect to spam tags. It can be improved by considering the user reputation.

The risk of recommendation techniques that address this criterion is the "over-weighting of certain tags that were associated with the resource first, even if they would not have arisen otherwise" [38]. However, this risk can be reduced by addressing criterion (c) suggesting users diverse and more appropriate annotations. Thus, while criteria (a) and (c) seem conflicting, they could be combined so as to obtain a whole description of resources but consistent, not redundant and agreed by most of the community's members.

3.3.1 Contribution of Recommendations to Web 2.0-Based Applications

Most of the instruments of the Web 2.0 paradigm (blogs, wiki, RSS feeds, tagging systems) are based on the addition of annotations to Web resources. Annotations can be added to Web objects such as bookmarks, photos, documents, blog posts, and portlets [42] but also to Web users. Users can indeed provide judgments on the quality of contents provided by other users but also judgments directly on users. They can specify their level of trust in other users, the relationship with other users, and also tag themselves and other users.

Many tagging systems provide some form of tag recommendation on the Web. The most typical form is suggesting popular tags. In the research community, several works started to experiment more elaborate algorithms. In the following we will analyze some of these works, classifying them according to the criteria in Table 3.1. Criteria (g) and (f) concerning the reduction of noise/spam/errors and the achievement of high coverage of annotated items, by reducing the annotation effort, are explicitly or implicitly addressed by all the systems that recommend tags. They are an intrinsic effect of tag recommendation, thus they will not be mentioned in the following description of systems, except when specific measures are adopted to address them.

Mishne [41] describes how adaptation techniques, and in particular techniques for recommendation based on collaborative filtering (see Sect. 3.2), can be applied to the suggestion of tags. With respect to our criteria of analysis, the main objective of recommendation is obtaining a community agreement on annotations (a). AutoTag, the system she presents in [41], is a tool that recommends tags for Web log posts. The author states that the blog posts "take the role of users, and the tags assigned to them function as the products that the users expressed interest in. In traditional recommender systems, similar users are assumed to buy similar products; AutoTag makes the same assumption, and identifies useful tags for a post by examining tags assigned to similar posts." Thus, most popular tags are suggested for most similar posts, increasing the probability that similar posts are annotated in a consistent way. To identify similar posts, she uses Information Retrieval measures based on document indexing. Moreover, as in traditional recommender systems, the recommendations are then further improved by incorporating external knowledge about the bloggers, the posts, or the tags. This feature addresses the issue of providing multifaceted annotations (c).

A similar approach is followed in the Smart Tag Recommender of Basile et al. [6], but with some important differences. As in AutoTag, the Smart Tag Recommender analyzes the new document that has to be annotated in order to find similar documents. However, the former carries out the analysis using Information Retrieval measures while the latter uses also a process of word sense disambiguation based on WordNet. Moreover, and most important with respect to our analysis, in the first case, the suggestion of tags mainly consists in ranking the tags associated to similar documents, while, in the second case, it considers the tagging history of the user, as stored in her user model. The result should be an increased probability for users to recover annotated resources (e). Indeed, as specified in Table 3.1, the underlying idea of this approach is to support the user in classifying resources according to her preferences and her organization model.

Jaschke et al. in [33] propose two algorithms for tag recommendation, and then evaluate them and show that "both provide better results than non-personalized baseline methods." The first algorithm is an adaptation of user-based collaborative filtering, while the second is FolkRank, an adaptation of the PageRank algorithm [14], which is based on the principle that a Web page is important if there are many pages linking to it, and if those pages are important themselves. The criteria they mainly address are (a), (c), and (e). The evaluation results are interesting especially with respect to the last-mentioned criterion, regarding the facility to recover annotated resources. Indeed the evaluation showed that "FolkRank is able to predict – additionally to globally relevant tags – the exact tags of the user which Collaborative Filtering could not." And "this is due to the fact that FolkRank considers [...] also the vocabulary of the user himself, which CF by definition doesn't do."

As a last example we describe the work of Xu et al. [68]. We already mentioned this work, since they identified a set of criteria for reaching a good quality of tags partially similar to our own. These criteria, identified through a study on real users in My Web 2.0, are then used to propose a collaborative tag suggestion algorithm that adopts such criteria to recommend appropriate tags of high quality. This work addresses most of our criteria in Table 3.1: it favors tags that are used by a large number of people with good reputation, trying to minimize the overlap of concepts among the suggested tags (a) and allowing for high coverage of multiple facets. Related to this criterion, it also includes the optional possibility to suggest content-based (and context-based) tags, by simply introducing a virtual user, and assigning her an authority score (c). It manages the problem of spam and noise (g), by using the mechanism of reputation, and addresses the issue of time-variable tags (d), even if by simply favoring more recent tags.

Finally, we just mention some works [e.g., 19, 43] that go further in the direction of tag recommendation, trying to automate the process of resources' annotation. In this way, criteria (f) and (c) are radically addressed, even if the appropriateness of tags can be compromised and annotations may not represent any more the community's view on resources. In [43], this problem is partially faced by making users' tags coexist with automatically generated annotations. Instead, P-TAG [19] follows a different approach and automatically generates personalized tags for Web pages on the basis of the content of the page and of the user's organization of data on her desktop, thus addressing in particular criterion (e).

3.3.2 Contribution of Recommendations to SW-Based Applications

The combination of the SW approach and adaptation techniques dates back to the first years of 2000, and the interest in this area is also demonstrated by the number of workshops that combine these fields of research (see, e.g., the workshops "SW Personalization"/2004/2006 and "Personalization on the SW"/2005).

As previously explained, the possibility to improve the quality of annotations, by exploiting recommendation techniques, mainly fits collaborative building of annotations. Thus, with respect to the SW, it especially fits the *collaborative building of ontologies* and the *collaborative annotation* of resources *on the basis of such ontologies*. It may regard the possibility of using assistive technologies for the process of metadata definition and the opportunity of building personalized ontologies for individuals or communities of users, as described in the work of Haase et al. [32].

The use of assistive technologies [29, 32, 35, 60, 63] addresses, above all, the issues of obtaining high coverage of annotated resources (f) and that one of reaching a community agreement on concepts/relations in the ontology and on annotations (a). It is particularly useful with *open corpora* of resources. As seen before, the community agreement on ontology's concepts and annotations is particularly relevant since it allows to overcome the problem of subjectiveness (the single point of view of the designer), typical in ontologies. As stated by Tempich et al. "ontologies often need to be built in a decentralized way, ontologies must be given to a community in a way such that individuals have partial autonomy over them and ontologies have a life cycle that involves an iteration back and forth between construction/modification and use"[5] [63]. The DILIGENT methodology they propose focus on these features and on that one of *guiding users*, who are not ontology engineering experts. The basic idea of the approach is to allow users to adapt an initial shared ontology according to their needs and then make these adapted ontologies converge on an agreed one. Since the process should be integrated seamlessly in the environment the user works in, they provide some hints about available technology to support each step. The support to users in adapting the ontology so that it reflects their needs is the most interesting feature with respect to our analysis. However, we have to notice that the authors do not mention specific techniques regarding adaptation and recommendation.

More relevant, from this point of view, is the work of Haase et al. [32], which regards the possibility of building personalized ontologies for individuals or communities of users, making use of recommendations provided by the system. In particular, they describe an approach for assisting users in the management

---

[5] This last issue addresses also criterion (d) regarding "time-variable annotations."

and evolution of their personal ontology, by providing suggestions about possible changes to a domain ontology they exploit in their activity. To this aim, they adopt a collaborative filtering algorithm. The objective is to determine the relevance of change operations over the personal ontology, based on the similarity of other users' changes over their ontologies. The final goal is to increase the probability of recovery and retrieval of resources – criterion (e).

3.3.3 Contribution of Recommendations to Combine Web 2.0 and SW Approaches

The most common way to combine Web 2.0 and SW technologies consists in the integration between folksonomies and ontologies. Comparing tags in a folksonomy to RDF triples, it has been observed that a tag in a folksonomy "is typically 2/3 of an RDF triple. The *subject* is known: e.g., the URL for the flickr image being tagged, or the URL being bookmarked in del.icio.us. The *object* is known as well: e.g., http://flickr.com/photos/tags/cats or http://del.icio.us/tag/cats. But the *predicate* to connect them is often missing."[6] Several projects try to fulfill this lack, with different approaches.

There are approaches that try to integrate ontologies' features into folksonomies and others that try to integrate folksonomies' features into ontologies. Flikr,[7] for example, the famous portal to tag and share photos, is developing a project to provide a new feature called "machine-tag" that allows users to be more precise in how they tag, and how they search, their photos. Machine-tags are tags that use a special syntax to define *extra information about a tag*. Very similar but more friendly than RDF, machine-tags have a namespace, a predicate, and a value.[8] What seems to lack is the possibility to easily build RDF Schema. Another example is GroupMe!,[9] described in Chapter 2 of this special issue. A folksonomy-based system that captures the semantics of every user interaction producing RDF tuples. To cover lacking information (see above, a tag in a folksonomy "is typically 2/3 of an RDF triple"), it uses ontologies consistent with the type of resource: FOAF, RSS, or Dublin Core metadata element. GroupMe! lets users tag resources and also allows them to organize resources into groups that can be tagged as well. Thus, the system is able to infer new relations between tags, by exploiting the relations between tags of resources that belong to the same group. This feature and the previous one provide both a semantic enrichment of resources, which evolves naturally while users are interacting with the system and improves the searching capabilities and the possibility of exchanges with other systems.

---

[6] http://www.w3.org/RDF/FAQ

[7] http://www.flickr.com/

[8] http://www.flickr.com/groups/api/discuss/72157594497877875/

[9] http://groupme.org/

On the other hand, as far as the integration of folksonomies into ontologies is concerned, much more projects exist since the typical approach for the combination of the Web 2.0 and the SW is exploiting Web 2.0 techniques for the development and extension of ontologies. The Workshop on Social and Collaborative Construction of Structured Knowledge[10] is a clear example of this approach.

Most of the systems that integrate Web 2.0 and SW technologies, using recommendation techniques, follow this approach. The work of Bateman et al. [8], in the domain of education, proposes a framework, CommonFolks, for integrating social tagging into a natural language ontology (WordNet). The objective is to allow students to easily annotate learning objects with metadata. The framework exploits techniques of recommendation to provide community support during authoring and a method to favor consensus on metadata (notice however that users are not forced to accept the system's suggestions, based on other users' annotations). With respect to criteria in Table 3.1, CommonFolks addresses three main objectives: reaching a community agreement on the ontology concepts and annotations (a), minimizing ambiguity and polysemy (b), and getting high coverage of annotated items, by involving students with creating machine-consumable metadata about learning objects (f). The aim of this approach is to overcome the problem of the lack of meaning in tags, by linking user metadata to structured knowledge, as much as possible. In this way, tags can be used to make inferences and intelligent agents can reason on them.

Van der Sluijs and Houben [65] offer another example of system in which the collaboration of users, supported by a mechanism of tag suggestion, is exploited to obtain ontological metadata. The module in charge of this task, called Matching Component, compares the set of tags a user entered to describe a resource with a set of ontologies or other tags previously accepted in the knowledge base. After this comparison, which uses syntactic and semantic techniques to connect tags to ontologies, the system provides a recommendation for alternative tags to the user. Every suggestion has a certainty factor, which represents the confidence of the system that the suggestion matches the user's original tag. The mechanism of suggestion is also improved by considering the user behavior with respect to the suggestions previously proposed by the system with other tags. Thus, similar to CommonFolks, recommendations are used to address the issues (a), (b), and (f) in Table 3.1. However, different from CommonFolks, the combination of the Web 2.0 and the SW is just aimed at improving the quality of tags and not at mapping tags to a general ontology. The higher quality of tags is a basis for providing improved services such as better search and navigation.

iCITY[11] [18] is a tagging system where tagged resources are the cultural events taking place in the city of Turin. Events are obtained from institutional RSS feeds and are annotated by means of a taxonomy that organizes them on the basis of their genre (event category). Users can tag the events and can post comments, additional information about the events, and new events. The class "events" of the taxonomy has a property (has_tags) that associates the resource to the tags the users inserted.

---

[10] http://km.aifb.uni-karlsruhe.de/ws/ckc2007/

[11] http://www.icity.di.unito.it/dsa/

Similar to CommonFolks and to the Matching Component of Van der Sluijs and Houben, iCITY aims at making tags meaningful and, to achieve this goal, it exploits a controlled vocabulary that allows correlating tags to the category to which the event belongs. This controlled vocabulary (more precisely an authority file) is used to suggest concepts when the user is tagging the event. Thus, when a user inserts a tag among those suggested by the system, the system is able to map it to the taxonomy and to derive the meaning of the tag (with the support of WordNet). In this case, the main criteria the system addresses are (c) and (b). Indeed, the objective is to provide users with more search keys (multifaceted annotations) than the simple event genre offered by the taxonomy (c). However, the objective is also the possibility to reason about these tags. As a consequence, they have to be as less ambiguous as possible and linked to the taxonomy (b).

To conclude this section concerning the improvement of annotations' quality, we will make some considerations about the opportunity to integrate the Web 2.0 and the SW and about the contribution of recommendations to it.

As discussed, both the approaches annotate resources and are complementary for most of their advantages and weaknesses. Therefore, to this aim, their combination could be useful, since the drawbacks of an approach could be mitigated by the other approach. However, these two approaches have also peculiarities that make them useful independently, in different situations. For example, comparing folksonomies to ontologies, Tim Berners-Lee states that they do not compete for the same space: ontologies are mainly tools for data integration, while folksonomies are mainly tools for information retrieval, an interesting variant on the keyword-search theme [12]. Others compare folksonomies to ontologies focusing on the domain of application, instead of on their functionality. Macgregor and McCulloch [37] emphasize the role of controlled vocabulary and taxonomical knowledge in formal domains (such as academic tasks, industrial research, corporate knowledge management and so on) and the role of folksonomies in informal domains (such as recreational research, personal information management, serendipity-based exploration prior to formal exploration, etc.). Shirky [55], who is very critic with respect to the ability of ontologies to properly classify data items, accepts them in small domains, with stable entities and formal categories.

Thus, we can say that, in some domains and for specific goals, folksonomies and ontologies do not need to be combined. Instead, their combination becomes necessary when opposite goals have to be reached at the same time, such as when the concurrent goals are as follows:

- Enriching resources with multifaceted annotations
- Allowing machines to *understand* the meaning of annotations, in order to reason on them
- Annotating open corpora of resources, thus requiring the collaborative building of annotations (a close corpus can be annotated by designers; an open corpus cannot)

Recommenders can significantly support this integration, since they can perform the necessary analysis to reach a good quality of annotation, as defined in the requirements, and provide users a set of possible tags among which they can choose the most fitting one. As seen, the automatic annotation of resources could be a cheaper alternative to tag suggestion, but it does not exploit the ability, which only human beings have, to assign meanings to resources and thus choosing the most fitting annotations.

3.4 Relevance of Annotation-Enriched Retrieved Resources

In this section, we analyze the second issue, that is, how adaptation and recommendation techniques can be deployed to improve the relevance of retrieved data in Web 2.0 and SW-based applications. For sake of brevity, we use the expression "retrieved data" to include both "retrieved" and "filtered" resources. More specifically, with this expression we mean the ordered list of resources that are displayed after the user clicks on a tag, or the ordered list that is automatically displayed when the user accesses a specific page. For example, in Web 2.0 tagging systems, retrieved resources are often ordered on the basis of their popularity, recency, etc. Adaptation techniques can be used to improve their ordering, according to their relevance to the user on the basis of her interests, her knowledge, her current location, and so on.

With respect to the previous section, where the role of recommendation techniques was localized and well defined, in this section it is more difficult to properly identify the contribution of adaptation and recommendation to the Web 2.0 and the SW, since Web 2.0 and the SW technologies bring contributions to adaptation techniques as well. In [64] we just analyzed the contribution of semantic techniques to the different tasks of an adaptive system and we can observe some overlap for the tasks of content adaptation and tag recommendation. Thus, the criterion we used in selecting papers was to limit the analysis to approaches that use recommendation techniques as an improvement to the system and not as a constitutive feature. In particular, we selected papers where the personalization component is an addition to the basic application. In this way, the contribution of recommendation techniques to Web 2.0, SW, and mixed approaches should emerge more clearly.

3.4.1 Contribution of Adaptation and Recommendation Techniques to Web 2.0-Based Applications

In this section we analyze just one system, since it is a particularly interesting example that shows how adaptation and recommendation techniques can be used to personalize the retrieval of resources in Web 2.0 tagging systems.

The work of Shepitsen et al. [54] proposes an algorithm for personalizing the retrieval of resources in folksonomies. Resources are represented as vectors of tags, calculated by using a folksonomy-adapted version of TF*IDF (see Sect. 3.2). When a user selects a tag in order to see the associated resources, as a first step, this single-tag query is matched against the tag vector of each resource, by using the Cosine Similarity measure. The *retrieved set of resources* is then *re-ranked according to* *the relevance* of these resources to the user. In this second step, the authors cluster tags on the basis of their similarity and use these clusters, instead of single tags, to model users and resources. To calculate the relevance of each resource to the user, they first calculate the user's interest in each cluster (user profiles represented as weighted vectors of tags' clusters), then they calculate each resource's closest clusters (resources represented as weighted vector of tags' clusters), finally they infer the user's interest in each resource that belongs to the set of retrieved resources, and this result is combined with the rank of retrieved resources coming from the first step.

The main contribution of the paper, with respect to this analysis, regards the effective application of standard content-based recommendation methods to tagging systems and the clear explanation of the importance of personalization techniques in folksonomies. As they state "while personalization has been shown to increase the utility of Web applications, the need for it in folksonomies is even more critical. Noise in the folksonomy such as tag redundancy and tag ambiguity obfuscate patterns and reduce the effectiveness of basic recommendation strategies."

3.4.2 Contribution of Adaptation and Recommendation Techniques to SW-Based Applications

The contribution of adaptation and recommendation techniques to the SW is an interesting issue. As known, the objective of the SW is to allow machines to understand data, in order to help users in their activities, such as the search for information with the highest relevance for the user, with the support of intelligent agents. This vision, aimed to provide end user support, enabling users to have the right information at the right time [10], implicitly emphasizes the importance of adaptation and personalization.

Current developments in the SW mainly focus on the first part of the SW vision: they focus on formalisms, languages, and reasoning frameworks, making available "an environment capable of enabling enhanced, efficient and user-centered applications, thus enabling the second part of the vision, and the goal of the SW."[12] In this scenario, adaptation and personalization techniques can play a relevant role: they can contribute to reach the ultimate goal of the SW.

The *Rule Level* is the place, in the SW architecture, enabling the natural implementation of adaptation and recommendation techniques. Coherently with that, the *adaptation model* of SW-based adaptive systems is often represented by means of semantically enriched rules, as described by Kravcík and Gaševic [36].

We previously stated that identifying the direction of the contribution, namely from these techniques to semantic technologies or vice versa, is not always easy and the most common situation is a reciprocal contribution. Even though the aim of this work is to analyze just one side of the relationship, showing how SW-based

---

[12] Introduction to the Workshop on SW Personalization, held in the Third European SW Conference. http://www.kbs.uni-hannover.de/~henze/swp06/

applications can use adaptation and recommendation techniques to better achieve their ultimate objective. In particular, we focus on the objective of improving the retrieval of annotated resources, by considering their relevance according to the user profile.

HERA [24, 67] is a methodology for designing SW-based information systems. The first version of the framework was integrated with an intelligent component to adapt the presentation to the user device capabilities and to the user preferences, on the basis of the AHA reference model (see Sect. 3.2). Data items are represented as instances of a domain ontology. Device features are defined by using the CC/PP and UAProf vocabularies, and user features are represented by extending CC/PP. Finally, the navigational aspects of the hypermedia presentation are defined by a navigation ontology. When a user submits a query, the user query is extended, covering a larger part of the domain ontology than the original query. Then, in the last transformation, the *retrieved set of data* is *personalized* according to the user profile. To this aim, the authors integrated the navigation ontology with some appearance conditions, which are *adaptation rules* represented as RDF properties. These rules specify conditions of appearance on the basis of device and user features. As a result, *resources* that the system infers as *relevant* to the user are emphasized in the final presentation. For example, resources estimated as relevant are displayed in "good" colors, nonrelevant resources in "bad" colors, and other resources are hidden.

Another example where adaptation techniques have been introduced to improve the relevance of retrieved resources is EPOS [51]. It is based on a previous system, called Semantic Desktop [50], which was aimed to support the user in her daily working activity and did not use any form of personalization. In EPOS, personalization is exploited in three specific desktop applications: a desktop search engine, a context-sensitive assistant, and a tool for filing new information. In [51], it is explicitly said that the results of EPOS show the "need of personalization in the SW." The basic idea of the new version of the system is that the support to knowledge workers cannot ignore the user's current actions, context, mental model, and personal information items. To this aim, the authors define a Personal Information Model Ontology (PIMO) and use it to represent documents according to the user's view; moreover, they try to infer the medium-term user's goals from a sequence of user actions. Considering for example the desktop search, when a user makes a query, the search "reaches across all parts of the PIMO framework, domain ontologies, native data sources, and the PIMO-User." Internally, the search engine represents the search results in a RDF graph model. Personalization rules are run on search results represented as RDF, before rendering them as HTML output. These rules are expressed using the Jena Rule syntax. Moreover, additional SPARQL queries can be called from within the rule engine and "personalized sets of these rules can be used to expand the search results (increasing recall values) or to filter out unwanted results (increasing precision). Thus, in the EPOS scenario, personalization rules were used to include defined ontology mappings," in order to adapt the search to the user's view of documents, and thus improve the relevance of retrieved data.

The examples above clearly highlight the contribution of adaptation, since the personalization component has been introduced over an existing nonadapted version. However, many other systems have been developed to improve the relevance of retrieved or filtered resources in different domains, such as e-learning [3, 4, 16, 20, 23], communities of practice [25], museums [5, 61], knowledge management [48], etc. Though in many cases it is difficult to define the direction of the contribution between adaptation and SW techniques, anyway all of the examples above show the importance of their synergy.

3.4.3 Contribution of Adaptation and Recommendation Techniques to Web 2.0 and SW

Up to now, just few systems exploit adaptation and recommendation techniques to improve the relevance of retrieved resources in mixed approaches. This is not surprising, since it is a subset of a set which itself is limited.

Movie Recommender of Szomszor et al. [62] integrates Web 2.0 annotations into a taxonomy and deploys adaptation techniques to recommend items. It is important to notice that, in this case, the adaptation functionality is a core component of the application (since it is a recommender system) and the contribution goes, more likely, from Web 2.0 and SW technologies to adaptation techniques than the contrary. Even if in the previous sections we tried to limit the analysis to systems that employ adaptation techniques as a supplementary component, and not a core one, we make an exception, since it is useful to compare it with another system, iCITY, described in Sect. 3.3.3 and pertinent to this section too. Movie Recommender is a system that provides predictions of rating for unseen movies. It is built combining a first data set containing *tags* from the Internet Movie Database and a second data set containing *ratings* about movies gathered from Netflix. Items to recommend are represented by an ontology of movies where, in the "movie class," they introduce the property "has_keywords," which associates each resource to tags coming from the Internet Movie Database. For the recommendation, the Movie Recommender exploits a *collaborative approach* based on *tags' similarities*. For each user, it computes the tag-cloud associated to each rating. The prediction of rating for a specific movie is calculated by a set of algorithms, which compare the movie's tags to the tag-cloud associated to each rating (using a TF*IDF-like approach) and predicting the rating with the highest match.

Similar to the Movie Recommender, iCITY [18] (see Sect. 3.3.3) defines a property of the "events class" (has_tags), which associates the resource to the tags the users inserted. However, in iCITY, tags are associated to the resource but also to the *user who inserted them*, and this approach allows including tags in the models of users and exploiting this information for the task of recommendation. Thus, iCITY implements mechanisms for improving both the quality of annotations (discussed in Sect. 3.3) and the relevance of resources to the user. And these features are connected, since the main reason to improve the quality of annotations regards the possibility to properly classify such annotations and use them in reasoning tasks for user modeling and recommendation.

3.5 Conclusions

In this paper we have analyzed the subject of resource annotation, as a process that brings to organize and add meaning to Web resources. It is not a linear and straightforward process and takes several forms, and different actors cope with it.[13] We have also observed that, besides the trend of adding semantics to Web resources, another spreading process is the personalization of these resources, in terms of contents, interface, and delivery. Both the Web 2.0 and the SW are connected to the concept of personalization, and probably each future development of the Web, and of the Internet of Things, will increasingly be.

The aim of this paper has been just to emphasize this concept. By analyzing current works in literature and describing some of them as examples, we tried to highlight the contribution of adaptation and recommendation techniques to the Web 2.0 and the SW, with a particular focus on:

- Their contribution to improve (1) the quality of annotations and (2) the relevance of retrieved resources in both the approaches
- Their contribution to the combination of the two approaches

With respect to this last issue, the reviewed examples show that an important role of adaptation and recommendation techniques is to favor the collaborative building of annotations, *combining advantages* of both the approaches in order to produce multifaceted annotations, with high consensus in the community of users. For example, CommonFolks, Matching Component, and iCITY are all applications that try to integrate Web 2.0 and SW technologies and use recommendations to achieve the combined goals of:

- Making tags more meaningful and less ambiguous (thus overcoming the major limit of folksonomies)
- Avoiding the subjectivity [1] of a single designer (a relevant limit of ontologies)

We could say that what they contribute to reach is a *nonrevolutionary SW*, obtained by adding simple meaning gradually into the documents and by exploiting the knowledge of crowd in this process. In other terms, we could say that they contribute to *guide users in the process of "Web semantization"* (and then they support users in obtaining relevant information in the *"semantized" Web space*).

As seen, guiding users by suggesting tags can be useful to combine the advantages of the Web 2.0 and the SW (or anyway, reducing their weaknesses), but it has also the effect of increasing the user participation, a prerequisite for achieving high coverage of annotated items. Several works [6, 38, 56] state that suggesting tags can improve the user experience and thus foster the users' participation.

---

[13] The most recent direction of research tries to apply these approaches not only to Web objects but also to objects in the real world. Indeed, it is becoming frequent to speak about the Internet of Things [27], in the sense that all things in the real world can become part of the Internet and thus requiring to be semantically described, similar to Web objects. See, for example, the Socialight (http://www.socialight.com) and Tag Your World (http://www.grapheety.com) projects.

The problem of user participation has been studied by many researchers [46, 57, 58] who investigated the reasons of active participation in online communities vs. passive attendance, often defined as lurking behavior. They found that, all conditions being equal, a positive user experience and easiness of interaction can increase the probability of participation [58]. The suggestion of tags makes (or should make) easier the action of tagging; moreover, it reduces the problem of the "post activation analysis paralysis" [56], which concerns the intellectually onerous task of deciding how a particular resource should be tagged.

However, guiding users can hide some risks, which are well exemplified by one of the systems we analyzed, CommonFolks. Among the reviewed systems, CommonFolks is the application with the highest integration between a Web 2.0 folksonomy and a SW ontology, since all the added tags are mapped on WordNet, using an RDF syntax. However, the impression is that the integration reached in CommonFolks risks to sort negative effects. The risk is that the approach they use, forcing users to disambiguate tags on the basis of a taxonomy of general terms, may inhibit users from using the system. This hypothesis is confirmed by one of the authors, who, in another work, states that "we came to believe the process required too much of the general user, and so we have abandoned this effort" [7].

More in general, the serious risk related to strict guides is to lose the benefits of Web 2.0, such as freedom of tagging, representation of the mental model of users, simplicity, and consequently user involvement. In this scenario, the automatic extraction of data from social software tools is sometimes seen as a solution [7]; however, as discussed in Sect. 3.3.1, it seems not able to satisfy all the criteria in Table 3.1, most of which require the cognitive capabilities of users. Rather, we think that the automatic annotation of resources could be effectively complemented by adaptation and recommendation techniques, which are required to provide contributions not only about the content of suggestions, but also about the modality to provide suggestions, so that each user can be guided in a personalized and appropriate way.

Acknowledgments This review has been supported by the Italian Ministry of Education, University and Research (MIUR), PRIN-05.

References

1. Abbott R (2004) Subjectivity as a Concern for Information Science: a Popperian Perspective, Journal of Information Science 30(1):95–106
2. Antoniou G, van Harmelen F (2004) A Semantic Web Primer. MIT Press
3. Apted T, Kay J, Lum A (2004) Supporting Metadata Creation with an Ontology Built from an Extensible Dictionary. In: Proceedings of Third International Conference on Adaptive Hypermedia and Adaptive Web-Based Systems, Springer
4. Aroyo L, De Bra P, Houben GJ (2004) Embedding Information Retrieval in Adaptive Hypermedia: IR meets AHA!, in Hypermedia 10(1):53–76, Taylor Graham Publishing

5. Aroyo L, Stash N, Wang Y, Gorgels P, Rutledge L (2007) CHIP Demonstrator: Semantics-Driven Recommendations and Museum Tour Generation. In: Proceedings of the 6th International SW Conference – ISWC 2007, Busan, Korea, November 11–15, 879–886

6. Basile P, Gendarmi D, Lanubile F, Semeraro G (2007) Recommending Smart Tags in a Social Bookmarking System. In: Proceedings of International Workshop on Bridging the Gap Between SW and Web 2.0, at 4th European SW Conference ESWC'07, 22–29

7. Bateman S (2007) Collaborative Tagging: Folksonomy, Metadata, Visualization, E-Learning, Master of Science Thesis, supervised by Gordon McCalla, Department of Computer Science, University of Saskatchewan, Saskatoon

8. Bateman S, Brooks C, McCalla G (2006) Collaborative Tagging Approaches for Ontological Metadata in Adaptive E-Learning Systems. In: Workshop on Applications of SW Technologies for E-Learning (AH 06), 3–12

9. Berners-Lee T (1998) Semantic Web Road Map, http://www.w3.org/DesignIssues/Semantic.html, Accessed 20 June 2008

10. Berners-Lee T (2002) The Future of the Web, in Scientific American, Special Online Issue, April 2002, 2:24–30

11. Berners-Lee T, Hendler J, Lassila O (2001) The Semantic Web, Scientific American

12. Berners-Lee T, Hall W, Hendler JA, O'Hara K, Shadbolt N, Weitzner DJ (2006) A Framework for Web Science. Foundations and Trends (R) in Web Science. Now Publishers Inc.

13. Beys P, Benjamins VR, van Heijst G (1996) Remedying the reusability–usability tradeoff for problem-solving methods. In: Gaines BR, Musen MA, eds. Proceedings of the 10th Banff Knowledge Acquisition for Knowledge-Based Systems Workshop, 2.1–2.20, Alberta, Canada. SRDG Publications

14. Brin S, Page L (1998) The Anatomy of a Large-Scale Hypertextual Web Search Engine. Computer Networks and ISDN Systems, 30(1–7):107–117

15. Brusilovsky P (1996) Methods and Techniques of Adaptive Hypermedia. User Modeling and User-Adapted Interactaction 6(2–3):87–129

16. Brusilovsky P, Sosnovsky S, Yudelson M (2004) Adaptive Hypermedia Services for E-Learning. In: AH 2004 Workshops proceedings, Eindhoven, the Netherlands, 470–479

17. Brusilovsky P, Kobsa A, Nejdl W, eds. (2007) The Adaptive Web. Methods and Strategies of Web Personalization, No 4321 LNCS, Springer

18. Carmagnola F, Cena F, Console L, Cortassa O, Gena C, Goy A, Torre I, Toso A, Vernero F (2008) Tag-Based User Modeling for Social Multi-Device Adaptive Guides. User Modeling and User-Adapted Interaction. DOI:10.1007/s11257-008-9052-2

19. Chirita P, Costache S, Nejdl W, Handschuh S (2007) P-TAG: Large Scale Automatic Generation of Personalized Annotation Tags for the Web. In: Proceedings of the 16th International Conference on World Wide Web (Banff, Alberta, Canada, May 8–12, 2007). WWW '07. ACM, New York, 845–854

20. Conlan O, Wade V (2004) Evaluation of APeLS – An Adaptive eLearning Service Based on the Multi-Model, Metadata-Driven Approach. In: Proceedings of AH2004, Eindhoven, The Netherlands

21. Cristea A, de Mooij A (2003) LAOS: Layered WWW AHS Authoring Model and Their Corresponding Algebraic Operators. In: Proc. of 12th WWW Conference, Budapest, Hungary, http://www2003.org/cdrom/papers/alternate/P301/p301-cristea.pdf, Accessed 10 June 2008

22. De Bra P, Houben G-J, Wu H (1999) AHAM: A Dexter-Based Reference Model for Adap-tive Hypermedia, In: Proc. International Conference on Hypertext '99, 147–156

23. Dolog P, Henze N, Nejdl W, Sintek M (2004) The Personal Reader: Personalizing and Enriching Learning Resources Using SW Technologies. In: Proc. AH 2004, LNCS, Springer, 85–94

24. Frasincar F, Houben G-J (2002) Hypermedia Presentation Adaptation on the SW, In: Adaptive Hypermedia and Adaptive Web-Based Systems, De Bra P, Brusilovsky P, Conejo R, eds. Second International Conference, AH2002, Malaga, Spain, Springer LNCS 2347:133–142

25. Garlatti G, Iksal S (2004) A Flexible Composition Engine for Adaptive Web Site. In: Proc. AH2004, Eindhoven, The Netherlands

26. Gendarmi D, Abbattista F, Lanubile F (2007) Fostering Knowledge Evolution Through Community-Based Participation. Proceedings of the 1st Workshop on Social and Collaborative Construction of Structured Knowledge at WWW'07
27. Gershenfeld N, Krikorian R, Cohen D (2004) The Internet of Things. Scientific American 291:44, 76–81
28. Golder S, Huberman BA (2006) Usage Patterns of Collaborative Tagging Systems. Journal of Information Science 32(2):198–208
29. Gomez-Perez A, Fernandez-Lopez M, Corcho O (2003) Ontological Engineering. Springer
30. Gruber T (2007) Ontology of Folksonomy: A Mash-Up of Apples and Oranges, in International Journal on SW and Information Systems, 3(1):1–11
31. Guy M, Tonkin E (2006) Folksonomies: Tidying up Tags? D-Lib Magazine, 12(1), http://www.dlib.org/dlib/january06/guy/01guy/htm, Accessed 13 June 2008
32. Haase P, Hotho A, Schmidt-Thieme L, Sure Y (2005) Collaborative and Usage-Driven Evolution of Personal Ontologies. In: Proceedings of the European SW Conference ESWC 2005, 486–499
33. Jaschke R, Marinho L, Hotho A, Schmidt-Thieme L, Stumme G (2007) Tag Recommendations in Folksonomies, in LNCS Knowledge Discovery in DataBases, vol 4702/2007:506–514, Springer, Berlin
34. Koch N, Wirsing M (2002) The Munich Reference Model for Adaptive Hypermedia Applications, In: Proceedings of the Second International Conference on Adaptive Hypermedia and Adaptive Web-Based Systems. London, UK, 213–222
35. Kotis K, Vouros GA, Alonso JP (2004) HCOME: Tool-Supported Methodology for Collaboratively Devising Living Ontologies. In: SWDB'04: 2. Int. Workshop on Semantic Web and Databases
36. Kravcík M, Gaševic D (2007) Leveraging the SW for Adaptive Education. Journal of Interactive Media in Education (Adaptation and IMS Learning Design, Special Issue, Daniel Burgos, ed), 2007/06. http://hdl.handle.net/1820/1080, Accessed 23 June 2008
37. Macgregor G, McCulloch E (2006) Collaborative Tagging as a Knowledge Organisation and Resource Discovery Tool, Library Review 55:291–300
38. Marlow C, Naaman M, Davis M, Boyd D (2006) Tagging Paper, Taxonomy, Flickr, Academic Article, ToRead. In: Press A, ed. In: Proceedings of Hypertext and Hypermedia, 31–40
39. Mathes A (2004) Folksonomies – Cooperative Classification and Communication Through Shared Metadata, USA. http://adammathes.com/academic/computer-mediated-communication /folksonomies.pdf. Accessed 9 June 2008
40. Mika P (2005) Ontologies Are Us: A Unified Model of Social Networks and Semantics. Proceedings of the 4th International SW Conference, LNCS, Vol. 3729 Springer, 522–536
41. Mishne G (2006) AutoTag: A Collaborative Approach to Automated Tag Assignment for Weblog Posts. In: Proceedings of the 15th international Conference on World Wide Web, Edinburgh, Scotland, May 23–26, ACM, New York, 953–954
42. Nauerz A, Pietschmann S, Pietzsch R (2007) Collaborative Annotation-Driven Adaptation in Web Portals, In: Proceedings of the 18th Conference on Hypertext and Hypermedia, Manchester, UK, September 10–12, 2007, ACM, New York
43. Nauerz A, Junginger M, Zhao S (2008) A Recommender Based on Automatic Metadata Extraction and User-Driven Collaborative Annotation, In: Proceedings of the International Workshop on Recommendation and Collaboration, at IUI '08, Canary Islands, Spain, Jan 13–16
44. O'Reilly T (2005) What Is Web 2.0, Design Patterns and Business Models for the Next Generation of Software. http://www.oreillynet.com/pub/a/oreilly/tim/news/2005/09/30/what-is-web-20.html. Accessed 4 June 2008
45. Pazzani M, Billsus D (2007) Content-Based Recommendation Systems, In: The Adaptive Web, LNCS 4321:325–341
46. Preece J, Nonnecke B, Andrews D (2004) The Top Five Reasons for Lurking: Improving Community Experiences for Everyone. Computers in Human Behavior 20(2):201–223
47. Quintarelli E (2005) Folksonomies: Power to the People, Proceedings of the 1st International Society for Knowledge Organization, Italy (ISKOI), UniMIB Meeting, June 24, Milan, http://www.iskoi.org/doc/folksonomies.htm. Accessed 22 June 2008

48. Razmerita L, Angehrn A, Maedche A (2003) Ontology-Based User Modeling for Knowledge Management Systems. In: LNCS 2702, Springer
49. Salton G, Buckley C (1988) Term-Weighting Approaches in Automatic Text Retrieval. In: Information Processing and Management, 24(5):513–523
50. Sauermann L, Bernardi A, Dengel A (2005) Overview and Outlook on the Semantic Desktop. In: Proceedings of the 1st Workshop on the Semantic Desktop at ISWC
51. Sauermann L, Dengel A, van Elst L, Lauer A, Maus H, Schwarz S (2006) Personalization in the EPOS Project. In: Proceedings of the International Workshop on SW Personalization, Budva, Montenegro, June 12, 42–52
52. Schafer JB, Frankowski D, Herlocker J, Sen S (2007) Collaborative Filtering Recommendater Systems, in The Adaptive Web, LNCS 4321:291–324
53. Shadbolt N, Berners-Lee T, Hall W (2006) The Semantic Web Revisited, IEEE Intelligent Systems 21(3):96–101
54. Shepitsen A, Gemmell J, Mobasher B, Burke R (2008) Personalized Recommendation in Collaborative Tagging Systems Using Hierarchical Clustering, In: International Conference on Recommender Systems 08, Losanna, October 23–25
55. Shirky C (2005) Ontology Is Overrated: Categories, Links, and Tags, http://www.shirky/com/writings/ontology_overrated.html. Accessed 10 May 2008
56. Sinha R (2005) A Cognitive Analysis of Tagging, http://www.rashmisinha.com/archives/05_09/tagging-cognitive.htm. Accessed 28 June 2008
57. Soroka V, Jacovi M (2004) The Diffusion of Reachout: Analysis and Framework for the Successful Diffusion of Collaboration Technologies. In: Proceedings of the 2004 ACM Conference on Computer Supported Cooperative Work. New York, NY, USA, 314–323
58. Soroka V, Rafaeli S (2006) Invisible Participants: How Cultural Capital Relates to Lurking Behavior. In: Proceedings of the 15th International Conference on World Wide Web. New York, USA, 163–172
59. Specia L, Motta E (2007) Integrating Folksonomies with the Semantic Web, The Semantic Web: Research and Applications, 4th European Semantic Web Conference, ESWC 07, LNCS 4519:624–639
60. Staab S, Schnurr HP, Studer R, Sure Y (2001) Knowledge Processes and Ontologies. IEEE Intelligent Systems 16
61. Stock O, Zancanaro M (2007) PEACH – Intelligent Interfaces for Museum Visits (Cognitive Technologies), Springer, New York
62. Szomszor M, Cattuto C, Alani H, O'Hara, Baldassarri K, Loreto V, Servedio V (2007) Folksonomies, the Semantic Web, and Movie Recommendation. In: Proceedings of 4th European Semantic Web Conference Innsbruck, Austria, 71–85
63. Tempich C, Pinto HS, Staab S (2006) Ontology Engineering Revisited: An Iterative Case Study. In: Proceedings of ESWC 06, 110–124
64. Torre I (2009) Adaptive systems in the era of the semantic and social web, a survey, User Modeling and User-Adapted Interaction, DOI 10.1007/s11257-009-9067-3
65. Van der Sluijs K, Houben G (2008) Relating User Tags to Ontological Information. In: Proceedings of UbiqUM 2008: Theories and Applications of Ubiquitous User Modeling Workshop at IUI '08, Canary Islands, Spain, Jan 13–16
66. Vander Wal T (2004) Folksonomy Coinage and Definition, http://vanderwal.net/folksonomy.html. Accessed 28 May 2008
67. Vdovjak R, Frasincar F, Houben G, Barna P (2003) Engineering Semantic Web Information Systems in Hera, Journal of Web Engineering, Vol. 2, No. 1/2:3–26
68. Xu Z, Fu Y, Mao J, Su D (2006) Towards the Semantic Web: Collaborative Tag Suggestions. In: Proceedings of Workshop on Collaborative Web Tagging, WWW 06, May 22–26

Chapter 4
Adaptive Reactive Rich Internet Applications

Kay-Uwe Schmidt, Roland Stühmer, Jörg Dörflinger, Tirdad Rahmani,
Susan Thomas, and Ljiljana Stojanovic

4.1 Introduction

Adaptive Hypermedia Systems (AHS) gained huge momentum in the mid-1990s
(for a survey of AHS research see [9]). The theory of AHSs provides models for the
adaptation of Web applications where people with different skills and knowledge as
well as with diverse and sophisticated working tasks are expected to interact with
the application. The goal of AHSs is to overcome the gap of available information
and information of interest to the current working environment (context) of the user.
One possible application of AHSs is the management of personalized views in information spaces [50,47]. Another application is the limitation of the navigation space
[32] and the presentation of the most relevant or similar links to follow [3,29]. For
instance online e-Government portals offer a huge amount of available online, services although only some of them might be currently interesting for users accessing
the portal. To fulfill their task, they only need access to a subset of the services.

Explicit user profiles are one possible solution for achieving this goal. But they
require permanent, manual updates and maintenance. On-the-fly implicit user modeling is the more convenient but less accurate counterpart to explicit user modeling.
Any kind of user inputs and interactions are collected and an up-to-date user model
is created every time the user visits the Web application from scratch or a historic
user model is updated in real time. Based on the user model, AHSs are able to infer
user goals, interests, or context information, which then can be used for the adaptation of the system. In conventional AHSs the tracking of user behavior, the inference
of the current user context and situation, as well as the adaptation itself take place

Kay-Uwe Schmidt, Roland Stühmer, Jörg Dörflinger, Tirdad Rahmani, and Susan Thomas
SAP Research CEC Karlsruhe, Vincenz-Prießnitz-Straße 1, 76131 Karlsruhe,
e-mail: {kay-uwe.schmidt, roland.stuehmer, joerg.doerflinger, tirdad.rahmani,
susan.marie.thomas}@sap.com

Ljiljana Stojanovic
FZI Forschungszentrum Informatik, Haid-und-Neu-Straße 10-14, 76131 Karlsruhe,
e-mail: ljiljana.stojanovic@fzi.de

V. Devedžić and D. Gašević (eds.), *Web 2.0 & Semantic Web*, Annals of Information
Systems 6, DOI 10.1007/978-1-4419-1219-0_4,
© Springer Science+Business Media, LLC 2010

on the server side. This limits the possibilities of behavioral user tracking to HTTP requests (GET or POST) [33], which are actually only a subset of the overall user click stream and thus of the user interactions. Furthermore, adaptation can only take place when a user explicitly requests a page, which then is adapted to his/her needs by a server application. On-the-fly adaptation, without reloading the whole page, is not possible to attain.

At the same time with the dawn of Web 2.0, a new technology for Internet applications appeared: AJAX [22]. Because of Web 2.0 and AJAX, Rich Internet Applications (RIAs) emerged from their shadow existence in the World Wide Web. AJAX, in contrast to Adobe Flash,[1] now enables RIAs running in browsers without the need for any additional plug-ins. Several Web 2.0 applications use AJAX heavily in order to provide desktop-like behavior to the user. Now the time seems right for RIAs, because of the broad bandwidth of today's Internet connections, as well as the availability of powerful and cheap personal computers. RIAs provide enhanced capabilities for user tracking and user interface adaptation. With RIAs the range of user actions that can be tracked is extended beyond just page requests. For example, scrolling, mouse clicks, and keystroke events can be tracked enabling a detailed recording of a user's actions on the client side. Additionally, the user's Web browsing behavior can be processed directly on the client, and the browser can react immediately to the recognized behavioral patterns. The advanced user tracking possibilities are also accompanied by sophisticated adaptation techniques formerly only seen in desktop applications, like fading windows. However, the rich variety of trackable user actions and dynamic user interface manipulation options can only be leveraged if they are meaningfully interpretable by the adaptation engine. This is where ontologies come into play because they provide, when linked to the RIA, a semantic model of the whole application.

In this paper we present a novel solution for the on-the-fly adaptation of RIAs that is named after a heroine of ancient Rome: ARRIA – Adaptive Reactive Rich Internet Application. We describe in this paper how to make RIAs adaptive and reactive. By adaptiveness we mean the ad hoc manipulation of the user interface according to the current user's context and by reactiveness our solution's ability to immediately respond to user actions. We introduce a holistic framework covering the whole adaptation loop, from obtaining adaptation rules, through ad hoc user modeling, to on-the-fly user interface adaptation. Compared to common AHSs, our approach goes two steps beyond as we introduce not only ontologies, for modeling the user's context, the Web application itself, and the application domain, and declarative rules, for carrying out the adaptation, but also advance the state of the art through a client-side implementation of real-time user tracking and portal adaptation. We consider the execution of the adaptation rules on the client-side one major research contribution of this paper, as it is the prerequisite to responsive user interfaces for ARRIAs. Client side rule processing has several advantages, such as the reduction of client–server communication to a minimum and the on-time response to user actions.

---

[1] http://www.adobe.com/products/flex

The acquisition of declarative adaptation rules is an indispensable prerequisite for dynamic client-side adaptation. Adaptation rules declaratively encode adaptation logic based on the user's behavior, i.e., based on the recorded interactions between a user and the ARRIA. Adaptation rules can be gathered by mining behavioral data like user access logs. With the help of ontologies, added to the Web application in advance, we present a semantic approach to Web usage mining in order to find common Web usage patterns. In turn, the most useful patterns can be directly modeled as adaptation rules, guiding the user while interacting with the ARRIA. The user interactions are interpreted as events and detected by complex event processing (CEP) algorithms and are used to build up the user model and to trigger the adaptation rules directly on the client-side. Whenever a rule fires, either the working memory is updated, further events are issued, or the user interface is manipulated directly as a response to a user interaction or to the lack of a user interaction. The user browsing behavior stored in the user model could be sent back to the server in order to make it persistent. Accumulated user models serve again as input to the collaborative filtering approach implemented by our semantic Web usage behavior mining.

The rest of the paper is structured as follows. In Sect. 4.2, an example is presented which motivates our work. In Sect. 4.3 we give an overview of the logical system architecture and illustrate the adaptation loop. Section 4.4 briefly gives an impression of the use of ontologies in our adaptation approach. Section 4.5 discusses our client-side event condition action rule language: JSON-Rules. The following Sect. 4.6 and 4.7 elaborate the details of the design-time and run-time architecture accordingly. An evaluation of our approach is given in Sect. 4.8, and in Sect. 4.9 we discuss related work. Sect. 4.10 contains the acknowledgments followed by Sect. 4.10: conclusions and prospects for future work.

4.2 Motivating Example

Searching for the right form is a widespread problem in portals especially in e-Government portals. Regarding the use of online services, the average user of an e-Government portal is usually not an expert but rather a novice. E-Government Web applications should be designed for end users who have no special knowledge or extra training. Two major requirements for e-Government Web applications are citizen-centric services and ease of use [48]. To meet these requirements a form of non-intrusive user guidance should be provided. So we established these two basic requirements for our motivating example. We want to recommend links related to the forms of the public services the user has already filled in. Let us consider the use case of a building application. The citizen officially has to apply for a building permit at the local department of housing and urban development. In an e-Government RIA the building permit can be filled in online and consists of several forms such as the main building permit application, the building license, the building description, and the start of construction, to mention just a few. We assume no predefined workflow determining the number and order of forms to be filled in. After completing the main form the user wants to know which form to fill in next. This can be accomplished by suggesting related forms based on the forms already filled in by the current user compared to the collaboratively filtered Web usage behavior of antecedent users. This use case was identified jointly with our end user partners from the Austrian town of Vöcklabruck[2] [20].

4.3 Logical System Architecture: The Adaptation Loop

Our architecture for Adaptive Reactive Rich Internet Applications (ARRIA) is a two-level approach consisting of three cycles constructing the adaptation loop. The design-time level and the run-time level logically divide the components of our architecture into off-line and online components, respectively. That is, the levels refer to the invocation time of the components. The three cycles, the modeling cycle on the left, the adaptation cycle on the right, and the larger transfer cycle in the middle of Fig. 4.1 illustrate the self-adaptive character of our architecture.

The modeling cycle stands for the design-time components in charge of constructing the adaptation rules. First of all appropriate adaptation ontologies have to be designed embracing the semantics of an ARRIA: user model ontology, event ontology, RIA design patterns ontology, and domain ontologies. Not all ontologies have to be designed from scratch. Only the domain ontologies disclosing the special knowledge of the application domain might be constructed individually. Also the domain ontologies can be reused for ARRIAs within the same domain. So, for instance, an e-Government ontology can be used in every ARRIA involving public services. Nevertheless, the design and implementation of the ontologies is only half of the modeling cycle. To take advantage of the formal semantic encoded in the ontologies, an ARRIA must be linked to the concepts. This process is known as annotation and can be accomplished by using an annotation tool as explained in [45]. After annotating the structure and the content of an ARRIA, the semantically enriched user access log data, collected in the past, can be mined for useful Web usage patterns. This is done by the semantic Web usage mining. Once useful patterns are found, they can be formulated as adaptation rules. The format of the rules is prescribed by our JSON rule language.

At design time the transformation cycle is also executed. In the case that the adaptation rules are formulated in any other rule language conforming to the ECA paradigm, an explicit transformation step is needed in order to translate the rules into the JSON-Rules format so that it becomes understandable by our client-side rule engine. The ontologies must be transformed from their native format to a serialization in JSON in order to be processed on the client side using only a little effort. At the end of the session the tracked user model is sent back to the server. All user

---

[2] http://www.voecklabruck.at

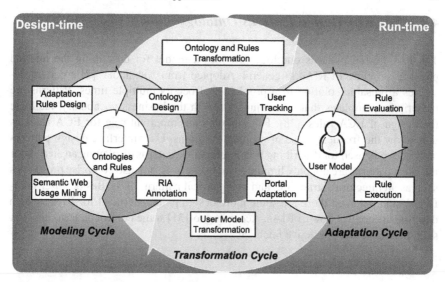

Fig. 4.1 Logical system architecture: the adaptation loops

models are then collected and fed back into the modeling cycle so as to mine new behavioral patterns. This gives an ARRIA a flavor of self-adaptiveness.

The rightmost cycle in Figure 4.1, the adaptation cycle, is executed, like the transfer cycle in the middle of the figure, at run-time. The aim of the adaptation cycle is to adapt the RIA based on the predefined adaptation rules and the current user model. The adaptation rules are obtained from the modeling cycle. When the user requests the Web site, the adaptation rules as well as the ontologies are transferred to the client together with all other application data. During the interaction with the user the user model is built up. Based on this the adaptation rules are evaluated, and fired, if the condition part holds. It is the task of the rule engine to carry out rule processing. If a rule fires, the corresponding actions are executed and the RIA adapts itself directly on the client side without server requests.

4.4 The Adaptation Ontologies: The Paving Stones of the Personalization Highway

The application domains, the user behavior, as well as the structure of ARRIAs are modeled as ontologies in order to provide the business vocabulary for the adaptation rules and to give the rules a formal foundation. First we introduce the ontologies valid across domains for all ARRIAs and then we show how to design a domain-specific ontology according to our motivating example. All ontologies are described using the Web Ontology Language (OWL) [4].

4.4.1 The RIA Design Patterns Ontology

The RIA design patterns ontology provides a model for describing the internal physical structure of RIAs in general. Adopted from Alexander [2] a pattern describes a reusable solution to a problem that occurs multiple times. Patterns are prescriptive templates that, in conjunction with the business vocabulary, facilitate the design of ECA rules [38]. Patterns play an important role for ECA rules as they allow the frequent reuse of problem solutions. User interface design patterns are frequently used for describing user interactions, such as displaying an alert. User interface patterns are not only limited to input controls, but also comprise prototypes such as architectural, structural, and navigational patterns [49]. Besides user interface design patterns, there are some more design patterns crucial for RIAs, which describe the control flow of RIAs. According to [31] some control patterns are RIA stub, fat client, and predictive fetch, etc.

4.4.2 The User Model Ontology

The user model ontology provides the relevant data structures in order to store relevant parts of user interactions at run-time. A detailed description of the user model ontology can be found in [39], where the user model ontology is explained in terms of a user ontology and a behavior ontology.

4.4.3 The Event Ontology

Events are first class objects in ARRIAs and therefore need a proper concept description. They include all possible user actions plus timer events plus external application events stemming, for instance, from streaming servers and including events fired by the ARRIA itself. We built an event hierarchy ontology[3] based on the work described in [12]. We adopted all of the hierarchy except the database events. Thus, we defined the event class as a super class having simple and complex events as direct subclasses. Simple events are atomic and not further divisible events, which might construct complex events. Complex events in turn are composed of simple or other complex events. The ECA rules are the guidelines of how to compose complex events from their constituting pieces. The simple event class is further subsumed by the explicit, user, application, and temporal event classes. Explicit events are issued by the ARRIA itself as one possible result of the executing of rules. User events are

---

[3] Our notion of an event hierarchy differs from David Luckham's as he denotes the complex event patterns, the first part of the ECA rules, as event hierarchy arguing that the complex event patterns constitute a hierarchy of events with the simple events at the bottom constructing the complex events at the top.

caused by user interactions like mouse movements or keystrokes. Application events are events received from external applications like stock quotes streaming servers or news feeds. Temporal events are issued by an internal clock. They are mainly used for defining time points and durations in ECA rules as well as for programming sliding windows. Absolute and relative events are subclasses of the temporal event. An absolute temporal event denotes a concrete point in time, and a relative temporal event indicates the duration of a time interval such as one lasting 5s.

4.4.4 The Domain Ontologies

The business vocabulary is coined in the domain ontologies. In contrast to the previously introduced ontologies that are common to all ARRIAs the domain ontologies describe a special application domain. We propose the use of faceted classification in order to flexibly classify application domains. According to our motivating example of an ARRIA for public administrations, the type of domain ontology required depends on the type of adaptation to be implemented: service or social. Service adaptation, because it concentrates on a service or set of services, is possible with a smaller, more focused ontology. Social adaptation, on the other hand, requires a more extensive ontology to discover significant relationships between users and content.

As documented by a number of studies [34], the usability of e-Government portals in general is substandard. Therefore, if a portal redesign is planned, it is worthwhile to consider developing an ontology that can serve multiple purposes namely, providing the semantics needed for social adaptation, as well as functioning as an information retrieval thesaurus. An information retrieval thesaurus can help address the major portal usability problems, two of which stand out from the rest. The first is poorly structured navigation. A common problem, seen on many portals, is to use the internal department hierarchy to organize the navigation hierarchy, rather than to use an organization that reflects the goals of the users. The second major problem is that the site uses civil-service jargon, i.e., language that is not easy to understand for most people. This is often related to the first problem because, for most users, department names and subdepartment names are jargon. Amongst information architects, the people responsible for designing portal navigation systems, it is accepted wisdom that an information retrieval thesaurus can serve as the backbone of an improved navigation system for a portal (cf. [8], p. 34; [37], p.221). An example of a portal with such a navigation system is http://www.direct.gov.uk. To construct the thesaurus, the method of faceted analysis as described in [8] can be used. This method provides three things: preferred names for concepts, which can be used as text labels in the portal, synonyms that can be used to improve search, and multiple hierarchies of concepts that can be used to create navigation hierarchies. Figure 4.2 shows schematically an example of multiple facets or hierarchies

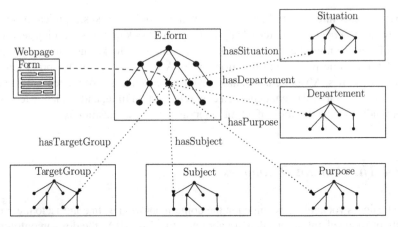

Fig. 4.2 Faceted ontology

of concepts that can be used to describe online forms. The most important are the target group and the subject, since they are optimal candidates for organizing forms on the portal into hierarchies.

The thesaurus ontology can also serve other purposes, thereby increasing its return on investment. It can be used to automatically create a folder structure in a Content Management System (CMS). For this purpose the departmental view might be most appropriate, since responsibility for content might be assigned by department. Another very important use is to annotate portal pages or elements of pages like links or buttons. This enables usage analysis at the semantic level. For example, as shown in Fig. 4.2, a page can be annotated with a concept for a type of form, and, thus, indirectly with target group, etc. Example types are the navigation page, the content page, the help page, and form page. Annotations can also be weighted to indicate to what extent the concept is applicable to the page. This can be useful if annotation is done automatically and could indicate the probability that the concept really applies.

To summarize the main uses of semantics based on faceted analysis: on the one hand, the faceted ontology can be used to improve the portal design and to organize CMS folders, and, on the other, it enables usage analysis at the semantic level, thus enabling on-the-fly social adaptation.

4.5 JSON-Rules: A Client-Side Rule Language

We propose a lightweight reaction rule language tailored to the needs of Internet applications, specifically applications that profit from or need complex event processing, condition evaluation on a working memory or variables, and rule actions written in JavaScript.

As a representation for our rules we use JSON, because it is almost directly usable within JavaScript. JSON can specify objects, arrays, and primitives. A rule object contains the three attributes `event`, `condition`, and `action`. The event part consists of Snoop operators [13]. The condition part uses logic expressions from RuleML [7]. The action part contains one or more JavaScript code blocks. For the rule action it is also possible to specify events that are to be triggered explicitly on the execution of a rule.

For the event part the usual Snoop operators are available: $Or(e_1, e_2)$: either of the two events must occur for the complex event to occur; $And(e_1, e_2)$: both events must occur; $Any(m, e_1, e_2, \dots)$: m of the specified events must occur; $e_1; e_2$: the strict sequence of the specified events (the constituent events are not allowed to overlap if they are complex themselves and detected over an interval of time); $A(e_1, e_2, e_3)$: the aperiodic event, it is signaled each time e_2 is detected within the time interval formed by the other two events; $A^*(e_1, e_2, e_3)$: the cumulative version of the former event, it is triggered at the end of the interval and accumulates all occurrences (if any) of event e_2; $P(e_1, TI[:\text{parameters}], e_3)$: the periodic event that is triggered regularly after the time interval TI, an optional list of working memory items or JavaScript identifiers may be given, the values of which are added to the event occurrences as parameters; $P^*(e_1, TI:\text{parameters}, e_3)$: the cumulative version of the former event, it is detected at the end of e_3 and accumulates all intervals with their parameters, the parameters are mandatory here, because a set of plain, past temporal events would in itself not be of any use; $Not(e_1, e_2, e_3)$: this event occurs if no e_2 is detected in the specified interval; $Plus(e_1, TI)$: it occurs at TI time after the detection of e_1. Also we propose an event operator $Mask(e_1, \text{condition})$, modeled after the event masks from ODE [26]. The mask enforces a condition on the event e_1. This allows, e.g., for fine-grained constraints of event types that may utilize the business vocabulary.

The event operators in our rule language are represented as tree nodes. The simple, atomic events form the leaves. This hierarchical representation allows a lean, abstract syntax without constructs from concrete syntax (like parentheses) compared to textual event expressions.

A condition in our language may use logical operators, comparison operators, identifiers from working memory or JavaScript and direct literal values. The condition part is a tree of operators with the leaves being identifiers or literals. Conditional operators are *And*, *Or*, and *Not*. Comparison operators are $<, >, =, <=,$ and $>=$. Identifier leaf nodes specify items from the working memory or global JavaScript variables if a match is not found in the working memory. The latter option, among other useful applications, provides access to the JavaScript Document Object Model (DOM) from within the condition. For this, no extra type of leaf node is needed.

Rule actions are JavaScript code blocks or events to be triggered on rule execution. A code block has access to the set of events that has led to the firing of the rule. Thus rule authors may create applications that do calculations on the parameters of the collected events. The use of the business vocabulary provides the necessary means for finding the event parameters and attributes of interest.

4.6 Design-Time Architecture

The design-time architecture consists of the components constituting the modeling as well as the transformation cycle as depicted in Fig. 4.1. These tools and components are executed off-line during the design, annotation, mining, design, and transformation phases.

4.6.1 Ontology Creation and Annotation of RIAs

Suitable ontologies are crucial for our ARRIA approach. We developed an approach amalgamating ontology learning [30], ontology refinement [43], and annotating RIAs into one coherent tool. The main ideas behind this approach are described in detail in [45]. Based on this approach we developed the adaptation ontologies elaborated in the previous section.

4.6.2 Semantic Web Usage Mining

Web usage mining is the application of data mining algorithms on Web server access logs to gain a better understanding of user behavior. Besides the access logs, metadata describing the Web resources and their content are conceptually helpful for data-mining analysis. The utilization of the metadata is strongly dependent on its organization and the way it can be combined with the log entries [15]. In recent years the research areas semantic Web and Web mining have become more important and have merged into a new research field called semantic Web mining, a field which has been deeply analyzed [6, 46]. In particular, semantic Web usage mining as a subcategory of semantic Web mining enables tracking of user behavior at a conceptual level.

Figure 4.3 shows the different stages of our semantic Web usage mining architecture. The first stage is the preprocessing stage. Here, the ontologies are designed, the Web resources are annotated, and the user sessions are reconstructed. Reconstructing user sessions is a difficult task, because of the lack of log-in data. The user sessions are reconstructed using common reconstruction methods as detailed in [42]. The available data sources for the second stage, the data mining step, comprise the reconstructed sessions, the annotated Web resources, and the domain ontology. The last two items form a knowledge base of available metadata. The Web usage mining algorithms used for this purpose are association rules, sequential rules, and multilevel rules based on a concept hierarchy. Moreover, clustering approaches that consider the user behavior as well as semantic contents are considered. More technical details are given in [44].

The results of the data mining step can be used for Web site optimization or online recommendation based on user behavior and semantic content. The new item

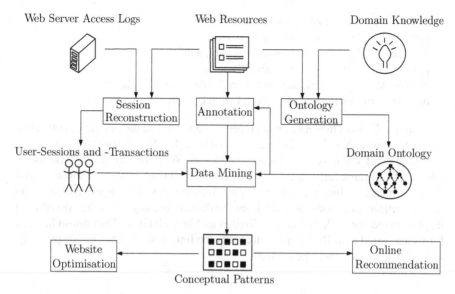

Fig. 4.3 Semantic Web usage mining architecture

problem illustrates the benefits of using semantics in Web usage mining. New items can be recommended directly after their annotation. That is possible, because our data mining approach, as well as our recommendation engine, work on concepts rather than concrete URLs or IDs. As an example, the following rule is considered: $C1 \wedge C2 \rightarrow C3$. This rule states that if pages annotated with $C1$ and $C2$ are visited, all pages annotated with concept $C3$ are candidates to be recommended. Now if a new Web resource annotated with $C3$ is introduced, it can be added to these candidates, because the rules are on the conceptual level.

4.6.3 Design of Adaptation Rules

After applying semantic Web usage mining to access log files, the discovered patterns need to be analyzed by an e-Government expert. The domain expert has to judge, whether or not the patterns are useful. Patterns that have been judged useful are then encoded into a rule format as adaptation rules. So, for instance, we discovered the following rule after evaluating the patterns found in the annotated access log file of the city of Vöcklabruck: 85% of all users that filled in the marriage certificate form and the wedding day form also filled in the birth certificate form.[4]

---

[4] support: 0,01; confidence: 0,85

Example 1 (Adaptation rule in SWRL).
   portal:Form(?*a*) ∧ portal:isVisited(?*a*, true) ∧
   domain:WeddingDay(?*b*) ∧ portal:isAnnotated(?*a*, ?*b*) ∧
   portal:Form((?*c*)) ∧ portal:isVisited(?*c*, true) ∧
   domain:MarriageCertificate(?*d*) ∧ portal:isAnnotated(?*c*, ?*d*) ∧
   domain:BirthCertificate(?*e*) → portal:showLink(?*e*)

Example 1 shows how an rule engineer could formulate the rule described above in the Semantic Web Rule Language (SWRL) [28]. Translated into English the rule states that whenever a form annotated with WeddingDay and a form annotated with MarriageCertificate were visited, show all links to forms annotated with BirthCertificate as link recommendations. WeddingDay, MarriageCertificate, and BirthCertificate are concepts taken from the domain ontology. The functionality of displaying recommended links is realized as an SWRL built-in. The built-in finds all forms annotated with BirthCertificate, reads the link from the appropriate property, and, finally, recommends these links.

4.6.4 Ontology and Rules Transformer

With the ontologies, annotations, and adaptation rules in place, the last step is depicted in the transfer cycle. It is the transformation of all of these parts into a client-readable format that can be executed by a browser's JavaScript engine. As an Internet browser on a client machine has only limited processing power and main memory capacity, both ontologies and rules must be translated beforehand in an easy-to-parse format that can be effortlessly executed on the client side. Because of the lack of a client-side reasoner, we materialize all ontologies at the server side. By using Pellet[5] as open source OWL DL reasoner [41], we check the consistency of the ontology at design-time, classify the instances, and infer the class hierarchy. There are two possibilities for representing ontologies on the client side: XML or JSON (JavaScript Object Notation) [14]. XML is very verbose and adds additional overhead to the payload. Furthermore, XML rules encoded in XML cannot be executed directly on the client, but have to be parsed, thus making an added expense. Therefore, we decided to represent ontologies, annotations, and rules in the compact and directly executable data interchange format JSON.

   Figure 4.4 shows what the JSON format looks like, after transforming the concept Button. As depicted in the concept hierarchy of Protege the class Button has several super and subconcepts. Additionally, there exists one instance of Button in the ontology. Not shown are the properties of the Button class, which in fact are *hasID* and *thisclass*. A class is represented as an object in JSON and its instances are collected in a property of type Array called *indi*. This array contains all instances as objects whereas the objects in turn hold their properties as attributes. The last attribute *thisclass* is a reference to the instantiated class and is automatically added

---

[5] http://pellet.owldl.org/

during the translation. The class hierarchy is stored directly in the JSON object representing the class as Array attributes: superclass and subclass.

Rules not encoded directly in our JSON-Rule format have to be translated into a client-executable format as well. The SWRL adaptation rule from the Example 1 is translated into the JSON-Rule format in Example 2. It consists of an object in curly braces having three attributes "event," "condition" and "action." The event part starts on line 02. It contains a complex event of type *And* with two children listening to user events from the DOM. The first event is triggered when the Web form #WeddingDay is submitted, the second is triggered when #MarriageCertificate is submitted. The condition part follows on line 17. It causes the preceding event to be only recognized when the condition is fulfilled. It is fulfilled if a working memory element of name "recommends" is found where the field "links" does not contain a value "BirthCertificate." On the occurrence of the event and the fulfilled condition, the action, starting on line 28, specifies that the value "BirthCertificate" is to be added to the links of the same working memory element of name "recommends." The action is formulated as a "MODIFY" operation on the named working memory element. A line of JavaScript is the modification.

Example 2 (Adaptation Rule in JSON-Rule Format).

```
01  {
02      "event": {
03          "type": "AND",
04          "children": [
05              {
06                  "type": "DOM",
07                  "selector": "#WeddingDay",
08                  "event": "submit"
09              },
10              {
11                  "type": "DOM",
12                  "selector": "#MarriageCertificate",
13                  "event": "submit"
14              }
15          ]
16      },
17      "condition": [
18          {
19              "name": "recommends"
20              "fields": [
21                  {
22                      "field": "links", "comparator":
                            "notContains",
23                      "literal": "BirthCertificate"
24                  }
25              ]
26          }
27      ],
28      "action": [
29          {
30              "type": "MODIFY",
31              "name": "recommends",
```

```
32        "modify": "this.links.push('BirthCertificate');"
33      }
34    ]
35  }
```

4.7 Run-Time Architecture

The core responsibility of the run-time architecture is to ensure the user-centric adaptiveness of the RIA. The run-time architecture is constituted by the adaptation cycle as depicted in Fig. 4.1. After transforming the ontologies, annotations, and adaptation rules into a client-readable format at design-time, they can be transmitted in answer to a client request at any point in time. When a user requests the RIA, not only content and layout data are sent to the client, but also the JSON representation of the ontologies, annotations, and rules. On the client side, the user model is built up and the portal is adapted by tracking user interactions and executing adaptation rules. Figure 4.5 shows the interplay of the constituent run-time components.

In a Web browser HTML pages are internally represented as a DOM. Whenever a user interacts with the Web page, the DOM fires appropriate events that can be

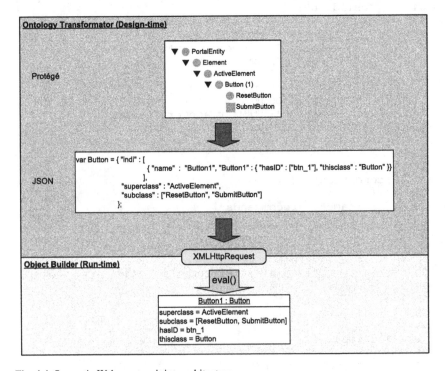

Fig. 4.4 Semantic Web usage mining architecture

caught by the event handler component. To catch events the event handler has to register first to specific event types. Each recognized event results in a call of the user tracking component and, in a second step, the invocation of the rule engine. The user tracking component resolves the relationships between the JavaScript events, the user interface elements, and their annotations. Furthermore, it records the events to the user model. In this way the user model materializes the browsing history of the current user on the level of JavaScript events. Based on the Web usage data stored in the user model, the rule engine evaluates the adaptation rules. The user model is periodically sent back to the server using the asynchronous communication facility of AJAX. The accumulated user models form the basis for a further modeling cycle.

For our implementation we chose JavaScript from the available Web programming languages. The data structures and program logic we implemented are roughly divided into the following areas: the adapters for the rule language and the remote event sources, the working memory, the condition representation and evaluation, and the complex event detection (see Fig. 4.5).

For complex event detection we are using a graph based approach as proposed in [13]. Initially the graph is a tree with nested complex events being parents of their less deeply nested subevents, down to the leaves being simple events. However, common subtrees may be shared by more than one parent. This saves space and time compared to detecting the same subevents multiple times and renders the former tree a directed acyclic graph. The graph is built starting at the leaves, bottom–up. The simple event types from the available rules are stored in a hash map and form the leaves of the tree. The hash keys are the event names. Each hash value (i.e., leaf) has a list of parents containing pointers to inner tree nodes. These in turn carry references to their parents.

When using the term *event*, the distinction must be drawn between event occurrences (i.e., instances) and event types, something which is usually done implicitly. In the detection graph the nodes are event types and they exist before there are any instances. Event instances exist after simple instances arrive and are fed into the graph at the leaves. Complex instances are then formed at the parent nodes, which in turn propagate their results upward. Every complex event occurrence carries pointers to the set of its constituent event occurrences, so that the events and their parameters can be accessed later. Once an occurrence is computed at a node that is attached to a rule, the evaluation of the associated condition is started.

A condition is also stored in a hierarchical structure, imitating the nesting of operators from the rule language. For each operator from the rule specification, a corresponding node is created that holds references to its child nodes. Every node has a Boolean function `evaluate()` that is specific to the corresponding operator and computes the value of its node from the values returned by the child nodes. This allows for recursive evaluation of subconditions, delegating the work to subnodes and propagating the results back to the root. At the leaves of the tree are literal values or identifiers that are queried from the working memory. The working memory may contain objects that are added, specifying an identifying string and a type from the set of classes in the business vocabulary. Thus, any working memory item can be found by its name or its type. Hash maps are used to implement fast lookup of the

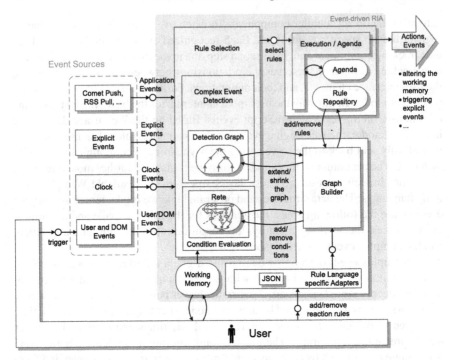

Fig. 4.5 Run-time architecture

objects by these criteria. Hash maps are also used to represent the *Is-A* relationship for types from the business vocabulary in order to find matches by supertype. We do not use object-oriented inheritance here because faceted classification is more expressive. Primitives may also be added to the working memory and autoboxed and unboxed to be handled transparently. Subsequently an item can be retracted, whereupon all references in the working memory are deleted. Our framework enables rule authors to directly access JavaScript features from their conditions.

Rule execution is done by inspecting the action parts in the rule specification. Explicit triggering of events and the direct execution of JavaScript code are possible. For every explicit event name that is specified, a new simple event occurrence is fed into the detection graph at the leaf of the corresponding event type. As the leaves are stored in a hash map, finding the leaf to a name is a simple hash lookup. For every JavaScript action that is specified in the action part of the rule, the code runs inside a new function that is created at run-time. The set of events that triggered the rule is then passed to the function. Thus, the rule action may employ the data from the constituent events in its computation. That includes the occurrence and duration times, the number and sequence of events, and the parameters carrying all values collected at the occurrence of the events.

Adapters had to be implemented in several components of our framework. Events have to be manifested into first class objects in order to propagate and store them in the detection tree. This is done by an adapter that constructs new objects for the events, adds the timestamp when it was received and parameters based on the type of event in accordance with the business vocabulary. The event is then fed into the detection graph. Adapters for other event sources may be added, e.g., to facilitate the polling of RSS feeds and the construction of event objects for the feed items or for detected changes in repetitive feed items.

Using the graph builder component another adapter converts the declarative rule language into internal data structures. The adapter dissects the rules. For the event part, the nodes are turned into nodes for the detection graph. The graph builder incorporates them into the graph, reusing common subtrees that it can detect among the newly added nodes and the existing graph. Among the detected similarities are identical subtrees, commutations of the children of operator nodes *And* and *Or*, identical temporal events, and identical simple events. For the condition part of a rule, the adapter creates the object tree to recursively evaluate a condition along the nested operator nodes as described previously in this section. The graph builder in turn stores the condition structures. For the JavaScript blocks in the action part, the adapter creates functions. As functions are first class objects in JavaScript, they need to be compiled only once and can be stored by the graph builder for later invocation.

4.8 Evaluation

The implementation of the conceptual framework was realized using Java libraries for the design-time code generation and AJAX for the run-time components. We evaluated our prototypical implementation at different levels. First, we evaluate our semantic Web usage behavior mining approach. Second, we looked at the time consumption of rebuilding the ontologies and executing the adaptation rules at run-time on the client side, and, finally, we evaluated our approach theoretically. That means we looked at the JSON format representing the ontologies.

The practical evaluation of the semantic Web usage mining was done based on the access log date of the e-Government portal of Vöcklabruck, whose service delivery mainly comprises electronic forms. These form pages, along with some other pages, were annotated using the faceted ontology that describes such forms according to their subject, target group, etc. Six months of Web server log data were analyzed, revealing 10011 sessions, in which form pages were accessed. We concentrated our analysis on searching for association rules related to the annotated form pages, specifically, types of forms that co-occurred in the same session. We hypothesized that an association rule involving two form types might mean one of two things: either the user confused the two forms or the two forms really are often used in the same session. The first case indicates that some help to disambiguate the forms is needed. The second indicates an opportunity to make the service more efficient by recommending the forms. We did, in fact, find a number of association rules involving two or more forms. Consultation with a domain expert revealed that one of them turned up an opportunity to streamline form processing. It related to people who want to remarry and who have to also provide information about a prior marriage. Either offering a combined form or offering the two forms together with an explanation of this case would improve the usability of the portal. We were also able to confirm that replacing URIs with concept names aids interpretation. Another general conclusion is that mining the concepts rather than the pages results in more rules being found, because multiple pages are often annotated with the same concept. Also, we tested multilevel mining and did find some rules at higher levels of generalization, when none were to be found at the more specific levels. As regards annotation, our experience was that after-the-fact annotation of a portal is somewhat time consuming and tedious. So, ideally, the annotation should be created as part of page creation.

The design-time modeling of ontologies and rules, as well as the subsequent translation into JSON, is the nontime critical part of the application. The transformation from RDF/XML syntax into JSON rules and the mapping of OWL concepts, instances, and relations into JSON occurs at design-time. But already at this stage optimization is a crucial issue. The preparation of the JSON file for later usage on client side requires an effective mapping method to keep the amount of data represented on the client to a minimum. As the result of translating ontologies, annotations, and rules, the compressed JSON format lets the file size shrink to 50% of its original size. The file size decreased from 42,1 KB (RDF/XML) to 20,3 KB (JSON).

The more time critical issues are the run-time tasks, such as the initial loading and creation of OWL concepts on the client side as well as the execution of rules and user interface adaptation on the client side. At the time of accessing the RIA the ontologies, annotations, and rules have to be uploaded to the client as a first step. The JSON file is executed using the JavaScript function *eval()*, and concepts, instances, and rules are represented as JSON objects on the client-side. An evaluation of this initial client-side concept creation is depicted in the following Figure 4.6a). The initial transfer and construction of the rules and ontologies does not affect the usability too much, since it takes place within the first couple of seconds a user accesses a new page, a time period of almost no interaction. As the diagram shows, the time consumption is below 200 ms for up to 10,000 concepts, something which is not recognized by the user when loading the page. During run-time the most important task is the execution of rules and the subsequent adaption of the user interface. The client-side rule engine is implemented using the Rete algorithm. Each rule is evaluated and, if all conditions hold, the body (action) of the rule is executed. In Fig. 4.6b) the performance of the rule execution is evaluated. As an evaluation constraint we let each rule fire, which means that all conditions of our evaluation rule set hold. Each rule manipulates the user interface of our exemplary ARRIA. The evaluation of each rule starts with loading the rules.

During the performance evaluation a slight distinction in the measurement results between the two tested Web browsers (Internet Explorer[6] and Mozilla Firefox[7]) has been determined. The diagrams are based on the average measurement results of both Web browsers.

---

[6] http://www.microsoft.com/windows/products/winfamily/ie/default.mspx

[7] http://www.mozilla.com/en-US/firefox/

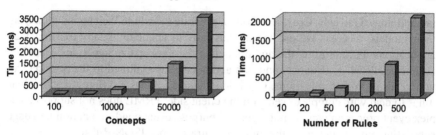

Fig. 4.6 Evaluation: (a) Client-side initial JSON concept creation; (b) rule execution time evaluation

We also evaluated the JSON format we created in order to represent OWL ontologies. Our JSON ontology serialization is conceived to minimize the time of accessing instances on the client side. The format puts some limitations on the representation of ontologies. On the other side, these limitations have no restrictive effects to the overall approach of client-side adaptation of RIAs as we solely rely on the concept taxonomy in our adaptation rules. By computing the subsumption hierarchy at design-time we can construct the entire class hierarchy graph. However, in doing so we lose all information regarding OWL class axioms such as equivalent classes and union or intersection class descriptions. All axioms and descriptions are mapped to a simple subclass relation. Also all information about relations are lost. Relations only appear as attributes in objects and are no longer represented as discrete entities. Only individuals are transformed without any information loss. But as already mentioned, because consistency checks are performed at design-time and the adaptation rules only rely on instances, their relations, and class hierarchy, there are practically no constraints to our approach.

4.9 Related Work

In [16], the integration of semantics in Web usage mining techniques is shown applied to a movie Web site. On the basis of a movie ontology and the user behavior, user profiles were constructed and used for online recommendations. In the center of our approach are e-Government Web sites consisting of forms, services, and information.

Comparing our work with standard models for adaptive hypermedia systems such as e.g., AHAM [36], we observe that they use several models: conceptual, navigational, adaptational, teacher, and learner. Compared with our approach, these models correspond to ontologies presented in Sect. 4, but miss their formal representation. Moreover, we express adaptation functionalities as encapsulated and reusable OWL-DL rules, while the adaptation model in AHA uses a rule-based language encoded in XML.

In the Web engineering paper [23] AWAC is presented, a prototype CAWE tool for the automatic generation of adaptive Web applications based on the A-OOH methodology. Garrigós, Cruz, and Gómez generate the whole Web application from their models, whereas we use the models only to annotate already existing Web applications. Furthermore, the authors define the Personalization Rules Modeling Language (PRML), an event condition action language tailored to the personalization needs of Web applications. Our rule language follows a different approach as it has to deal with complex events on the client side. PRML does not support complex event processing and is not a general purpose event condition action language supporting more than personalization, in contrast to our JSON-Rules.

The ECA-Web language suggested in [17] is an enhanced XML-based event condition action language for the specification of active rules, conceived to manage adaptiveness in Web applications. Our JSON-Rules are different to that approach as we, as stated in the name, relay on JSON as exchange and execution format. Moreover, we incorporated an event algebra for specifying complex events based on Snoop. Besides that, the whole adaptation approach is quite different as we support real-time adaptation directly on the client compared with the server-side adaptation and rule execution approach of ECA-Web.

The Personal Reader [18] constructs a framework for designing, implementing, and maintaining Web content readers, thus providing personalized enrichment of Web content for each individual user. The adaptive local context of a learning resource is generated by applying methods from adaptive educational hypermedia in a semantic Web setting. Similarly [21] focuses on content adaptation, or, more precisely, on personalizing the presentation of hypermedia content to the user. However, neither approach focuses on the online discovery of the profile of the current user. This, though, is one of the main features of our approach. Another difference between our approach and others would be the self-adaptivity.

In [19], the authors suggest the use of ontologies and rules in order to find related content on the Web, based on the content currently displayed to the user. We enhance this work by adapting the content based on accumulated Web usage data. Furthermore we show how to link semantics and content. Still, the main difference remains the introduction of the autonomous client, as we are dealing with Rich Internet Applications and not with common dynamic Web applications executed on a Web server.

The Web Accessibility Initiative – Accessible Rich Interactive Applications (WAI-ARIA) [40] is an applications suite defining how to make Web content and Web applications more accessible to people with disabilities. It focuses on dynamic content creation and advanced user interface controls developed with Ajax, HTML, JavaScript, and related technologies. The WAI-ARIA approach is also based on the annotation of RIAs with ontologies in order to capture the semantics of the single parts of the Web application. Our paper provides an approach that transforms OWL ontologies to a JSON format in order to access the semantic annotations directly on the client side. Furthermore, we also demonstrate how to declaratively present the adaptation logic. Making Web applications accessible is a subset of it. In addition, we showed a convenient and reactive way of achieving on-the-fly user interface adaptation.

Although the idea of combining CEP, production rules, and formal business vocabulary in RIAs is new, we built our approach on work that already exists. Most, if not all, languages for event specification have been developed for use in active databases so as to realize complex and composite trigger functionality. Apart from their original purpose, e.g., describing transactions or watching method calls in object oriented databases or the like, these languages are universal in their capabilities of building complex expressions from an arbitrary set of simple events. Over the last decades, several event detection strategies have been developed, strategies such as graph-based approaches [13], finite state automata [27], and colored petri nets [25]. The number of complex event pattern languages is also tremendous: COMPOSE [27], ODE [26], SAMOS [24], Snoop/SnoopIB [1], or Reaction RuleML [35]. Our work was very much inspired by Snoop and Reaction RuleML. The definition of complex event patterns of our JSON-Rules ECA language is to a large extent based on the SnoopIB operators. The structure of our JSON-Rules language follows a slightly modified structure of Reaction RuleML. Our detection algorithms for complex events are graph-based as proposed in [13].

In [10] an event-based architecture, which is very close to a streaming Web architecture, is proposed for RIAs. In this paper RIAs have the ability to receive events and to react to those events. Our solution goes one step further as we equip RIAs with the ability to construct complex events from simple ones. This architecture makes our solution more powerful, flexible, and open for personalization. The main difference is that we moved the detection of complex events from the server to the client.

In [39], an architecture for adapting RIAs based on production rules is proposed and in [38] the drawbacks of production rules and the need for complex event processing on the client side are explained. Our current work grasps and lifts the ideas to a higher level by adding complex event processing capabilities to RIAs.

4.10 Conclusions and Outlook

In this paper we presented the conceptual foundations of ARRIAs – Adaptive Reactive Rich Internet Applications. We elaborated our novel approach that holistically combines page annotations, semantic Web usage mining, user modeling, ontologies, complex event processing, and rules to adapt RIAs. We showed and evaluated how our concept of an autonomous client works. With our prototypical implementation we demonstrated the proof of concept, and our motivating example taken from the e-Government domain emphasized the practical relevance of our work. We proposed a lightweight reaction rule language tailored to the needs of ARRIAs. Our JSON-Rule language is a general purpose event condition action rule language capable of declaratively expressing client-side application logic. We used this language in order to encode the mined adaptation rules. In conjunction with our client-side rule engine this led to a highly responsive and on-the-fly adaptable user interface.

Currently, we are planning an end user evaluation. Recently, we started to re-design and annotate the e-Government portal of Vöcklabruck. Our evaluation plans comprise the whole adaptation loop, that is, from the design of the ontologies and adaptation rules to the real-time personalization of the user interface of the ARRIA. User questionnaires will be evaluated as well as benchmarks for the online execution of the adaptation rules directly on the client side.

Acknowledgments The work is based on research done within the FIT project - Fostering self-adaptive e-Government service improvement using semantic technologies. The FIT project is cofunded by the European Commission under the "Information Society Technologies" Sixth Framework Program (2002–2006).

References

1. R. Adaikkalavan and S. Chakravarthy. Snoopib: Interval-based event specification and detection for active databases. *Data Knowl. Eng.*, 59(1):139–165, 2006.
2. C. Alexander, S. Ishikawa, M. Silverstein, M. Jacobson, I. Fiksdahl-King, and S. Angel. *A pattern language*. Oxford University Press, 1977.
3. R. Armstrong, D. Freitag, T. Joachims, and T. Mitchell. Webwatcher – a learning apprentice for the world wide web. In *AAI Spring Symposium*, 1995. AAAI Spring Symposium.
4. S. Bechhofeer, F. van Harmelen, J. Hendler, I. Horrocks, D. McGuinness, P. Patel-Schneider, and L. A. Stein. Owl – web ontology language reference. Recommendation, W3C, 2004.
5. B. Benatallah, F. Casati, D. Georgakopoulos, C. Bartolini, W. Sadiq, and C. Godart, editors. *Web Information Systems Engineering – WISE 2007, 8th International Conference on Web Information Systems Engineering, Nancy, France, December 3–7, 2007, Proceedings*, volume 4831 of *Lecture Notes in Computer Science*. Springer, 2007.
6. B. Berendt, A. Hotho, D. Mladenic, M. van Someren, M. Spiliopoulou, and G. Stumme. A roadmap for web mining: From web to semantic web. In *Web Mining: From Web to Semantic Web*, volume 3209, pages 1–22, Heidelberg, Springer,2004.
7. H. Boley. The rule markup language: Rdf-xml data model, xml schema hierarchy, and xsl transformations. In Oskar Bartenstein, Ulrich Geske, Markus Hannebauer, and Osama Yoshie, editors, *INAP (LNCS Volume)*, volume 2543 of *Lecture Notes in Computer Science*, pages 5–22. Springer, 2001.
8. V. Broughton. *Essential Thesaurus Construction*. Neal-Schuman, 2006.
9. P. Brusilovsky. Methods and techniques of adaptive hypermedia. *User Model. User-Adapt. Interact.*, 6(2–3):87–129, 1996.
10. G. T. Carughi, S. Comai, A. Bozzon, and P. Fraternali. Modeling distributed events in data-intensive rich internet applications. In Benatallah et al. [5], pages 593–602.
11. S. Casteleyn, F. Daniel, P. Dolog, M. Matera, G.-J. Houben, and O. De Troyer, editors. *Proceedings of the 2nd International Workshop on Adaptation and Evolution in Web Systems Engineering AEWSE'07, Como, Italy, July 19, 2007*, volume 267 of *CEUR Workshop Proceedings*. CEUR-WS.org, 2007.
12. S. Chakravarthy. Sentinel: An object-oriented dbms with event-based rules. In Joan Peckham, editor, *SIGMOD '97: Proceedings of the 1997 ACM SIGMOD International Conference on Management of Data*, pages 572–575. ACM Press, 1997.
13. S. Chakravarthy, V. Krishnaprasad, E. Anwar, and S. K. Kim. Composite events for active databases: Semantics, contexts and detection. In Jorge B. Bocca, Matthias Jarke, and Carlo Zaniolo, editors, *20th International Conference on Very Large Data Bases, September 12–15, 1994, Santiago, Chile proceedings*, pages 606–617, Los Altos, CA 94022, USA, 1994. Morgan Kaufmann.

14. D. Crockford. Rfc4627: Javascript object notation. Technical report, IETF, 2006.
15. H. Dai and B. Mobasher. Using ontologies to discover domain-level web usage profiles. In *2nd Semantic Web Mining Workshop at ECML/PKDD-2002*, 2002.
16. H. Dai and B. Mobasher, editors. *Using Ontologies to Discover Domain-Level Web Usage Profiles*, 2002.
17. F. Daniel, M. Matera, A. Morandi, M. Mortari, and G. Pozzi. Active rules for runtime adaptivity management. In Casteleyn et al. [11].
18. P. Dolog, N. Henze, W. Nejdl, and M. Sintek. The personal reader: Personalizing and enriching learning resources using semantic web technologies. In *International Conference on Adaptive Hypermedia and Adaptive Web-Based Systems (AH 2004)*, August 2004.
19. A. Ankolekar, D. Thanh Tran, and P. Cimiano. Rules for an ontology-based approach to adaptation. In *1st International Workshop on Semantic Media Adaptation and Personalization*, Athen, Greece, December 2006.
20. D. Feldkamp, K. Hinkelmann, B. Thönssen, and S. Marie Thomas. D5: As-is-analysis. Technical report, FIT consortium, http://www.fit-project.org/Documents/D5.pdf, September 2006.
21. F. Frasincar and G.-J. Houben. Hypermedia presentation adaptation on the semantic web. In Paul De Bra, Peter Brusilovsky, and Ricardo Conejo, editors, *AH*, volume 2347 of *Lecture Notes in Computer Science*, pages 133–142. Springer, 2002.
22. J. James Garrett. Ajax: A new approach to web applications. *http://www.adaptivepath.com/publications/essays/archives/000385.php*, 2005.
23. I. Garrigós, C. Cruz, and J. Gómez. A prototype tool for the automatic generation of adaptive websites. In Casteleyn et al. [11].
24. S. Gatziu and K.R. Dittrich. Events in an Active Object-Oriented Database System. In N.W. Paton and H.W. Williams, editors, *Proc. 1st Intl. Workshop on Rules in Database Systems (RIDS)*, Edinburgh, UK, September 1993. Springer, Workshops in Computing.
25. S. Gatziu and K. R. Dittrich. Detecting composite events in active database systems using petrinets. In *Proc. Fourth International Workshop on Active Database Systems Research Issues in Data Engineering*, pages 2–9, 1994.
26. N. H. Gehani, H. V. Jagadish, and O. Shmueli. Event specification in an active object-oriented database. *SIGMOD Rec.*, 21(2):81–90, 1992.
27. N. H. Gehani, H. V. Jagadish, and O. Shmueli. Compose: A system for composite specification and detection. In *Advanced Database Systems*, pages 3–15, London, UK, Springer, 1993.
28. I. Horrocks, P. F. Patel-Schneider, H. Boley, S. Tabet, B. Grosof, and M. Dean. Swrl: A semantic web rule language combining owl and ruleml. Technical report, W3C Member submission 21 May 2004.
29. C. A. Kaplan, J. Fenwick, and J. Chen. Adaptive hypertext navigation based on user goals and context. *User Model. User-Adapt. Interact.*, 3(3):193–220, 1993.
30. A. Maedche and S. Staab. Semi-automatic engineering of ontologies from text. In *Proceedings of the 12th International Conference on Software Engineering and Knowledge Engineering*, 2000.
31. M. Mahemoff. *Ajax Design Patterns*. O'Reilly, 1. ed. edition, 2006.
32. N. Mathe and J. R. Chen. User-centered indexing for adaptive information access. *User Model. User-Adapt. Interact.*, 6(2-3):225–261, 1996.
33. B. Mobasher, R. Cooley, and J. Srivastava. Automatic personalization based on web usage mining. *Commun. ACM*, 43(8):142–151, 2000.
34. J. Nielsen and H. Loranger. *Prioritizing Web Usability*. New Riders, Berkeley, CA, 2006.
35. A. Paschke, A. Kozlenkov, and H. Boley. A homogenous reaction rules language for complex event processing. In *International Workshop on Event Drive Architecture for Complex Event Process*, 2007.
36. C. Romero, S. Ventura, C. Herváas Martinez, and P. De Bra. Extending aha! In *Proceedings of the Fifth International Conference on Human System Learning, ICHSL*. Europia, November 2005.
37. L. Rosenfeld and P. Morville. *Information Architecture for the World Wide Web: Designing Large-Scale Web Sites*. O'Reilly, August 2002.

38. K.-U. Schmidt and L. Stojanovic. From business rules to application rules in rich internet applications. In Witold Abramowicz and Dieter Fensel, editors, *BIS*, volume 7 of *Lecture Notes in Business Information Processing*, pages 447–458. Springer, 2008.

39. K.-U. Schmidt, L. Stojanovic, N. Stojanovic, and S. Thomas. On enriching ajax with semantics: The web personalization use case. In *Proceedings of the European Semantic Web Conference, ESWC2007*, volume 4519 of *Lecture Notes in Computer Science*. Springer, July 2007.

40. R. Schwerdtfeger and J. Gunderson. Roadmap for accessible rich internet applications(wai-aria roadmap). World Wide Web Consortium, Working Draft (WAI-ARIA Roadmap), 2006.

41. E. Sirin and B. Parsia. Pellet: An owl dl reasoner. In Volker Haarslev and Ralf Möller, editors, *Description Logics*, volume 104 of *CEUR Workshop Proceedings*. CEUR-WS.org, 2004.

42. M. Spiliopoulou, B. Mobasher, B. Berendt, and M. Nakagawa. A framework for the evaluation of session reconstruction heuristics in web usage analysis. *INFORMS Journal of Computing, Special Issue on Mining Web-Based Data for E-Business Applications*, 15, 2003.

43. L. Stojanovic, J. Ma, and N. Stojanovic. D9: Methods and tools for semi-automatic learning of a domain ontology that models the content of a front office. Technical report, FIT consortium, http://www.fit-project.org/Documents/D9.pdf, January 2007.

44. L. Stojanovic, J. Ma, J. Yu, N. Stojanovic, K.-U. Schmidt, S. Thomas, and T. Rahmani. D18: Methods and tools for mining the log data by taking into account background knowledge. Technical report, FIT consortium, http://www.fit-project.org/Documents/D18.pdf, July 2007.

45. L. Stojanovic, N. Stojanovic, and J. Ma. An approach for combining ontology learning and semantic tagging in the ontology development process: egovernment use case. In Benatallah et al. [5], pages 249–260.

46. G. Stumme, A. Hotho, and B. Berendt. Semantic web mining: State of the art and future directions. *Web Semantics: Science, Services and Agents on the World Wide Web*, 4(2):124–143, June 2006.

47. C. G. Thomas. Basar: A framework for integrating agents in the world wide web. *IEEE Computer*, 28(5):84–86, 1995.

48. S. Thomas and K.-U. Schmidt. D4: Identification of typical problems in e-government portals. Technical report, FIT consortium, http://www.fit-project.org/Documents/D4.pdf, July 2006.

49. J. Tidwell. *Designing Interfaces*. O'Reilly, 1. ed. edition, 2006.

50. J. A. Waterworth. A pattern of islands: Exploring public information space in a private vehicle. In Peter Brutsilosky, Piet Kommers, and Norbert A. Streitz, editors, *MHVR*, volume 1077 of *Lecture Notes in Computer Science*, pages 265–278. Springer, 1994.

Section 3: Knowledge Representation and User Interfaces

Chapter 5
Towards Enhanced Usability of Natural Language Interfaces to Knowledge Bases

Danica Damljanović and Kalina Bontcheva

5.1 Introduction

One of the most prominent benefits gained from the emergence of Semantic Web technology is the possibility to access data more efficiently, through the use of ontologies [18]. Querying such data requires using formal languages such as SeRQL [7] or SPARQL [39]. However, the syntax of these formal languages tends to be too "artificial" and complex, especially for domain experts who are unfamiliar with such machine-like languages.

To minimise the learning curve mandatory for the access of such data, many user-friendly interfaces have been developed. Some of them provide a graphical interface where users can browse the data (e.g., Protégé [36]), others offer a form-based interface for performing search whilst hiding the complexity of formal languages, e.g., KIM Platform [31]. The most sophisticated ones provide a simple text box for a query, which takes full-blown questions or a set of keywords as an input, and return answers in a user-understandable form.

According to the interface evaluation conducted in [28], systems developed to support Natural Language (NL) interfaces are perceived as the most acceptable by end-users. This conclusion is drawn from a usability study, which compared four types of query language interfaces to knowledge bases and involved 48 users of general background [28]. The full-sentence query option was significantly preferred to keywords. However, using keywords for querying was preferred to menu-guided, or graphical query language interfaces.

On the other hand, evaluation of CHESt [40] – a system about computer history that accepts both keywords and NL queries as input – revealed user's preference for keywords unless the full-blown questions yielded better results. Namely, when asked if they would accept typing full blown questions instead of keyword-based

Danica Damljanović and Kalina Bontcheva
University of Sheffield, Department of Computer Science, Regent Court, 211 Portobello Street, S1 4DP, Sheffield, UK, e-mail: {D.Damljanovic,K.Bontcheva}@dcs.shef.ac.uk

V. Devedžić and D. Gašević (eds.), *Web 2.0 & Semantic Web*, Annals of Information Systems 6, DOI 10.1007/978-1-4419-1219-0_5,

queries, 22% of users answered positive, 69% said they would accept only if this yielded better results, and 8% of users disliked this option.

The development of accurate Natural Language Interface (NLI) systems is "very complex and time-consuming task that requires extraordinary design and implementation efforts" [28, p.281]. According to [22], a major challenge in building NLIs is to provide the information the system needs to bridge the gap between the way the user thinks about the domain of discourse and the way information about the domain is structured for computer processing. In the case of Natural Language Interfaces to Knowledge Bases (NLIs to KBs), the domain knowledge is in the knowledge base. The knowledge base is typically created by instantiating classes defined in the domain ontology and relating them as per ontology definitions. Therefore, it is very important to consider the ontology structure and content when building NLIs to KBs.

Another big challenge is building a robust NLI due to the very difficult task of automatically interpreting natural language [11]. NLIs are also typically difficult to port to other domains [11]. *Portable* or *transportable* NLIs are those that can be adapted easily to new domains (e.g., from software engineering to cultural heritage). Although they are considered as potentially much more useful than domain-specific systems, constructing transportable systems poses a number of technical and theoretical problems as many of the techniques developed for specialised systems preclude automatic adaptation of the systems to new domains [22]. Moreover, portability affects retrieval performance: "the more a system is tailored to a domain, the better its retrieval performance is" [28, p.281].

This paper explores how these challenges are addressed by different existing NLIs to KBs, with emphasis on their usability and the overall retrieval performance. The usability of NLIs to KBs is observed from the two aspects: that of the developer who is customising the system for a new domain and that of the user who is using it for querying. More specifically, we are presenting the survey of the state of the art, in order to:

- Compare usability of existing customisation methods used to port NLIs to KBs to new domains
- Compare usability of methods for assisting the user in getting the right answers (e.g., assistance while formulating the query)

By conducting this survey we are expecting to answer the question of how existing NLIs to KBs can increase the performance without a significant additional cost for customisation and further, which methods are efficiently used to assist the user, in order to reach better user–system interaction and consequently better performance.

The paper is organised as follows. In Sect. 5.2 challenges for NLI development are discussed, followed by usability measures used for evaluation of such systems, and the aim of the survey is presented in this paper. Section 5.3 discusses the usability of NLIs from the perspective of application developers in charge of system customisation. We review different NLIs to KBs and present their evaluation results, concluding with a discussion on how the performance of the reviewed systems can be improved (see Subsect. 5.3.9). Next, Sect. 5.4 covers usability from an end-user point of view – specifically methods for assisting end-users when formulating the query and the impact of such methods on performance. Based on this, we draw recommendations for NLI system design in Subsect. 5.4.6. Overall conclusions are discussed in Sect. 5.5.

5.2 Natural Language Interfaces to Knowledge Bases

Natural Language Interfaces to structured data allow users to interact with a system using written or spoken language (e.g., English) to perform tasks that usually require knowledge of a formal query language. The intention behind building NLIs to structured data is enabling users with no knowledge of formal languages to use them with minimal, ideally, no training. From end-users' point of view, natural language is easy to use, considering that it is used everyday in human to human communication [37].

Research in the area of NLIs has been around for more than three decades. Most of the developed NLI systems are created to serve as an interface to relational databases (e.g., [23, 38, 47] and many others). Recently, these evolved towards interfaces to semantically richer data in the form of ontologies/knowledge bases. The third popular group of NLI systems are concerned with accessing semi-structured data from documents. NLIs are also used for dialogue and tutoring systems [11], e.g., a chat bot called Asimov, which answers simple questions in English (asimov-software.com). Lastly, a few NLI systems are developed for purposes other than knowledge access, such as a replacement for a programming language, e.g., see the NLC system [6].

In this paper we focus on NLIs to ontologies/knowledge bases and their usability. If an ontology consists of a finite list of terms and the relationships between them (TBox) [1], a knowledge base is a set of interconnected instances, which are created based on defined concepts and relations from the ontology (ABox). As a knowledge base in this case always relies on an ontology (contains references to the ontology), we will use the term knowledge base to refer to the instantiated ontology and ontology at the same time. Therefore, we say that the focus in this paper is on NLIs to KBs. Such NLIs accept natural language queries as input, generate formal queries behind the scene, execute them against an ontology/knowledge base, and present the results to the user.

5.2.1 Habitability

NLIs were invented to assist the communication between users and computers. However, some studies ([10, 32]) show that users behave differently when communicating with computers than with humans. In the latter case, their conversation relies heavily on context, whereas with a computer the language they use is restricted as they are making assumptions about what computers can and cannot understand [37].

One particular approach to the human–computer communication problem is to keep it brief and use restricted natural language syntax [34]. However, a big challenge when restricting the vocabulary of an NLI system is to consider habitability.

Habitability indicates how easily, naturally, and effectively users can use language to express themselves within the constraints imposed by the system. If users can express everything they need for their tasks, using the constrained system language, then such NLIs are considered *habitable* [37]. In other words, habitable languages are languages that people can use fluently [19]. According to [19], a language is habitable if (1) users are able to construct expressions of the language that they have not previously encountered, without significant conscious effort; and (2) users are able to avoid easily constructing expressions that fall outside the bounds of the language. Another way of viewing habitability is the mismatch between the users expectations and the capabilities of an NLI system [5].

5.2.2 Usability

The habitability of an NLI system correlates directly to its usability. According to Brooke [8], *usability* can be defined as "being a general quality of the appropriateness to a purpose of any particular artefact." In other words, usability is evaluated in the context in which an NLI system is used, by measuring its appropriateness for that context. First, it is important to identify the system's target users, and second – the tasks that these users will have to perform [8].

NLIs to KBs are used by:

- *Application developers* who are responsible for porting the systems to a specific domain and whose task is to customise the system to work with that domain (if the system requires customisation)
- *End-users* who are querying the customised system in order to retrieve domain knowledge (e.g., domain experts).

Therefore, the usability of NLI systems to knowledge bases should be evaluated from two different aspects: (1) that of the user who is customising the system, and (2) that of the user who is querying the system. According to ISO 9241-11, measures of usability should cover [8]:

1. *Effectiveness* – the ability of users to complete tasks using the system and the quality of output of these tasks
2. *Efficiency* – the level of resource consumed in performing tasks
3. *Satisfaction* – the user's subjective reaction to using the system

Effectiveness: customisation issues. As discussed in Sect. 5.3 next, the task of the user who is customising the system is usually to create a domain-specific lexicon. The quality of the output of this task can be evaluated by measuring the performance of the system when it is ported from one domain to another. As this task does not involve actual end-users, performance can be measured in the abstract through the *coverage* of the system. Given a set of questions collected from a real-world application, the percentage of those that are answerable (e.g., covered by the domain lexicon or/and by the knowledge base) can be summarised as coverage. In other words, coverage here refers to the number of questions that would be successfully answered by the system, assuming that the questions are successfully parsed. The richer the lexicon is, the higher value for the coverage. This term should not be mixed with the *language coverage*, which usually refers to the complexity of questions covered by an NLI system.

Effectiveness: end-user's point of view. As we are mainly interested in effectiveness in terms of quality of the retrieved answers; typically NLI systems are evaluated in terms of precision and recall, which are measured adapted from information retrieval (see [35,38]). *Recall* is defined as the number of questions correctly answered by an NLI system, divided by the total number of questions.[1] Excluded from these are often questions with errors or which are ungrammatical or clearly out of the scope of the queried knowledge base [11]. *Precision* measures the number of questions correctly answered divided by the number of questions for which the answer is returned at all [11].

Efficiency. Efficiency refers to the level of resource consumed in order to perform the specific task. In other words, efficiency reflects how fast a user can accomplish a task. In case of NLI users, this is usually reported by the time needed to customise the system for a specific domain (the developer's point of view), or by the time needed to successfully find the particular information (the end-user's point of view). In the latter case, the efficiency is usually expressed by the execution time for the queries of various complexity.

User satisfaction. There is no unique way of measuring user satisfaction. The most common methodology is to engage users into a session with the system and ask them to fill a questionnaire where they can express their views on the different features of the system. One of the most popular questionnaires used for evaluating different interfaces is SUS – System Usability Scale – a simple ten-item scale giving a global view of subjective assessments of usability [8].

5.2.3 The Aim and the Scope of the Survey

The goal of the survey presented in this paper is to explore methods for building habitable and usable NLIs to KBs. We review usability, based on evaluation measures discussed above, from the two aspects: that of the users in charge of customising the system and that of the users who are querying the system. These two aspects are independently discussed in Sect. 5.3 and 5.4.

---

[1] Sometimes, recall is interpreted as the number of questions answered by an NLI system, divided by the total number of questions.

Section 5.3 reviews existing NLIs to KBs, with regards to the performance and customisation issues. We must emphasise that comparing the performance of the different NLIs to KBs is not a trivial task, due to the variation in evaluation conditions (e.g., ontologies used) and measures used. To begin with, the datasets used to evaluate the different systems are not the same and their size, coverage, and quality varies. In addition, the benchmark queries are of different complexity [37]. Overall, these differences make comparative system evaluation somewhat unreliable, because the evaluation metrics and, consequently, the reported system results are heavily dependent on which datasets are used and how difficult the queries are. Nevertheless, in our view, these results still provide enough evidence of where the major problems lie and where additional improvements can be made, in order to achieve usable and easily portable NLIs to knowledge bases.

Section 5.4 reviews methods for assisting the end-users when formulating the queries and therefore is mainly concerned with the ways to address habitability. We clearly stated methods used for achieving habitable systems from the end-users' point of view, and based on the evaluation results of various systems we have reported how the application of such methods can affect the retrieval performance.

By conducting this survey we expect to answer several questions, such as: which methods can affect the retrieval performance of NLIs to KBs; if existing methods can be combined; and which method is suitable for which situation/domain; which new methods need to be researched and applied.

5.3 Customisation and Retrieval Performance

In this section, we review several NLIs to KBs and report on their performance and customisation issues. To give as objective comparison as possible, we show on which dataset was the system evaluated, how the process of customisation is performed, and the recall and precision values. This section only covers a sub-set of NLIs to KBs, i.e., those that reported evaluation results.

A brief overall summary is shown in Table 5.1, subdivided by dataset, as no reliable comparison of precision and recall can be made across different datasets. The main conclusion to be drawn from this table is that although systems with zero customisation tend to have reasonable performance, it varies significantly across systems – in general, the more complex the supported queries are, the lower the performance is.

5.3.1 ORAKEL

ORAKEL is an NLI to knowledge bases [11], which supports factual questions, starting with wh-pronouns such as who, what, where, etc. Factual here means that answers are ground facts as found in the knowledge base, but not complex answers

Table 5.1 Natural language interfaces to knowledge bases

Dataset	System	Precision (%)	Recall (%)	Portability
	PANTO	88.05	85.86	0 customisation
Mooney: geography	Querix	86.08	87.11	0 customisation
	NLP-Reduce	70.7	76.4	0 customisation
Mooney: restaurants	PANTO	90.87	96.64	0 customisation
	NLP-Reduce	67.7	69.6	0 customisation
Mooney: jobs	PANTO	86.12	89.17	0 customisation
Software engineering	QuestIO	82.14	71.87	0 customisation
ontology	AquaLog	86.36	59.37	0 customisation
Geographical facts about Germany	ORAKEL	80.60–84.23	45.15–53.7	Customised
Library data	E-librarian	97%	–	–
Biology	CPL	38%	–	–
Chemistry	CPL	37.5%	–	–
Physics	CPL	19%	–	–

to *why* or *how* questions that require explanation. The most important advantage of ORAKEL in comparison to other such systems is its support for compositional semantic construction, i.e., the ability to handle questions involving quantification, conjunction and negation.

ORAKEL has a domain-independent component with a shared *general lexicon*, where for example words such as *what*, *which*, etc. are stored. A part of the *domain-specific lexicon* is created automatically from the domain ontology and is called *ontological lexicon*. Another part of the domain-specific lexicon is created manually and contains mappings of subcategorisation frames to relations, as specified in the domain ontology. Subcategorisation frames are essentially linguistic argument structures, e.g., verbs with their arguments, nouns with their arguments, etc. For example, a verb *write* requires a subject and an object, as it is a transitive verb. This "triple" of subject–verb–object in this case could be considered a subcategorisation frame, and could be mapped to an ontology relation *writes*. Subcategorisation frames are created by the person in charge of customising the system, who is usually the domain expert. He does not have to be familiar with computational linguistics, although he is expected to have a very basic knowledge of subcategorisation frames. The adaptation of the NLI is performed in several iterative cycles in the user interaction sessions, based on the questions that the system fails to answer. In this way, the *coverage* of the lexicon is being increased each time. The evaluation reported in [11] indicates that users preferred creating the lexicon during these interaction sessions, rather than from scratch.

In the user study carried out in [11] the question was if it is feasible for users without expertise in NLP to customise the system without significant problems. The evaluation knowledge base contained geographical facts about Germany, covering 260 entities in total. The experiment was conducted with 27 users. Three persons had to customise the lexicon, while the remaining 24 users who did not have any background knowledge in computational linguistics received brief instructions for the experiment: the scope of the KB was explained to them and they were asked to explicitly say if the received answer was correct or not; each user had to ask at least ten questions.

Only one of the three people in charge of creating the domain lexicon was very familiar with the lexicon acquisition tool (user A), while the other two users (user B and user C) were not and received 10 min of training on the software (FrameMapper tool [11]) and 10 min of explanation about the different subcategorisation types, illustrated with examples. User A constructed the lexicon in one iteration, whereas users B and C constructed it in two rounds, each lasting 30 min. In the first round they created the model from scratch, while in the second round they were presented with those questions that the system had failed to answer after the first round of four sessions with different users. Overall, users B and C had 1 h each to construct the lexicon.

The results showed that querying system that used lexicons created by users B and C gives comparable precision and recall to that of using the lexicon created by the user A. Namely, after the second iteration, recall for users B and C was 45.15% and 47.66%, respectively, in contrast to the recall when user A created the lexicon (53.67%). Precision was in the range from 80.95% (user B) to 84.23% (user A). The customisation system of ORAKEL is designed so that in each iteration, the created lexicon is more accurate and thus gives better performance. Consequently, the more time users spend customising the system, the better the performance of the system is.

5.3.2 AquaLog

AquaLog [33] is a portable question-answering system, which takes queries expressed in natural language and an ontology as input and returns answers drawn from one or more knowledge bases, which instantiate the input ontology with domain-specific information. With a controlled language, such as that used by Aqua-Log, users can create factual queries beginning with *what*, *which*, *who*, and the like. The types of supported queries are classified into 23 groups. Questions not belonging to one of these 23 types will not be answered as this system heavily relies on its controlled language.

Although the customisation of AquaLog is not mandatory (except providing the URL of the different ontology), it can increase the performance of the system [33]. The role of a person who customises the system is to associate certain words with relevant concepts from the ontology. For example, *where* needs to be associated with ontology classes that represent a location such as *City* and *Country*; similarly, *who* needs to be associated with, e.g., classes *Person* and *Organisation*. Additionally, it is possible to add the so-called *pretty names* to the concepts or relations in case that the term that is used when referring to a concept is not in the knowledge base. For example, if the property *locatedIn* is usually lexicalised as *in*, this will be added as a pretty name for that property. AquaLog also uses WordNet [20] for extending the system vocabulary.

During evaluation reported in [33], ten users who are not familiar with the KMi knowledge base[2] or AquaLog generated questions for the system. They were given an introduction about conceptual coverage of the ontology pointing out that its aim is to model the key elements of a research lab such as people, publications, projects, research areas, etc. They were also told that temporal information is not handled by AquaLog and that the system is not a conversational system, as each question is resolved on its own without references to the previous questions.

From the 69 collected questions, 40 of them were handled correctly [33]. However, this includes seven queries with conceptual failures that happen when the ontology does not cover the query (e.g., the ontology is not designed properly, lack of appropriate relation or term to map with, or having instances instead of classes) and 10 questions for which the answer was not in the knowledge base.

To evaluate portability, AquaLog was also trialed with the wine ontology.[3] To customise the system to work with the new domain, first words like *where*, *when*, and *who* were associated with relevant ontology resources, and then synonyms for several ontology resources were manually added. As the authors point out in [33], this step was not mandatory, but due to the limitations of WordNet coverage, it increases the recall. Overall, the system was able to handle 17.64% of questions correctly. The system failed to answer 51.47% of questions due to the lack of knowledge inside the ontology.[4] However, the lack of knowledge was not the only cause of low performance, as many problems arose due to the *problematic* ontology structure, which is designed so that it contains a lot of restrictions over properties. To be handled properly by AquaLog, the ontology should have simpler hierarchy structure; also, the terms in a query should be related by no more than two direct relations. For example, if the query would be *which cities are located in Europe*, *cities* might refer to the ontology class *City*, whereas *Europe* might refer to an instance of the class *Continent*. If these concepts are related so that a *City* is located in a *County* and a *County* is located in a *Country*, where *Country* is located in a *Continent*, this query would not be handled by AquaLog. However, if in this chain *County* would not exist, and there would be direct relation between *City* and *Country* (located in), the query would be processed and answered as the number of relations between the terms *City* and *Europe* (as a continent) is 2. In addition, all resources should be accompanied by labels inside the ontology [33].

5.3.3 E-Librarian

E-librarian [40] system accepts a complete question in natural language and returns a set of documents in which a user can find the answer. A dictionary with only domain-specific words is designed and used instead of external sources such as

---

[2] KMi knowledge base is populated based on AKT ontology http://kmi.open.ac.uk/projects/akt/ ref-onto/ and they are both a part of KMi semantic portal: http://semanticweb.kmi.open.ac.uk

[3] http://www.w3.org/TR/2003/CR-owl-guide-20030818/

[4] Note that these numbers do not refer to the precision or recall as defined in this paper.

WordNet. There is no evaluation on how expensive it is to build this dictionary; however, it needs to be built manually [40].

The E-librarian service was applied in two applications: one is CHESt – about computer history, and the other is about fraction in mathematics – MatES. The performance of MatES is evaluated with 229 questions created by a mathematics teacher who was not involved in the implementation of the prototype. The system returned the right answer for 97% of the questions; however, the paper does not present sufficient information on the complexity of those questions.

5.3.4 CPL

Computer Processable Language (CPL) [14] is capable of translating English sentences to formal Knowledge Representation (KR). KR is Knowledge Machine (KM) language – a mature, advanced, frame-based language with well-defined semantics.

CPL was evaluated by two users in three domains: biology, physics, and chemistry. They all received 6 h of training individually, followed by 1 week using the question-answering system. Our understanding is that the domain knowledge was created using the CPL language; however, in [13], there is no information about how much time was needed to create the domain knowledge used in the evaluation. In Physics 131 questions were asked, and the correctness of answers was 19.%[5] This low figure is due to the fact that some questions were very complex, comprising several sentences. The total number of questions in biology was 146, and the average correctness was 38%. In chemistry, 86 questions were answered with 37.5% correctness.

Examination of the system failures revealed that one-third was caused by the fact that the user did not create the query that was understandable for the system (some common sense facts were not expressed explicitly enough), so the question was unanswerable. Another third was because the knowledge base did not have an answer and the last third was caused by mistakes of the CPL interpreter that misinterpreted CPL English, so the system failed to find the solution.

5.3.5 PANTO

PANTO [49] is a portable NLI to Ontologies. From [49] there is no evidence of what types of questions are supported, but as they claim that the system correctly parsed 170 questions taken from AquaLog's Web site we can assume that PANTO supports a set of questions that is similar to that supported by AquaLog. Similar to AquaLog, WordNet is used for the vocabulary extension, and the user lexicon is

---

[5] It is important to point out that although Table 5.1 shows these measures as precision, this result is calculated on the overall set of questions, whereas most other systems removed the questions for which the answer was not in the KB before calculating precision.

configurable – there is no need to manually customise the system unless the user is interested in adding associations to the ontology resources in order to improve system performance.

PANTO was evaluated with test data provided by Mooney,[6] which have been used widely to evaluate NLIs to databases. This dataset covers three domains: geography, restaurants, and jobs. As shown in Table 5.1 precision and recall for this dataset is quite high, although it contains relatively simple queries.[7] In addition, the range of supported NL queries is limited to those handled by SPARQL, e.g., questions starting with *how many* are not supported. Additionally, they do not report if the answer of the question was found in the knowledge base, as is the case with most other systems, but rather if the generated SPARQL query was correct. They also do not comment on customisation issues and if the system was customised prior experimenting with three different domains.

5.3.6 Querix

Querix [30] is another ontology-based question answering system that translates generic natural language queries into SPARQL. However, [30] does not make it clear what types of questions are supported by the system. When Querix was evaluated on Mooney geography domain (215 questions) the precision was 86.08% and recall 87.11%. Similar to the performance of PANTO, if the answer was returned by the system, it was almost always correct. The majority of unanswered queries required handling of negation, which is not supported by Querix. As the system vocabulary is derived from the ontology vocabulary, there is no need for customisation. The downside of this approach is that the quality of the ontology strongly affects the system's performance.

5.3.7 NLP-Reduce

NLP-Reduce is a naive domain-independent natural language interface for the Semantic Web [29]. It accepts full sentence queries, sentence fragments, or keywords in a text field. However, the performance of the system differs when used with different knowledge bases. This indicates that the quality of data and the complexity of the queries on these knowledge bases is not always the same and that the performance of the system relies on it.

---

[6] http://www.cs.utexas.edu/users/ml/nldata.html

[7] Note that the recall here is calculated with *number of answered* questions, even if they are not all correct.

5.3.8 QuestIO

Similar to NLP-Reduce, QuestIO (Question-based Interface to Ontologies) [17] is quite flexible in terms of complexity and syntax of the supported queries. Both keyword-based searches and full-blown questions are translated to SeRQL (or SPARQL) queries and executed against the ontology in order to return answers to the user. Customisation of this system is performed automatically from the ontology vocabulary. In evaluation reported in [17], QuestIO and AquaLog systems were trialed with the GATE knowledge base,[8] which contains data about GATE source code, documentation, manuals, and the like. A set of questions was extracted from the GATE mailing list where users are enquiring about different GATE components. None of the two systems were customised for this experiment [17]. Reported results are used to calculate precision and recall shown in Table 5.1.

5.3.9 Summary and Discussion

Most of the mentioned systems rely on lexical matching from the ontology. Few of them use external sources to extend the vocabulary such as WordNet. However, the more technical the domain gets, the less is the chance that one can rely on lexical matching alone. In fact, it is not expected that the complete lexical knowledge necessary for very technical domains is present in general resources such as WordNet [12]. That is why domain lexicons, which contain only domain-specific vocabulary, tend to be also used by systems such as E-Librarian or ORAKEL (see Figure 5.1). Manually engineering a lexicon as in the ORAKEL system certainly represents an effort, but it allows to control directly the quality and coverage of the lexicon for the specific domain [12]. Moreover, it has been shown that the more time users spend customising the system, the better performance.

If we accept the fact that "there is no free lunch" [12], we then have to accept that, in order to build a NLI to KB with a reasonable performance, while not affecting portability, the system needs to be customisable easily by their users.

However, as we saw that the performance of the systems can be degraded by the problematic ontology structure (see Subsect. 5.3.2), there is potential in avoiding system failures caused by the ontology design. Moreover, scope of the knowledge base (e.g., the number of ontology resources defined) can affect the overall coverage of the system. Experts for customising NLI systems usually have to manually add descriptions or labels to the relevant terms (e.g., ontology resources). If an ontology would be created so that each concept and relation is accompanied by a human understandable label or description, the automation of domain-specific knowledge creation would be feasible, as during the automatic processing of the knowledge base, all human understandable text attached to the ontology resources would be processed and added to the lexicon.

---

[8] http://gate.ac.uk/ns/gate-kb

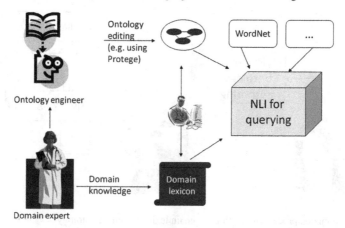

Fig. 5.1 Process of creating a domain lexicon manually, using an ontology

On the other hand, creating formal data is a high initial barrier for individuals wishing to create ontologies with existing ontology authoring tools such as Protégé as these often require specialist skills in ontology engineering. Therefore, using Natural Language for ontology authoring might be a solution. CLOnE – *Controlled Language for Ontology Editing* ([21, 45]) allows users to design, create, and manage information spaces without knowledge of complicated standards (e.g. OWL) or ontology engineering tools. CLOnE is implemented as a simplified natural language processor that allows the specification of logical data for semantic knowledge technology purposes in normal language, but with high accuracy and reliability. The components are based on GATE's existing tools for Information Extraction and Natural Language Processing [15]. CLOnE is designed either to accept input as valid (in which case accuracy is generally 100%) or to reject it and warn the user of their errors [21]. Many systems similar to CLOnE have been developed with the idea to enable ontology authoring using natural language (e.g., ACE [26], Rabbit [24]).

If the domain expert who is in charge of customising the system uses NLIs for ontology authoring instead of using the tools for customisation (see Figure 5.2), the time for training and learning language-specific terminology can be reduced. For example, if an NLI for ontology authoring allows construction like *Who is usually referring to a person* that will add an additional *label* to the class *Person*, and in this way, the approach used by some of the presented systems (AquaLog, PANTO) for manually customising the lexicalisations of ontology terms would be eliminated. Consequently, the system will "know" that when the user starts a question with *who*, it needs to be associated with a person.

However, in order to create NLIs to KBs with reasonable performance, not only quality customisation is essential, but there is a need to assist end users in the process of query construction. The next section discusses existing methods and how they can affect the overall performance of the system.

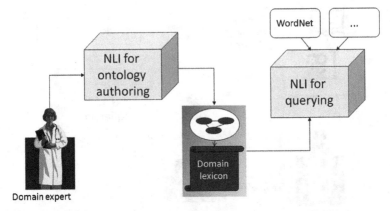

Fig. 5.2 Automated process of creating a domain lexicon from an ontology

5.4 Enhanced usability of Natural Language Interfaces: end-users' point of view

This section reviews methods for assisting the end-users during the search process with NLIs to KBs.

According to the traditional information retrieval, during the search process, the user poses a query based on an existing information need, and after retrieved results are shown, decides to stop or to reformulate the query in a way that promises to improve the result [44]. This is repeated until the "perfect" answer is found. As this traditional model is adequate only for simple cases, a so-called berry-picking model [2] has been proposed where users take some of the results and move on to a different topic area. This model assumes that the user starts off with a query on a particular topic and based on the results, he can either explore the result set or re-scope the search by re-defining the information need and posing a new query [44]. Although different users behave differently during the search process, it has been shown that majority prefer interactive methods, where the system performs the search, gives the feedback to the user, and lets him decide about the next steps [44].

In the context of NLIs to KBs, from the point of view of end-users, the search process is very similar. The main difference is related to the system design as a big challenge is to address habitability problem. One of the ways to address this problem is to support simple and explicit semantic limitations [19]. One way to achieve this is by restricting the supported vocabulary and grammar.

5.4.1 Vocabulary Restriction

A Controlled Language (CL) is a subset of a natural language that includes certain vocabulary and grammar rules that have to be followed. On one hand, a CL provides a simple way to retrieve data without extensive training for the end-user, whilst on the other has less expressiveness than the formal languages typically used for accessing structured data [17].

The biggest challenge when designing a controlled language is restricting the natural language so that it still remains intuitive and does not require much training for the end-user. However, applications in industry prove that, actually, CLs can be learnt and used in practise. For example, AECMA Simplified English [48] has been used by the aviation industry since 1986.

Another example is from CPL's evaluation [13], which found that, although users have to be very familiar with CPL in order to use it correctly, they do not have much trouble working with its grammar restrictions, as only a small number of the failures were due to violation of the CPL grammar. Some of the failures were due to the user language: the expressions were not explicit enough for the system (i.e., common-sense facts were not made explicit). The conclusion is that the system would benefit from showing the user the derived query interpretation and any mistakes made. As it is pointed out "a challenge for languages like CPL is to devise methods so that these corrective strategies are taught to the user at just the right time e.g., through the use of good system feedback and problem-specific on-line help" [14, p.510].

According to [37], constraining a user to a limited vocabulary and syntax is inappropriate, as users should be free, but the constraints should come from the task and the domain instead. However, allowing the task and the domain to constrain the language still does not prevent the user from creating ambiguous queries. As natural language itself is ambiguous even in human to human communication, controlled languages have a role to play in reducing the ambiguity and allowing a smooth exchange of information between humans and computers. This exchange can be improved by moving NLI systems towards conversational systems, which means that the system should provide the means of giving feedback to the user, by showing its interpretation of the user's query, so that the user can validate or reject it. Having a limited vocabulary, coupled with a feedback mechanism, means easy training from the end user's point of view [50].

As shown in Figure 5.3, to design habitable NLI system, the system's vocabulary has to be aligned to that of the user. In this paper we will discuss the effect of *feedback* (Sect. 5.4.2) and *guiding the user* (Sect. 5.4.3) through the available questions in order to assist this adaptation (red circle). In addition, as was discussed in Sect. 5.3, system vocabulary is often extended from external sources (e.g., Word-Net). For more personalised systems, this extension can be user-centric, as the user vocabulary can be used for extending the system vocabulary (Sect. 5.4.4). Once the user is familiarised with the system vocabulary, the opposite adaptation needs to take place, as the user vocabulary needs to be in line with that of the system (yellow circle). Methods for assisting the user in that adaptation are those that are used to solve *ambiguity* problem and are discussed in Sect. 5.4.5.

An alternative approach to restricting the vocabulary is to support both keyword-based and question-based queries. This allows some flexibility in a way that if the user is not familiarised with the full expressiveness of the controlled language, he can try with keywords, while for more advanced users there is option of using

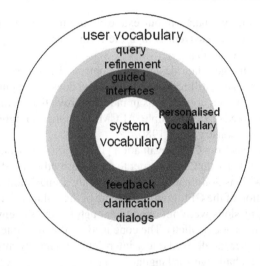

Fig. 5.3 Synchronizing the vocabulary of the user and the system

full-blown questions. Examples of such systems are QuestIO [17] or NLP-Reduce [29], which would give the same result for both "capital France" and "what is the capital of France?" queries.

5.4.2 Feedback

Showing the user the system's interpretation of the query in a suitably understandable format is called feedback. Several early studies ([41,50]) show that after getting a feedback, users are becoming more familiar with the system interpretations and the next step is usually that they are trying to imitate the system's feedback language. In other words, returning feedback to the user helps them understand how the system is transforming the queries, therefore motivating them to use the similar formulations and create queries that are *understandable* to the system.

In the evaluation of Querix and three other interfaces for semantic Web [30], this system was preferred to all others because it returned the answer in a form of a sentence, in contrast to the list of answers returned by the other three systems. For example, the question *How many rivers run through Colorado?* was answered by Querix as: *There are 10* [30], while the other three systems returned a list of rivers and the number of results found. Because of the way Querix replied to the questions, users had the impression that the system really understood them and trusted the system more [30].

The main drawback of controlled languages is their rather steep learning curve. For example, in order to formulate correctly questions using CPL, users need to know "a bag of tricks" [13]. That is one of the reasons why in CPL an interactive process of question-asking was introduced. After the user poses the question, their

Advice System detects CPL errors and returns reformulation advice. There are 106 different advice messages triggered when, for example, the user's question contains grammar rules that are outside the scope of CPL, although correctly interpreted in English; or when the user omits words, such as a unit of measure after the number [13]. The feedback is not using the input text from the user, but rather detecting the error and giving an advice from a static list of feedback sentences. As the authors point out in [13], automatic rewording would be very challenging, especially with longer, complex sentences. In addition to the Advice System, an *Interpretation Display System* is applied, which shows the user how the question is interpreted by the system. It works so that after posing the question, the system generates a set of English paraphrases and shows them to the user. In addition, it generates a graph where nodes are objects or events from the question, and arcs are relationships between them. If the user detects an error in the graph or English paraphrases, it is possible to rename nodes and arcs, or to reformulate the whole question and inspect the interpretation by the system again. In their evaluation with users in [13], this graphical representation was chosen as the most useful.

Although it might be annoying for users, it is not unusual that systems fail to answer the question, due to an unsupported query syntax, even though that same query could be answered if re-formulated. Adding support for extra linguistic coverage is not always easy due to the need to balance expressivity with ambiguity [33]. For instance, the evaluation of AquaLog on the KMI ontology [33] shows that 27.53% (19 of 69) of the questions could be handled correctly by AquaLog if re-formulated, which means that 65.51% of failures could be avoided. Reformulating in this case entails stating the queries in Aqualog's controlled language so that unsupported linguistic failures are avoided, as well as nominal compounds, or unnecessary functional words like *different, main, most of.*

Closer look at user's queries and behaviour during evaluation of CPL from [13] revealed that users rarely "got it right" the first time. The number of attempts of reformulating the query by the user, before either getting a satisfactory answer from the computer, or giving up, was counted. In physics and chemistry, this number was 6.3 and 6.6, respectively, as the questions were usually very complicated, while for biology the number of reformulated queries was 1.5, as the most common questions where very simple, such as "what is an X?," in contrast to the "story" questions as they call them posted in physics, and the algebraic questions posed in chemistry. Further analysis of the frequency of actions taken for reformulating the query, and the types of these actions, showed that the biggest problem for users was to find the right *wording* that enabled the system to answer the question. For example, in chemistry one of the question was whether a compound is *insoluble.* Users tried several words to express solubility: *soluble, dissolve, solution, insoluble,* until finally hitting on *solubility,* for which the system was able to give the answer.

Summary. By providing the user with the feedback in the form of system's interpretation of the query, users can learn how to generate queries more efficiently. For example, showing the user which words were understandable and which were not helps users to familiarise themselves with the system's vocabulary more quickly and avoid repeating mistakes.

In cases when the system is not able to interpret the query, the system could provide the user with a suggestion of how this query could be reformulated in order to be answered (e.g., by showing examples of supported types of queries adapted for the particular domain).

5.4.3 Guided Interfaces

According to [3], a major problem with query interfaces is how to guide the user in what queries are supported by the system. Users need knowledge about what it is possible to ask in a particular domain. In [3], relations between concepts are used to assist users by expressing what is possible to ask about the concept which is typed in – this way only meaningful questions can be posted.

According to Bullock [9] there is a need for lucidity in information systems – a system should supply the user with an idea as to what is available and which next steps can be taken. In [3], Description Logic (DL) is used to help supporting flexible querying and navigation through the information space, by using the tools for manipulation and construction of DL expressions or queries. These tools are driven by constraints known as *sanctions*, which are added to the DL model and which describe the meaningful compositions that can be built. Sanctions are used for lucidity or guidance for creating suggestions. Suggested manipulations are *restriction* – specialising the query by adding more criteria, *widening* – removing criteria from a composite query, *replacement* – replacing the topic by a more specific query, and *sibling replacement* – replacing subqueries with sibling concepts. All these manipulations are controlled by sanctioning, ensuring that only reasonable queries are built.

Ginseng [4] is a guided input natural language search engine for the semantic Web. This system allows access to knowledge bases in OWL through NL. The evaluation of Gingseng [4] reported 92.8% precision and 98.4% recall, which indicates that, although the user is limited in the way questions can be asked, this is counterbalanced by high performance–thanks to the offered support. The evaluation of its descendant GINO [5] with six users proves that the use of guided entry overcomes the habitability problem that hampers users' ability to use most full NLIs. The GINO system offers guidance to the user as they formulate a quasi-English query step by step, ensuring that only valid queries are posed.

Another option for guiding the user through the domain and available concepts is by using autocompletion. Traditional autocompletion is based on matching input strings with a list of the words in a vocabulary, sorted by different criteria, e.g., popularity, user preferences, etc. For ontology-based systems, this concept can be extended to the semantic level so that in addition to traditional string similarities, relations between ontology resources are used in order to predict the next valid entry [25]. The proposed *semantic autocompletion* is described in [25] and applied in information retrieval, specifically for multi-faceted search. For example, the semantic portal MuseumFinland[9] uses semantic autocompletion on request. The search keywords are matched not only against the actual textual item descriptions, but also the labels and descriptions of the ontological categories by which they are annotated and organised into view facets. As a result, a new dynamically created facet is shown on the user request and it contains all categories whose name or other configurable property value, such as alternative labels, matches the keyword. These categories describe the different interpretations of the keywords and the roles with respect to the search items. For example, if the user types in *EU countries*, the system would show list of countries from which the user can choose.

Summary To familiarise the user with the system's vocabulary and capabilities, methods for guiding the user through the space of allowed questions could be used. On one hand, the user is limited as the number of questions is limited, but on the other, the performance of such a system is rather high. This means that once the user formulated the query, it is very likely that he will get the answer. A more flexible option is the use of semantic autocompletion, so that users can choose, rather than know the names and type them in. This approach, contrary to fully guided interfaces, leaves the freedom to the user. On the other hand, if the user's input is not fully controlled, the habitability problem could arise nevertheless.

5.4.4 Personalised Vocabulary

As it has been discussed in Sect. 5.3, many NLIs to KBs use external vocabularies such as WordNet in addition to the domain lexicon. However, the vocabulary of the user could be a good source for extending the system vocabulary, as non-known words could be learned by the time, and used to enrich the lexicon and vocabulary used by the system.

The AquaLog [33] is backed by a learning mechanism, so that its performance improves over time, in response to the vocabulary used by the end-users. As already discussed in Sect. 5.3, when porting AquaLog to work with another domain, it is possible to configure its lexicon by defining "pretty names." During runtime, when the system is interpreting user's input ambiguously, it asks the user to help by choosing from several possible interpretations. The user's selection is then saved as a "pretty name" for future disambiguation of the same type. For example, in the evaluation they noticed that when referring to the relation *works-for* users use words like: *is working, collaborates, is involved in* [33]. When the system does not know that *collaborates* can be interpreted as referring to the property *works-for*, it will prompt the user with the available options and "learn" the user's choice. In addition to learning a new term, AquaLog records the context in which the term appeared. The context is defined by the name of the ontology, the user information, and the arguments of the question. Arguments of the question are usually the two arguments

---

[9] http://www.museeosuomi.fi

of the triple, namely two classes or two instances in the ontology connected by a relation.

To evaluate how the Learning Mechanism (LM) affects the overall system performance and the number of user interactions, two experiments are conducted and results are reported in [33]. First, AquaLog is trialed with LM deactivated. In the second experiment two iterations are performed. First, the LM is activated at the beginning of the experiment in which the database containing learned concepts is empty. The second iteration is performed over the results obtained from the first iteration.

The results show that using LM improves performance from 37.77% of answered queries to 64.44%. Queries that could not be answered automatically (i.e., required at least one iteration with the user) are quite frequent (35.55%) even if the LM is used. This is because the LM is applied only to relations, not to terms. For example, if the term in the query is a name *Peter*, the user would have to choose in the first iteration from the list of people with names *Peter Scott*, *Peter Whalley*, etc. Finally, the number of queries that require two or three iterations are dramatically reduced with the use of the LM system.

In conclusion, AquaLog LM can improve the performance even for the first iteration from 37.77% to 40% as it uses the notion of context to find similar but not identically learned queries. This means that LM can help to disambiguate the query even if it is the first time this query is presented to the system.

Summary: Although external sources such as WordNet can enrich the system vocabulary, as well as the domain lexicon that is created individually for each domain, the user-centric vocabulary can play a significant role in increasing the performance of the system over time.

In addition to maintaining the user vocabulary, the AquaLog's approach can be extended to allow users to see and modify the created lexicon at any time. Moreover, in cases when the system cannot offer any options based on the existing user-centric vocabulary, the vocabularies of other users could be used. For example, if the user A asks "Who works for the University of Sheffield?," the system can recognise *The University of Sheffield* as an *Organisation*, and *Who* as a *Person*, but the construction *works for* could be unknown and not similar to any of the existing ontology relations between classes *Person* and *Organisation*. If there are several relations between these concepts, the system can prompt the user (as would be the case with AquaLog) to choose from the list of available options. If the user chooses relation *employedIn*, the system will remember that *works for* can be related with the relation *employedIn* and would add this to the user-centric vocabulary. If now the user B asks the same question, and there is no data about *works for* construction in his user-centric vocabulary, the vocabulary of the user A could be used to automatically give the answer to the user B, or to rank the *employedIn* relation on the top of all others suggested by the system. In an ideal case, the users A and B should be recognised as *similar*. For determining similar users, user profiles need to be modeled. However, modeling user profiles requires a good understanding of the user interests, needs and behaviour as well as understanding the domain knowledge. According to the number of systems that use ontologies to model user profiles (e.g., [16]), it is likely that their nature has a great potential in creating quality user profiles.

Another direction of improving the personalised feature is related to the presentation of options: recommendations offered to users are usually the names of potential ontology resources, e.g., names of properties, and these sometimes do not sound natural. For example, properties usually consist of at least two words, such as *has-Brother* or *has-brother*. Simple processing of such names can help deriving more natural words such as *has brother*. However, the way ontology resources are named is definitely not standardised, and this feature would have to be customised for each system dependently on the domain.

5.4.5 How to Deal with Ambiguities?

Although controlled languages reduce natural language ambiguities to some extent, some issues, specific to domain knowledge, still remain. For example, if the knowledge base contains two instances of a class *Person* with the same name, e.g., *Mary*, the system is not able to predict in which one the user is interested in. The way this problem is usually solved is (1) using heuristics and ontology reasoning to implement ranking algorithms to solve ambiguities automatically or/and (2) by asking the user for clarification (clarification dialogues). In cases when the cause of ambiguity is a vague expression of the user information need, query refinement can be used to improve the system performance.

Automatically solving ambiguities. E-librarian [40] system uses focus function algorithm in case of ambiguities. A focus is a function that returns the best interpretation for a given word in the context of the complete user question. If there is more than one best interpretation, they are all shown, although the experience with the system revealed that the users generally enter simple questions where the disambiguation is normally successful [40].

OntoNL is an ontology-based natural language interaction generator for multimedia repositories [27]. This system combines domain knowledge with user profiles, both represented in standards such as MPEG-7 and TV-Anytime to resolve ambiguities and rank results, thus avoiding clarification dialogues. Their system is domain-specific and oriented towards digital libraries.

In QuestIO [46], relation ambiguities are resolved automatically, based on *string similarity metrics* (comparison of the user input and the name of the ontology relation) in addition to the *position of the relation, its domain and range classes inside ontology hierarchy*. The more specific the relation, its domain and range classes are, the better chance that it will be ranked high.

Clarification dialogues. In case of ambiguities Querix [30] send them to the user for clarification. In this process users need to disambiguate the sense from the menu with system-provided suggestions, in order to get better retrieval results. For example, if the user enters *population size* and the system cannot decide if the user is interested in the property with name *population density* or *population*, it will ask the user to choose from the two.

Similar to Querix, the AquaLog system [33] relies on clarification dialogues when ambiguity arises. In comparison to Querix, AquaLog is backed by the learning mechanism discussed above (see Sect. 5.4.4), so it saves the results for future sessions.

In general, clarification dialogues can help users resolve ambiguities caused by the content inside the repository. However, if the suggestions provided by the system are not satisfactory, it is likely that the user's need was not expressed precisely, which is the main pre-requisite for retrieving relevant information from the knowledge base (see Figure 5.4).

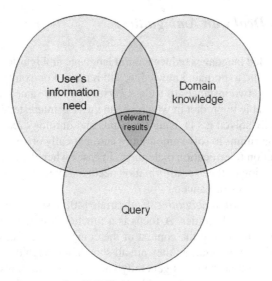

Fig. 5.4 Retrieving relevant result with NLI systems

According to [42], there is usually a gap between the information need and the query which is expressing that need, which is caused by "the usage of short queries, whose meaning can be easily misinterpreted". The indicator of this gap, which is called *query ambiguity* [43], can be reduced by the process of query refinement.

Query refinement. Changing or refining the query in order to obtain results that are more relevant is called *query refinement*. When refining the query it is important to know the precise information need as well as which part of the query to change/refine [42]. Refining usually means adding more constraints to the query, until the quality of the results corresponds to the user expectation.

Librarian Agent [42] – a system created to replace the human librarian when helping users to find the appropriate books in the library – uses the query refinement technique proposed by Stojanovic [43]. The agent measures query ambiguities regarding the ontology structure (structure-related ambiguity) and the content of the knowledge base (content-related ambiguity). Ambiguities are interpreted from the point of view of the *user's need*, which are implicitly induced by analysing the user's behaviour. Modeling user's need is not trivial especially when users are anonymous as the model of the user behaviour has to be developed implicitly, i.e., by analysing *implicit relevance feedback* whose main idea is to infer the information need by analysing the user interaction with the portal [42].

The agent further defines the neighbourhood of the user's query, which is identified by the query constraints and the ambiguity of each word. Query neighbourhood includes determining:

1. *A more specific query.* The query is refined so that the set of answers is more specific.
2. *A more generic query.* The query is refined so that the set of answers is bigger.
3. *Equivalent query.* When the query is rewritten so that the returned results are the same, but this is initiated for other reasons, e.g., optimising the execution time.
4. *Similar queries.* The query is refined so that its results are partially overlapped with the initial query.

The query refinement process is treated as the process of moving through the query neighbourhood in order to decrease its ambiguity regarding user's need [42].

In Librarian Agent, the ontology lexical layer contains about 1,000 terms, and the information repository (KB) contains about 500 information resources (Web pages about persons, projects, etc.). Each information resource is related to an instance in the ontology. The query refinement system is implemented as an additional support in the searching process so that it can also be switched off. When it is switched on, the user gets the query neighbourhood after posting the query.

For evaluation the authors selected 20 questions. They cannot be expressed precisely using the defined ontology vocabulary, but the answers are contained in the information repository, e.g., "find researchers with diverse experiences about the semantic web." Six computer science students with little or almost no knowledge about ontologies or the domain, and with no knowledge of the system, were asked to retrieve resources for 10 questions in one session, using the two retrieval methods. Users were asked to explicitly confirm when they get relevant result.

For each search they considered four measures: success, quality, number of queries, and search time. Results revealed that *success* and the *quality of the session* were significantly higher (57/85.7%; 0.6/0.9), while the *number of queries* and the *search time per session* was significantly lower for the system with query refinement switched on (10.3/5.2; 2023/1203s). Stojanovic concludes that if the system can discover and measure ambiguities in a query and support the user in resolving these ambiguities efficiently, the precision and recall of the retrieval process will increase.

Summary. In some cases it is not convenient for users to control the output either because they are not interested to do so, or the system might have enough data to efficiently solve ambiguities automatically. However, this is strongly related to the domain and the system functionality. The more specific the domain and the simpler the system, the more feasible automatic ambiguity resolution is.

Deriving all possible calculations from available sources could assist in solving the ambiguity problem without user's help. However, it is important to show these decisions to the user in an understandable way as they might not be satisfied with the system's decision and wish to change it. Letting the user choose and express weights of relevant topics/items is a good idea, as this gives users the power of controlling the system's output.

Clarification dialogues are good solutions if they can help system understand what the user is aiming at, whereas in cases of imprecise information needs, query refinement is likely to be a good solution. However, it is important to observe the user, their actions and behaviour during the process of refinement.

5.4.6 Summary and Discussion

Design of habitable NLI systems includes adapting the system vocabulary to that of the user. This adaptation minimises required users' training, which in ideal cases can be eliminated. Methods to achieve this are as follows:

Feedback.   Providing the feedback to the user by showing the system's interpretation of a query, the user can learn how to generate queries efficiently. Moreover, if the user uses words that are "unknown" to the system, feedback can be combined with *clarification dialogues* where the user is prompted by the system provided suggestions. The user's selected option can be further used to build a *personalised vocabulary* of the user. In cases when the system is not able to interpret the type of a question, the user could be prompt by the suggestion, e.g., the list of the supported questions for specific domain. However, the inspection of the queries posted by the user for the specific domain might be useful when defining a way of giving the feedback.

Guided interfaces.   For small domains, it is possible to provide guided interfaces to the user, which are fully controlled by the system. This means that the user does not have the freedom to enter a query of any length and form. However, as the performance of such systems can be high, and the habitability problem can be eliminated, this might be a preferred solution for domains for which the set of questions that could be asked is limited. A more flexible way of guiding the user is by showing autocomplete options.

Personalised vocabulary.   NLI systems can benefit from designing a user vocabulary, so that if the term used in a query is unknown to the system, that term can be "learnt" i.e, saved into a user-centric vocabulary that will be used in future. This vocabulary should be *controllable* by the user, so that advanced users can enrich the system vocabulary easily.

After the user is familiar with the system capabilities and the domain, adapting user's vocabulary to that of the system is necessary. However, ambiguity can arise either because of undefined information need, or due to the structure of the knowledge base. Methods for assisting the user include the following:

Clarification dialogues. Ontology reasoning as well as heuristics should be used in order to calculate ambiguities. In cases when the calculations are not leading to the one unambiguous solution, the user should be prompt by the *clarification dialogues* to choose from the system provided options.

Query refinement. Deriving similar queries, more specific and more generic queries can help users understand the scope of the system and might help in expressing the need more precisely. Ontologies play a significant role in predicting the query refinement process, e.g., defining a set of similar queries, as they contain semantics of the concepts and relations between them.

Controlling the relevance. Allowing users to define what does it mean relevant and also allowing them to assign relevance of retrieved results.

Ranking suggestions. Ranking popular and relevant queries and suggesting them before any other queries. By relevant queries we assume those that users specified to have satisfying results. Consequently, this means that the users have to be able to define what does it mean to be relevant.

Defining similarity. Although NLI systems should have the default measures to express similarity between concepts, it would be great to allow users to define what is similar in cases they want to dig deeper into the power of expressiveness, or in cases they want to have more control over the system output.

All of these five methods can be employed (and potentially improved) in combination with quality user profiles. However, creating and maintaining quality user profiles requires analysing the domain space (e.g., available domain knowledge) and user space (e.g., user interests and preferences) and making the connection between the two. The nature of ontologies is convenient for designing and intersecting these two spaces. Using "semantic web" language for creating user profiles would require the following:

1. *Creating domain space.* creating domain ontology with defined concepts and relations between them so that they explain the domain precisely. Instantiating the concepts and creating relations between the instances.
2. *Creating user space.* creating user ontology with defined concepts and relations between them so that they explain user interests, preferences and activities precisely. Instantiating the concepts and creating relations between the instances.
3. *Intersection of two spaces.* connecting the two spaces would result in defining user profiles. In practise, this would mean defining relations between concepts from the domain and user space, i.e., domain and user ontologies.

5.5 Conclusion

We have reviewed different NLIs to Knowledge Bases and their usability from the point of view of (1) users (developers) who are customising the system, and (2) end-users who are querying the system. Although systems that require zero customisation have reported high performance, the main concern is the strong dependence of performance on the quality of the ontology. Additionally, several other systems give better performance when manual customisation is enabled, in order to create associations between the user and the system vocabularies. To address this problem we have proposed using natural language interfaces for ontology authoring, in addition to querying, in order to enhance the quality of the data in the ontology and also to eliminate the process of manual customisation.

Based on the classification of methods used for assisting the users when formulating the queries, we have drawn the recommendations for building habitable and usable NLIs to KBs, from the end user's point of view. These recommendations contain the answer on questions such as when the certain method should be used, which methods could be combined with others and for which domain which method is suitable.

Comparison of NLIs to KBs in this paper reveals that there is the need to standardise the evaluation methods of such systems. Different systems use different datasets (e.g., ontology size), questions of various complexity, and even different evaluation measures. For example, in one case measuring recall might consider only correct queries (e.g., ORAKEL), while in the other case it might be the number of queries for which the system generated an output (e.g., PANTO). The third group often refers to the number of *answered queries* as performance (e.g., AquaLog), although it is not clear if the answers are correct. Moreover, in some cases, queries that return no results due to the knowledge base not containing the answer are counted as correctly handled and as such contribute to the overall performance of the system (e.g., AquaLog). From the evaluation results reported in such way no reliable conclusions can be made with regard to comparison of such systems.

To obtain a progress in the field of NLIs to KBs there is an emergent need to obtain the clear methodology of how these systems need to be evaluated, so that it would be feasible to compare how a method used in one system can affect the performance in another. Only then, when these systems follow the same rules and report on the same measure (evaluated with the same set of queries, the same knowledge base, and under the same conditions) the clear and precise conclusions of how to work on improvement of such systems can be reliable.

Acknowledgments This research is partially supported by the EU Sixth Framework Program project TAO (FP6-026460).

References

1. Grigoris Antoniou and Frank van Hermelen. *A Semantic Web Primer*. MIT Press, 2nd edition, 2008.
2. Marcia J. Bates. The design of browsing and berrypicking techniques for the online search interface. *Online Review*, 13(5):407–424, 1989.
3. S. Bechhofer, R. Stevens, G. Ng, A. Jacoby, and C. Goble. Guiding the user: an ontology driven interface. *User Interfaces to Data Intensive Systems, 1999. Proceedings*, pages 158–161, 1999.

4. A. Bernstein, E. Kaufmann, and E. Kaiser. Querying the semantic web with gingseng: a guided input natural language search engine. In *15th Workshop on Information Technologies and Systems, Las Vegas, NV*, pages 112—126, 2005.

5. Abraham Bernstein and Esther Kaufmann. GINO—A guided input natural language ontology editor. In *5th International Semantic Web Conference (ISWC2006)*, 2006.

6. A.W. Biermann, B.W. Ballard, and A.H. Sigmon. An experimental study of natural language programming. *International Journal of Man-Machine Studies*, 18:71–87, 1983.

7. Jeen Broekstra and Arjohn Kampman. Serql: a second generation rdf query language. In *In Proc. SWAD-Europe Workshop on Semantic Web Storage and Retrieval*, pages 13–14, 2003.

8. J. Brooke. SUS: a "quick and dirty" usability scale. In P.W. Jordan, B. Thomas, B.A. Weerdmeester, and A.L. McClelland, editors, *Usability Evaluation in Industry*. Taylor and Francis, London, UK, 1996.

9. J. Bullock. *Informed Navigation: description Logic Based Hypermedia Linking*. PhD thesis, University of Manchester, UK, 1999.

10. D. Chin. An Analysis of Scripts Generated in Writing Between Users and Computer Consultants. *National Computer Conference*, pages 637–642, 1984.

11. Philipp Cimiano, Peter Haase, and Jörg Heizmann. Porting natural language interfaces between domains: an experimental user study with the orakel system. In *IUI '07: Proceedings of the 12th international conference on Intelligent user interfaces*, pages 180–189, New York, NY, USA, 2007. ACM.

12. Philipp Cimiano, Peter Haase, Jorg Heizmann, Matthias Mantel, and Rudi Studer. Towards portable natural language interfaces to knowledge bases âĂŞ the case of the orakel system. *Data and Knowledge Engineering*, 65(2):325–354, May 2008.

13. Peter Clark, Shaw-Yi Chaw, Ken Barker, Vinay Chaudhri, Philip Harrison, James Fan, Bonnie John, Bruce Porter, Aaron Spaulding, John Thompson, and Peter Yeh. Capturing and answering questions posed to a knowledge-based system. In *Proceedings of the 4th International Conference on Knowledge Capture (K-CAP'07)*, 2007. http://www.cs.utexas.edu/users/pclark/papers/kcap07.ppt.

14. Peter Clark, Philip Harrison, Thomas Jenkins, John Thompson, and Richard H. Wojcik. Acquiring and using world knowledge using a restricted subset of english. In Ingrid Russell and Zdravko Markov, editors, *Proceedings of the 18th International FLAIRS Conference (FLAIRS'05)*, pages 506–511. AAAI Press, 2005.

15. H. Cunningham, D. Maynard, K. Bontcheva, and V. Tablan. GATE: a Framework and graphical development environment for robust NLP tools and applications. In *Proceedings of the 40th Anniversary Meeting of the Association for Computational Linguistics (ACL'02)*, 2002.

16. Danica Damljanović and Vladan Devedzic. Applying semantic web to e-tourism. In Zongmin Ma and Huaiqing Wang, editors, *The Semantic Web for Knowledge and Data Management: Technologies and Practices*. Information Science Reference (IGI Global), 2008.

17. Danica Damljanović, Valentin Tablan, and Kalina Bontcheva. A text-based query interface to owl ontologies. In *6th Language Resources and Evaluation Conference (LREC)*, Marrakech, Morocco, May 2008. ELRA.

18. J. Davies, D. Fensel, and F. van Harmelen, editors. *Towards the Semantic Web: ontology-driven knowledge management*. Wiley, 2002.

19. Samuel S. Epstein. Transportable natural language processing through simplicity—the PRE system. *ACM Trans. Inf. Syst.*, 3(2):107–120, 1985.

20. Christiane Fellbaum, editor. *WordNet – An electronic lexical database*. MIT Press, 1998.

21. A. Funk, V. Tablan, K. Bontcheva, H. Cunningham, B. Davis, and S. Handschuh. Clone: controlled language for ontology editing. In *Proceedings of the 6th International Semantic Web Conference (ISWC 2007)*, Busan, Korea, November 2007.

22. Barbara J. Grosz, Douglas E. Appelt, Paul A. Martin, and Fernando C. N. Pereira. TEAM: An experiment in the design of transportable natural-language interfaces. *Artificial Intelligence*, 32(2):173 – 243, 1987.

23. Catalina Hallett, Donia Scott, and Richard Power. Composing questions through conceptual authoring. *Computational Linguistics*, 33(1):105–133, 2007.

24. Glen Hart, Martina Johnson, and Catherine Dolbear. Rabbit: developing a control natural language for authoring ontologies. In *Proceedings of the European Semantic Web Conference ESWC 2008, Tenerife, Spain*, pages 348–360. Springer, June 1-5 2008.
25. Eero Hyvnen and Eetu Mkel. Semantic autocompletion. In *Proceedings of the first Asia Semantic Web Conference (ASWC 2006), Beijing*. Springer, New York, August 4-9 2006.
26. Kaarel Kaljurand. Writing OWL ontologies in ACE. Technical report, University of Zurich, August 2006.
27. Anastasia Karanastasi, Alexandros Zotos, and Stavros Christodoulakis. The OntoNL framework for natural language interface generation and a domain-specific application. In *Digital Libraries: Research and Development*, pages 228–237. Springer, Berlin (2007).
28. Esther Kaufmann and Abraham Bernstein. How useful are natural language interfaces to the semantic web for casual end-users? In *Proceedings of the Forth European Semantic Web Conference (ESWC 2007)*, Innsbruck, Austria, June 2007.
29. Esther Kaufmann, Abraham Bernstein, and Lorenz Fischer. NLP-Reduce: A âĂIJnaÂíÄśveâĂİ but domain-independent natural language interface for querying ontologies. In *Proceedings of the European Semantic Web Conference ESWC 2007, Innsbruck, Austria*. Springer, June 4-5 2007.
30. Esther Kaufmann, Abraham Bernstein, and Renato Zumstein. Querix: A natural language interface to query ontologies based on clarification dialogs. In *5th International Semantic Web Conference (ISWC 2006)*, pages 980–981. Springer, November 2006.
31. A. Kiryakov, B. Popov, D. Ognyanoff, D. Manov, A. Kirilov, and M. Goranov. Semantic annotation, indexing and retrieval. *Journal of Web Semantics, ISWC 2003 Special Issue*, 1(2):671–680, 2004.
32. J. Krause. Natural language access to information systems. An evaluation study of its acceptance by end users. *Information Systems*, 5:297–319, 1980.
33. Vanessa Lopez, Victoria Uren, Enrico Motta, and Michele Pasin. Aqualog: An ontology-driven question answering system for organizational semantic intranets. *Web Semantics: Science, Services and Agents on the World Wide Web*, 5(2):72–105, June 2007.
34. A. Malhotra. Design criteria for a knowledge based english language system for management: An experimental analysis. Technical report, Massachusetts Institute of Technology, Cambridge, MA (1975).
35. Raymond J. Mooney. Using multiple clause constructors in inductive logic programming for semantic parsing. In *In Proceedings of the 12th European Conference on Machine Learning*, pages 466–477, 2001.
36. N.F. Noy, M. Sintek, S. Decker, M. Crubézy, R.W. Fergerson, and M.A. Musen. Creating Semantic Web Contents with Protégé-2000. *IEEE Intelligent Systems*, 16(2):60–71, 2001.
37. William Ogden and Philip Bernick. Using natural language interfaces. In M. Helander, editor, *Handbook of Human–Computer Interaction*. Elsevier Science, North-Holland, 1996.
38. Ana-Maria Popescu, Oren Etzioni, and Henry Kautz. Towards a theory of natural language interfaces to databases. In *IUI '03: Proceedings of the 8th international conference on Intelligent user interfaces*, pages 149—157, New York, NY, USA, 2003. ACM.
39. E. Prud'hommeaux and A. Seaborne. Sparql query language for rdf. W3C recommendation – 15 january 2008, W3C, 2008. URL http://www.w3.org/TR/rdf-sparql-query/.
40. Christoph Meinel Serge Linckels. Semantic interpretation of natural language user input to improve search in multimedia knowledge base. *it – Information Technologies*, 49(1):40–48, 2007.
41. B.M. Slator, M.P. Anderson, and W. Conley. Pygmalion at the interface. *Communications of the ACM*, 29:599–604, 1986.
42. Nenad Stojanovic. On the query refinement in the ontology-based searching for information. *Information Systems*, 30(7):543–563, 2005.
43. Nenad Stojanovic. On the role of a users knowledge gap in an information retrieval process. In *Proceedings of the Third International Conference on Knowledge Capture*, October 2005.
44. Heiner Stuckenschmidt, Anita de Waard, Ravinder Bhogal, Christiaan Fluit, Arjohn Kampman, Jan van Buel, Erik M. van Mulligen, Jeen Broekstra, Ian Crowlesmith, Frank van

Harmelen, and Tony Scerri. A topic-based browser for large online resources. In Enrico Motta, Nigel Shadbolt, Arthur Stutt, and Nicholas Gibbins, editors, *EKAW*, volume 3257 of *Lecture Notes in Computer Science*, pages 433–448. Springer, 2004.

45. V. Tablan, T. Polajnar, H. Cunningham, and K. Bontcheva. User-friendly ontology authoring using a controlled language. In *5th Language Resources and Evaluation Conference (LREC)*, Genoa, Italy, May 2006. ELRA.

46. Valentin Tablan, Danica Damljanović, and Kalina Bontcheva. A natural language query interface to structured information. In *Proceedings of the 5h European Semantic Web Conference (ESWC 2008)*, Tenerife, Spain, June 2008.

47. Craig W. Thompson, Paul Pazandak, and Harry R. Tennant. Talk to your semantic web. *IEEE Internet Computing*, 9(6):75–78, 2005.

48. Mike Unwalla. Aecma simplified english. Communicator, Winter 2004.

49. Chong Wang, Miao Xiong, Qi Zhou, and Yong Yu. Panto: A portable natural language interface to ontologies. In *The Semantic Web: Research and Applications*, pages 473–487. Springer, 2007.

50. E. Zolton-Ford. Reducing variability in natural-language interactions with computers. In *Proceedings of the Human Factors Society 28th Annual Meeting*, pages 768–772. The Human Factors Society, 1984.

Chapter 6
Semantic Document Model to Enhance Data and Knowledge Interoperability

Saša Nešić

6.1 Introduction

The Semantic Web aims at providing an environment in which both humans and software agents can unambiguously determine the meaning of resources and make better use of them [2]. Moreover, data and knowledge stored within a resource should be easily accessible across application, enterprise, and community boundaries. In traditional desktop architectures, applications are isolated islands with their own data, which are unaware of related and relevant data in other applications [9]. Heterogeneous, application-specific document formats, which keep data into schema-specific elements, do not allow data interoperability between the applications. In a similar way, there is no standardized architecture for interoperation and data exchange between the desktops of different users. To achieve data interoperability on local desktops and its seamless integration with other resources of the Semantic Web, the first step is the organization of local desktops as complete RDF and ontology-based environments. This brings us to the notion of the Semantic Desktop [3] – the driving paradigm for desktop computing in the area of the Semantic Web. In other words, local desktops should become the Semantic Web for a single user.

Digital desktop documents (e.g., Word, PDF, and PowerPoint) hold a significant part of the data and knowledge stored on local desktops and hence they play an important role in the vision of the Semantic Desktop and the Semantic Web. However, in order to fully participate in this vision traditional desktop documents need to be adapted first. The large variety of application-specific document formats hampers the interoperability of document data. Document data are kept into schema-specific elements and are hardly accessible across application boundaries. In the last few years several XML-based document formats have been developed, such as the Open

Saša Nešić
Faculty of Informatics, University of Lugano, Via G. Buffi 13, Lugano, Switzerland, e-mail: sasa.nesic@lu.unisi.ch

V. Devedžić and D. Gašević (eds.), *Web 2.0 & Semantic Web*, Annals of Information Systems 6, DOI 10.1007/978-1-4419-1219-0_6,

135

Document Format for Office Applications (ODF) [16] and Microsoft Open Office XML (OOXML) [5], which opened a way toward easier document transformation and data exchange. Yet, the development of export/import functions is a difficult and costly process, as it requires detailed knowledge of both the input and output formats.

The variety of application-specific document formats is not the only issue that impacts the interoperability of document data. To be discovered and then reused, document data need to be semantically annotated. So far, several document annotation frameworks [23] that apply one of the two annotation storage models, the Semantic Web model and Document-Centric (word processor) model, have been developed. In the first model, annotations are stored separately from the source document. An advantage of this model is that no changes to a document are required. However, this model is rarely applied to desktop documents because an efficient solution of the maintenance of links between document content and annotations still does not exist. The Document-Centric model stores annotations inside the internal document representation and has been used as the dominant annotation model for desktop documents (e.g., Word, PDF, PowerPoint) [4, 6, 22], mainly because it overcomes the problem of keeping annotations and documents consistent. However, storing annotations inside a document usually require the extension of the document format schema, which is not always possible. The other problem of the document annotation is the lack of appropriate schema elements for the annotations of document CUs of different levels of granularity (e.g., sections, paragraphs, images, tables). The majority of existing document schemas provide elements for document annotations at the level of a whole document, while document CUs of lower granularity remain unannotated. This is primarily because document schemas do not define document CUs as uniquely identified and addressable entities that can hold their own annotations. Accordingly, the discoverability and reusability of document CUs is significantly decreased.

Moreover, the existing desktop documents are suited primarily for humans, so that knowledge modeled within them is not represented in a form that allows intelligent software agents to discover and use it. Document annotation with ontologies, known as "Semantic Document" approach [6], is as an attempt to conceptualize document knowledge. However, we believe that the term 'Semantic Document' should not denote only documents annotated with ontologies, but rather a new category of documents that can fully contribute in the environment envisioned by the Semantic Web. To be a part of the Semantic Web resources, digital desktop documents need to be adapted first. This adaptation will lead to a new generation of documents that we call semantic documents. We have identified following four principles, which can be considered as the basis of semantic documents:

1. Document content should be completely queryable, with addressable elements (i.e., CUs) of different granularity
2. A whole document and all its CUs should be uniquely identified with URIs (Unique Resource Identifiers)
3. A document as a whole, as well as document CUs should be annotated with substantial sets of metadata

4. Human-understandable knowledge that is modeled in document CUs should be also represented in a form that can be processed by machines (i.e., software agents)

In accordance to these principles we have developed Semantic Document Model (SDM), which turns digital documents into semantic documents. The model takes the existing digital documents as human-readable (HR) instances of the semantic document and integrates it with the newly created machine-processable (MP) instance. We have taken existing digital documents as the HR instances in order to let users continue to use well-established document formats and because of the development of new document authoring systems, which is an expensive investment that is not likely to happen.

This paper is organized as follows. In the next section, we discuss the document evolution starting from paper-based documents then digital documents to the envisioned semantic documents. In Sect. 6.3, we first present the SDM, then propose an RDF and ontology-based solution for the MP document instance, and conclude the section with the explanation of how semantic documents are stored and organized. In Sect. 6.4, we first explain the notion of the Social Semantic Desktop (SSD) paradigm and outline the architecture of the NEPOMUK SSD [9] as a real example of the SSD. Then we explain the Semantic Document Management System (SDMS) that we have developed on the top of the SDM, and how it can be integrated into the NEPOMUK SSD platform. In Sect. 6.5, in order to illustrate semantic documents in real use, we present some application examples (i.e., MS Office add-ins) that take advantage of the SDMS services. In Sect. 6.6, we identify some shortcomings of the presented work and continue with related works in Sect. 6.7. Discussion of future work and final remarks conclude the paper.

6.2 From Paper-Based and Digital to Semantic Documents

A document is a bounded physical representation of a body of information designed to convey informatio n. Documents play a key role in the construction of social reality [1] and therefore play a part in accounts of every important aspect of human society and culture. The form of documents has been changing over time following the development of human society. One of the key changes happened with the introduction of "Digital Era," which led to the main classification of documents into the paper-based and digital documents. Despite many differences between these two forms of documents, the purpose of documents remained unchanged. Both the paper-based and digital documents serve as a medium for the information sharing between humans. The next form of documents, which is inspired by the notions of the Semantic Web and the Semantic Desktop, aims at enabling document data and knowledge to be shared and understood not only by humans but also by machines. In the rest of the section, we discuss the main features of the three forms of documents: paper-based, digital, and semantic.

The principal differences between paper-based and digital documents come from different types of physical medium that is used for document storage and from the way in which documents are created, managed, and communicated among people. Paper-based documents are created and managed completely manually or by using some mechanical devices (e.g., a typewriter) and communicated among people in the same manner as any other mobile physical object. Throughout history, there have been used different materials such as clay tables, parchment, and papyrus as the physical medium for the storage of paper-based documents. Nowadays, paper is the most common medium for this form of documents and hence the name paper-based documents. In contrast to paper-based documents, digital documents are stored on digital mediums such as hard disk drives (HDDs), CD-ROMs, external hard drives, and DVDs. Digital documents are computer supported in all phases of their life cycle, starting from the creation and utilization to the archival and destruction. The most popular ways of communicating digital documents are document publishing on the Web and sending documents by e-mails.

Besides these principal differences, digital documents differ in many other ways from paper-based documents. Prominent examples of digital documents such as word processor documents, slide presentations, spreadsheets, and PDF documents are structured documents, which have a visual layer separate from their logical structure. The logical structure of digital documents enables direct access to particular document parts, thus making the granularity in digital documents smaller than in paper documents. By using named anchors, document parts can be linked to external resources (e.g., other documents, Web pages, and people). Moreover, readers can add extra information at a particular point of document without making changes to document content. This extra information is known as an annotation and may help other readers to better understand document content. Logical document structure, combined with possible annotations, opened the way for structuring and acquisition of document knowledge, which can turn a digital document into a widespread knowledge model. Digital documents have some drawbacks as well. They are less stable in time (i.e., their content can change at any point in time) than paper documents and can be cited only if they are managed by trustworthy sources.

Digital documents render a significant part of the knowledge base stored on local desktops and as such they are important potential resources for the Semantic Desktop and the Semantic Web. However, digital documents in a current form do not meet the requirements demanded of the Semantic Web resources. The Semantic Web resources have to be uniquely identified resources with easily accessible content and annotated with machine processable metalevel descriptions. The content of current digital documents is usually locked into specific schema elements and is not always addressable and accessible from the outside of the documents. Moreover, knowledge modeled within documents is represented in a HR form and cannot be discovered and processed by machines. The transformation of digital documents into the Semantic Web resources leads to the semantic documents as a new form of documents. Several existing technologies, in particular ontologies and RDF, can be taken as basis for semantic documents. Annotating digital documents with ontologies [23] has been the most common strategy to adapt digital documents to the

Semantic Web. However, in our opinion the ultimate goal of semantic documents is not merely to provide annotations for documents, but to integrate two representations of the same knowledge: human readable (HR) and machine processable (MP) and to create platform/tool independent, unified view of document data.

Semantic documents will even more differ from digital documents than digital documents differ from paper documents. If we consider a paper document as a hard copy of a digital document, then a digital document can be seen as human-readable form of a semantic document. Therefore, the generation of semantic documents can be equated with the generation of the MP document form and its integration with the existing digital documents (i.e., HR document instances).

6.3 Semantic Documents

In accordance to four principles that we stated in Sect. 6.1, we give the following definition of semantic documents:

> A Semantic Document is a uniquely identified and semantically annotated composite resource. It is built of smaller resources (CUs), which can be either composite or atomic and which are also uniquely identified and semantically annotated. Each document CU is characterized by its content (data) and knowledge, which are represented in a form understandable to both humans and machines. CUs can be put in different kinds of relationships with other, uniquely identified resources (e.g., other CUs, Web Pages, people, institutions, etc.). Hierarchical and navigational relationships among CUs are used to define document logical structure.

Based on the given definition, semantic documents are resources, which exist independently of their concrete implementation. The two categories of possible users (i.e., humans and machines) determine the two possible forms of the semantic document implementation: human-readable (HR) and machine-processable (MP). Both forms are persistent, with the difference that there is only one MP document instance and that can be zero or several HR instances. The same document CUs in the MP and HR instances are identified with the same URIs, establishing in that way the links between the two document instances. These links allow users to take advantage of new features enabled by the introduction of the MP document instance. Therefore, the MP instance plays the key role in our vision of the semantic documents.

The MP document instance is universal, platform independent, and completely queryable. It enables the annotation of the semantic document and its CUs with different kinds of annotations and lets the HR instances to be intact by the annotations. Over the links between the MP and HR instances users can query the MP instance to get the annotations. Moreover, the MP instance holds conceptualized document knowledge, thus enabling users to deploy some software agents in discovering documents, CUs based on their knowledge rather than performing full-text search. The MP instance also provides mechanisms for versioning of CUs and formal representation of changes made to CUs over time. In addition, universal and platform independent MP instance, which can be rendered into different platform-tool-specific HR instances, serves as a transformation bridge between platform-tool-specific document formats.

6.3.1 Semantic Document Model (SDM)

We have developed the Semantic document model (SDM) in accordance to the given definition and being partially inspired by the Abstract Compound Content Model (ACCM) [14] and the Abstract Learning Object Content Model (ALOCoM) [11], which both have roots in the IBM's Darwin Information Architecture (DITA) [18]. The ACCM model defines CUs of different levels of granularity as well as the content aggregation architecture that organizes CUs for content deliverables. From the prospective of the ACCM, digital documents can be regarded as instances of the content aggregation architecture in which document parts are considered as CUs. The ALOCoM has served as the basis for supporting learning content personalization as well as learning content authoring. Unlike ALOCoM, which is an abstract content model for learning content, the ACCM is applicable to any kind of digital content.

We have chosen ontologies to formally describe the SDM because they are promising solutions to both: modeling document logical structure and document knowledge representation. Ontologies provide a number of useful features for intelligent systems, knowledge representation in general, and for the knowledge engineering process. Although the major purpose of ontologies is knowledge sharing and knowledge reuse by applications [21], in the last decade, ontologies have also emerged as one of the most popular modeling approaches to taxonomies, classifications, and other structures used in information systems (IS). The ontological foundation of the SDM consists of the document ontology, annotation ontology, and change ontology. We have developed all the three ontologies as OWL ontologies by using ProtŐgŐ ontology editor and they are available at [24].

6.3.1.1 Document Ontology

The document ontology formally describes the SDM by providing definitions of possible types of document CUs as well as architectural elements that organize CUs into document logical structure. Figure 6.1 gives the graphical representation of the document ontology in a form of a Resource Description Framework (RDF) graph. The ontology contains two groups of concepts: content elements and architectural elements.

The first group, that is content elements, contains concepts that define document CUs as uniquely identified resources, which hold pieces of document content and can be extracted form document context and reused in other documents. The main concept in this group is *ContentUnit (CU)* concept, which has two subconcepts: *ContentFragment (CF)* and *ContentObject (CO)*. The *CF* represents *CUs* in their most basic form (i.e., raw digital resources) and can be further specialized into *DiscreteCF* (e.g., *Graphic* and *TextFragment*) and *ContinuousCF* (e.g., *Audio*, *Video*, and *Simulation*). The *CO* represents *CUs* (e.g., *Paragraph*, *Table* and *Slide*), which aggregate *CFs* and other *COs* by using the *hasPart* property and add navigation among them by the *hasOrdering* property.

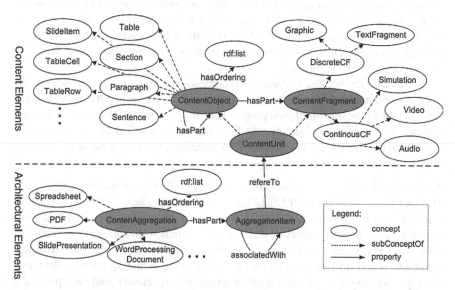

Fig. 6.1 Document ontology

The second group, that is, architectural elements contains concepts that define elements of the document logical structure. Two core concepts are *AggregationItem (AI)* and *ContentAggregation (CA)*. The *AI* holds a reference to an instance of the *CU* concept via a *refersTo* property and represents the appearance of the *CU* within a document. The *CA* defines logical structure of a document by establishing relationships among the *AIs*. Besides aggregational relationships, which are expressed with a *hasPart* property, the *ContentAggregation* defines navigational and associative relationships via the *hasOrdering* and *associateWith* properties. The aggregational and navigational relationships enable sequencing and structuring of the document content in a form of the tree structure. On the other hand, the associative relationships enable links among *AIs* based on the given criteria (e.g., this can be used for modeling hyperlinks inside a document).

6.3.1.2 Annotation Ontology

One of the main objectives of our semantic document model is to enable software agents to easily discover, access, and reuse document CUs of different levels of granularity without affecting the document as a whole. However, prior to the access and reuse, document CUs have to be discovered, which demands their semantic annotation. To enable infrastructure for semantic annotation of document CUs, we have developed the annotation ontology.

Our intention with the annotation ontology was not to cover all possible kinds of annotations, but to provide common interface (e.g., classes and properties) for adding annotations to the document CUs. Considering document CUs as constitutive blocks of document context on the one hand, and isolated pieces of content on the other hand, we have identified two types of possible annotations: (1) annotations that belong to CUs independently of the document (i.e., *context-free* annotations) and (2) annotations that belong to CUs when they are parts of the document (i.e., *context-dependent* annotations).

The annotation ontology relates the context-free annotations to instances of the content elements defined by the document ontology. For this purpose, the ontology introduces the *hasAnnotation* property and the *ContentUnitAnnotation* concept, which act as a metadata binding to a CU. We have identified three categories of context-free annotations: (a) standardized metadata, (b) usage metadata, and (c) subject-specific metadata.

Standardized metadata is described by internationally recognized vocabularies like Dublin Core[1] (DC) [6] or IEEE Learning Object Metadata[2] (LOM) [14], which are designed to describe any kind of resources, that is, anything that has identity. We have chosen a subset of this metadata which is meaningful for document CUs: `dc:creator`, `dcterms:created`, `dc:format`, `dc:language`, `dc:title` and `dc:description` referring to the author(s), creation date, media type, language(s), title, and short description, respectively, and incorporated it in the annotation ontology.

Usage metadata tracks information about the usage of document CUs in different contexts by different users. Since one of our goals is to enable users to share their documents by interacting (e.g., visiting, modifying, and reusing) directly with the document CUs, we have extended the annotation ontology with a set of properties and concepts to capture this interaction (Fig. 6.2). There are three new concepts: *Modification, Reuse*, and *Visit* and three new properties: *numOfVisits, numOfMod-ifications*, and *numOfReuses*. All the three introduced concepts are characterized by the time of the interaction and person who is involved in it. The *Modification* and *Reuse* concepts also track information about deployed applications during the interaction. Every time the user interacts with the document CU, the interaction metadata are added to the CU. This metadata are primarily used to determine how some document CUs correspond to the userÕs preferences (e.g., if the user prefers recently modified CUs or CUs reused many times, etc.) and has an important role in the ranking algorithm for document CUs that we have presented in [13].

---

[1] Dublin Core Metadata Initiative: http://dublincore.org/

[2] IEEE standard for learning object metadata: http://ltsc.ieee.org/wg12

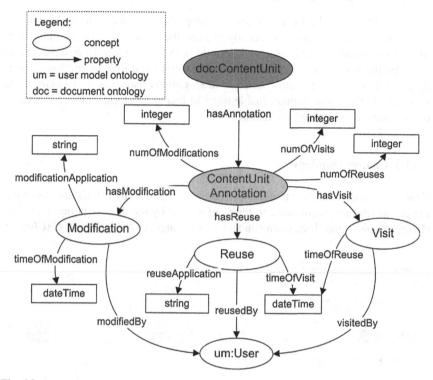

Fig. 6.2 Annotation ontology - usage metadata

Subject-specific metadata of the CU are ontological metadata [20], which conceptualize the same subjects as those described by the CU. The annotation ontology uses the dc:subjectproperty to add the subject-specific metadata to the CU. These metadata are actually a set of ontological concepts, which can be regarded as the conceptualization of knowledge/phenomena modeled by the CU. Since one of our goals with the SDM is to represent document knowledge not only in human-readable but also in machine-processable form, these metadata play an important role in our approach. It allows intelligent software agents to manipulate with conceptualized document knowledge. On the other hand, it also enables humans to use software agents in locating document CUs based on the knowledge modeled within them. There are two approaches to obtaining these metadata, that is, to finding and relating appropriate ontological concepts to document CUs. One is the manual annotation based on the domain expertÕs knowledge and the other is automatic annotation based on the information extraction (IE) and natural language processing (NLP) techniques.

The context-dependent annotations characterize the CUs only when they are parts of the document context. The annotation ontology relates these annotations to the instances of the *AggregationItem* concept defined by the document ontology, which refer to the CUs and represent their appearance within the document. For this purpose, we have introduced the *ItemAnnotation* concept that serves as a metadata binding around the AggregationItem. Currently, we use the context-dependent annotations for adding rhetorical and cognitive descriptions [8, 11] to CUs. To achieve this we extended the annotation ontology with two new concepts: *RhetoricalElement* (e.g., *Abstract*, *Overview*, and *Introduction*) and *CognitiveElement* (e.g., *Definition* and *Procedure*). These annotations enable users to include rhetorical and cognitive aspects when they search for document CUs.

6.3.1.3 Change Ontology

Change ontology (Fig. 6.3) tracks possible changes to document CUs and document logical structure in accordance to their definitions by the document ontology. The change ontology has three main concepts: *CFChange*, *COChange*, and *CAChange*.

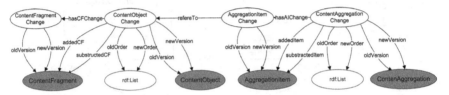

Fig. 6.3 Change ontology

The *CFChange* is a change made to a CF, which creates a new version of the CF. Since the CF is an atomic CU that can not be disaggregated into smaller units, a *CFChange* can only be determined by comparing the old and new versions of the CF. To keep track of this kind of changes, the presence of both the old and new versions of the CF is necessary. Thereby, we defined the *oldVersion* and *newVersion* properties, to link the old and new versions of the CF to the instance of the *CFChange* concept. By deleting the old version, we lose all the information about the changes that translate this version into the new version.

The *COChange* is a change made to a CO, which creates a new version of the CO. Based on the CO definition, we have identified the following possible types of the CO modifications: (1) addition of CFs, (2) subtraction of CFs, (3) reordering of CFs, and (4) changes to CFs which are part of the CO. The first two are modeled by the *addedCF* and subtractedCF properties which link added and subtracted CFs to COChange. The third is modeled by the *newOrder* and *oldOrder* properties, which link instances of the *rdf:List* concept to the *CFChange*. The instances of the rdf:list keep the new and old order of CFs in the CO. If the modification to the CO is a result of changes to CFs, which are part of the CO, then instances of the *CFChange* are linked to the *COChange* by the *hasCFChange* property. In contrast to the *CFChange*, the *COChange* does not necessarily need to keep link to the old version of the CO. In the case of losing the old version of the CO, it can be rebuilt based on the new version and captured changes by the *COChange*.

Besides changes to document CUs, the change ontology also captures possible changes to document logical structure. The logical structure of a document can be changed either by adding, subtracting, or reordering references (i.e., *Aggregation-Items*) to the document CUs. The ontology defines the *CAChange* concept and the *addedItem*, *subtractedItem*, *oldOrder*, and *newOrder* properties to model changes to document logical structure.

6.3.2 The MP and HR instances of semantic documents

Semantic documents can be instantiated into HR and MP forms. Both forms are persistent with the difference that exists only one MP instance and zero or several HR instances. Actually, a new HR instance can be rendered from the MP instance at any time when humans want to browse or edit the semantic document. Changes to a HR instance are not necessarily changes to the semantic document. Only the author and a set of authorized users have rights to change the semantic document by incorporating changes from HR instances. The MP and HR instances are stored separately without restricting each other, but well linked in order to ensure consistency and synchronous evolution of data and knowledge modeled by the semantic document. Figure 6.4 gives the illustration of the semantic document by showing the couple of its MP and HR instances and the application range of the document, annotation and domain ontologies within the document. From the human point of view the advantage of this coupling is that users can continue to work with documents as before, but now they can also use different services provided by software agents, which are capable to process the MP document instance. For example,

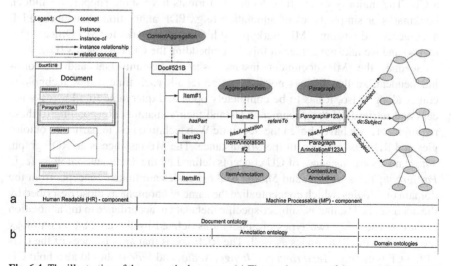

Fig. 6.4 The illustration of the semantic document: (a) The two instances of the semantic document HR and MP; (b) The range of the document, annotation, and domain ontologies

the ontology-based software agents can be used to locate and retrieve document CUs, which model the desired knowledge (i.e., CUs to which are related ontological concepts that conceptualize the desired knowledge). From the machine point of view the advantage of the coupling, that is, the advantage of the existence of the MP document instance is that intelligent software agents can "understand" and use document knowledge in reasoning and answering to some domain-specific questions.

We have identified following principles, which act as the basis of the MP and HR document instances and define the correlation between them:

- The use of existing document formats as a HR instance
- Universal, platform-independent, and queryable MP instance
- Bidirectional links between the MP and HR instances
- Semantic annotations stored only into the MP instance

First, the use of existing, well-established document formats, as a HR document instance is preferred because the development of new formats and tools for their management requires expensive investment and it is not likely to happen. Therefore, the success of the SDM demands the use of existing document formats as the HR instances of the semantic document. Accordingly, new services introduced by the model should be implemented through extensions to the existing document management environments. Currently, there are numerous document formats, many of which have format schemas that are very strict and difficult to extend. This actually means that the possibility of storing some metalevel descriptions into internal document representation is limited to the ability of a format's schema to be extended. In our approach, we do not face this problem, since we store the MP document instance separately from the HR instances. Changes to documents (e.g., PDF and MS Office documents) are minimized: specifically, the only necessary change is embedding CU URIs and CU version IDs (VIDs), which are used to uniquely identify a CU. The majority of existing document formats have some support for hidden bookmarks or simple types of annotation (e.g., PDF annotation element for PDF documents and custom XML markup and hidden bookmarks for MS Office documents) and we take advantage of this for embedding the CU URIs and VIDs.

Second, the MP document instance should be universal and platform-independent, so that it does not have to be rebuilt each time a new technology comes along. Also, it has to be completely open and queryable to allow easy access and retrieval of the document CUs and their semantics. Responding to these requirements, we have chosen the Semantic Web technologies, in particular ontologies and RDF, as the basis of the MP instance. The MP instance is an RDF graph, whose nodes are instances of CU concepts defined by the document ontology (e.g., *Paragraph*, *Table*, *Image*, and *Slide*). To these nodes are linked concepts from the domain ontologies, which conceptualize the same phenomena as those described by the document CUs, that is, subject-specific metadata in accordance to the annotation ontology. The other two types of annotations defined by the annotation ontology are linked to the RDF nodes as well. The RDF nodes that are instances of the CUs of the CF type (e.g., *TextFragment*, *Image*, *Audio*, and *Video*) should also hold CU binary content (data). However, current RDF repositories are not meant to store large chunks of binary data so that the content from CUs is placed into binary data stores and linked to RDF nodes. In addition, the relationships between the nodes that are defined by the properties from the document ontology model the document logical structure. Traditionally, a document structure is considered as a tree-like structure, although some document formats (e.g., MS Office) support hyperlinks between non-parent–child document CUs. In accordance to our definition of semantic documents, a document logical structure is a graph structure, which enables not only parent–child navigation but also other navigation paths through the document. Therefore, the RDF vocabulary, which is defined primarily to describe resources as interlinked graph nodes, is a promising solution to modeling document logical structure.

Third, as mentioned before, the MP instance of the document has an RDF node for each document CU. Each node is identified with the URI and Version Identifier (VID). While rendering the HR instance from the MP instance, copies of these identifiers are embedded in the HR instances, thus forming the link between the same CUs of the two instances. Via these links, humans can obtain the additional information of the CUs, which is stored only into the MP instance. On the other hand, the links between the HR and MP instances also enable users to edit the document by editing its HR instances. By using appropriate services, the authorized users can incorporate changes they made to the HR instances into MP document instance.

Fourth, semantic annotations of the semantic documents are stored only into the MP instance, thus enabling the semantic annotation model to be unconstrained by the specifics of different document format schemas. The majority of existing desktop document annotation models [6, 22, 23] store annotations inside the internal document representation. Such annotation storage model has been used mainly because it overcomes the problem of keeping annotations and documents consistent. However, storing annotations inside a document usually demands the extension of the document format schema, which is not always possible. Thus, the possibility of the annotation depends on the ability of a document format schema to be extended. In our approach, we simplify the annotation process by adding annotations to RDF nodes of the MP instance instead of embedding them into the internal document representation of the HR instances. The semantic document annotation becomes independent of the HR document format. Through links between the MP and HR instances the user can access annotations of each document CU while browsing its content. In the same way, the user can edit existing or add new annotations to the semantic document.

6.3.3 Storage and Organization of Semantic Documents

After the transformation of digital documents into semantic documents, the HR instance (i.e., a digital document with embedded CUs' URIs) can stay on the same location in the file system as it was before the transformation or can be moved somewhere else. The embedded document's URI is unaffected by the location of the document in the file system. Moreover, by making a copy of the document or by changing the document's name, the document remains the same resource. If the user changes content of the already transformed digital document, the system, which manages semantic documents, should initiate process of updating the MP instance.

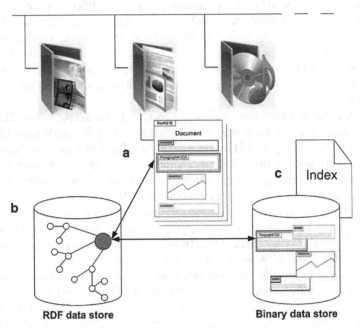

Fig. 6.5 Semantic Document Store: (a) Digital documents with embedded CUs' URIs (HR instances); (b) RDF data store (MP document instances); (c) Binary data store (CUs' binary content)

The MP instance is stored in an RDF repository. Conceptually each RDF node can store string data in an `xsd:string` datatyped literal and binary data in an `xsd:base64Binary` datatyped literal. However, current RDF repositories are not meant to store larger chunk of binary data [10]. When a large amount of data has to be managed, queries in structured query languages such as SPARQL [19] are not always powerful enough. The MP instance does not approach such problem since it is not meant to store the CU's content. The content stays in the source digital document and can be accessed via links made by embedded URIs. For example, if logical structure of the digital document is described by XML, access to content of the document CUs can be realized by using XPointer[3] references. However, in order to speed up the access to the content while utilizing the MP instance, we extract the content of each CU and store it in a binary store during the transformation process. Content from textual CUs is placed into plain text files, while content from media CUs is placed in appropriate media files. Names of these binary files encrypt the URIs of document CUs and establish the link between the CUs and their binary

---

[3] XPointer Framework: http://www.w3.org/TR/xptr-framework/

content. Files stored in the binary store are only accessible through the system's services. The binary content is indexed and enables full-text search as supplement to structured queries over RDF data. Figure 6.5 illustrates stores of semantic document components (i.e., HR and MP instances) and relations between them.

6.4 Social Semantic Desktop (SSD)

There are several new technologies, which could provide a means to build the semantic bridges necessary for data exchange and application integration as well as dramatically impact a way in which people interact and collaborate: the Semantic Web, peer-to-peer computing, and online social networking. Stefan Decker presented in [3] a vision of how these different thrusts will evolve and produce the social semantic desktop (SSD) The main goal of the SSD is to transform the conventional desktop into a seamless, networked working environment, by loosing the borders between individual applications and the physical workspace of different users [20]. The SSD adopts some of the ideas of the Semantic Web. The aims of allowing data to more easily be shared could be considered as a subset of those of the Semantic Web, but extended to a user's local computer, rather then just files stored on the Internet.

Formal ontologies that capture a shared conceptualization of desktop data, and RDF as a common data representation format, can be used to unify all forms of data and allow data to be accessed in a format-independent way. Our aim in building the semantic document model (SDM) on these principles is to enable data from digital desktop documents to take part in the vision of the SSD. Since the SSD is regarded as a building block of the Semantic Web [3], by including semantic documents into the SSD they will also become resources of the Semantic Web. To test the developed model and to explore its advantages and drawbacks in a real use, we chose the NEPOMUK SSD [9] platform. In the rest of this section we first outline the architecture of the NEPOMUK SSD platform and then discuss the integration of semantic documents into the platform.

6.4.1 Architecture of the NEPOMUK SSD

The NEPOMUK SSD is made up of the user's individual desktops, which are organized in a peer-to-peer (P2P) fashion. The NEPOMUK architecture is organized in three layers: Network Communication Layer, NEPOMUK Semantic Middleware, and Presentation Layer.

The role of the Network Communication Layer is to enable the communication between peers (i.e., networked desktops). This layer provides (1) the Event-Based System for distribution of the events between NEPOMUK peers, (2) the Messaging System for routing messages, and (3) the Peer-To-Peer File Sharing System, which enables the shared information space.

On the top of the Network Communication Layer is the NEPOMUK Semantic Middleware. The role of this layer is to provide core services of the NEPOMUK SSD, to enable the interservice communication and to establish the infrastructure for possible platform extension with new services. To operate within the platform, services first need to be registered at the Service Registry. Based on the operating system (e.g., MS Windows, Mac OS, and Linux), different communication techniques such as SOAP over HTTP, OSGI[4] [20], or D-Bus[5] [3] can be used for interaction between the services. The core services are divided into two subsets. The first subset contains services that are more specific in terms of purpose such as *Data Wrapping*, *Context Elicitation*, *Mapping and Alignment*, and *Text Analytics*. The second subset contains *Data Services*, which are more general and usually called by services from the first subset. *Data Services* are also important for our work, and the services that we have developed and added to the NEPOMUK SSD take advantage of them. The *Data Services* control the insertion, modification, and deletion of resources in the NEPOMUK SSD. A resource can be any digital or nondigital entity that is identified with a URI and described by RDF descriptions. For local queries and offline work, the RDF descriptions and resource binary data are stored by the *Data Storage* services in the NEPOMUK RDF data store and NEPOMUK binary data store, respectively. If a user wants to share a resource with other users, the RDF descriptions of the resource need to be uploaded to the distributed index of the peer-to-peer file sharing system (i.e., distributed RDF data store). The *Data Search* services can either issue a local search in the local store or a distributed search in the underlying peer-to-peer system or both.

The top layer of the architecture is the Presentation Layer, which provides a user interface to the services provided by the NEPOMUK Semantic Middleware. The aim of the layer is not to build completely new applications and systems for managing different types of resources that can be stored on the NEPOMUK SSD, but to extend existing popular applications, such as Office applications, Email clients, and Web browsers so that they can take advantage of the middleware services.

6.4.2 Semantic Document Management System (SDMS)

To integrate semantic documents into NEPOMUK SSD we have developed the semantic document management system (SDMS) as a set of services that can be integrated into NEPOMUK Middleware. The SDMS enables the transformation of digital documents into semantic documents and storage of MP instances into NEPOMUK RDF data store. Moreover, it provides support for different functionalities, which are enabled by the introduced SDM. The SDMS consists of the following services: *Transformation, Annotation, Indexing, Change-Tracing, Ranking*, and *Terms-Mapping*.

---

[4] OSGi Alliance: http://www.osgi.org/

[5] D-Bus: http://www.freedesktop.org/wiki/Software/dbus

The Transformation service scans the structure of a digital document to be transformed, recognizes document CUs, and generates the MP document instance as defined in the SDM. For each CU (e.g., paragraph, image, and table), the MP instance contains instances of appropriate concepts from the document ontology (e.g., *Paragraph*, *Image*, and *Table*). The service generates a URI for each of those instances and embeds them into the source digital document as hidden bookmarks. Moreover, the service extracts all textual, audio, and video data from the CUs and stores them into the NEPOMUK binary data store. For each identified CU, the *Transformation* service also calls the *Annotation* service to semantically annotate the CU. At the end of the transformation, the MP component is generated and the NEPOMUK *Data Storage* service stores it either into local NEPOMUK RDF data store if the user does not want to share the document or into distributed RDF data store.

The Annotation service performs semantic annotation of the CUs with annotations defined in the annotation ontology. It relates them to the RDF nodes within the MP instance. The annotation process, is fully automated. Values of standardized metadata are derived from the documentÕs metadata or generated based on the available formatting information. Some metadata are just literally copied from the document's metadata like `dc:creator`, `dcterms:created`, `dc:format`, and `dc:language`, referring to the author(s), creation date, media type, and language(s), respectively. A value of a dc:title element is generated based on the formatting information. For example, a text fragment with a font style (e.g., *title* or *heading1*) is used as a value for the `dc:title` element of all successive CUs up to the next formatted text fragment. A value of a `dc:description`element is generated out of the values of previously explained elements using the following text pattern: "A content unit of `dc:format` media type with a title `dc:title` authored by `dc:creator`; creation date `dcterms:created`" [9]. The usage metadata come from capturing interaction between the users and CUs over time. Always when the users interact with the CUs the annotation service generates the usage metadata and relates it to RDF nodes that represent the CUs. Moreover, the service generates the subject-specific metadata by performing the ontology-based information extraction from the CUs. The service first queries a set of specified domain ontologies to find labels of their concepts and then for each found label it generates a set of synonyms (the synonyms are obtained through a lexical ontology such as WordNet). After that, for each CU the service checks if the CU contains some of the labels or their synonyms and if so, relates the labeled concepts to the CU. Although, in the current implementation of the annotation service we are primarily focused on the automatic CU annotation, we want to stress that the semantic annotation model that we propose does not make any difference between manually and automatically generated annotations. In the near future we plan to enhance the annotation module with support for the manual CU annotation. Moreover, document CUs become sharable resources which can be annotated with unstructured vocabularies (e.g., collaborative tags) as well.

The Indexing service does text indexing of all textual data from the document CUs. The data are indexed after the transformation service places it into binary files. The

SDMS maintains a single index, which is updated always when a new document is transformed. The index stores inverse mappings for pairs (CU's URI, CU's text). Text indexing is included in order to supplement structured queries (e.g., SPARQL, RQL and RDQL) on RDF data with full-text search. For the index implementation we use the Apache Lucene[6] [1] IR Library.

The change-tracing service inspects the HR document instance and if there are some changes to document CUs creates a change-log as an instance of the change ontology. For changed CUs, the service creates a new VID and relates it to the ontological instance of the CU in the MP document instance. The VID is also added to the CU's hidden-bookmark within the HR instance and along with the CU's URI uniquely identifies the CU.

The terms-mapping service maps a set of terms with a set of domain concepts. The service queries the domain ontology for concepts whose labels contain some of the specified terms or their synonyms. Ideally, there is only one ontology for each domain. In reality, however, we are faced with many ontologies of partially overlapping domains (e.g., FOAF, SIOC and hCard for the description of the Web users). The NEPOMUK Semantic Middleware provides the Mapping service that can be used to find related or equivalent concepts from different ontologies. The Terms Mapping service takes advantage of the Mapping service in resolving potential redundancy within the found set of domain concepts. The Terms Mapping service is mostly used as a part of the ontology-based search for document CUs, which are annotated with ontological concepts.

The ranking service ranks the document CUs within a set of CUs that is retrieved by the Data Search service. The applied ranking algorithm is based on the user's preferences regarding CUs, such as number of CU's versions and occurrences in different documents, which are specified as a part of the user's profile, and weighting schemas, which we have developed for each preference [13]. By applying the weighting schemas, the service first calculates the weight of each CU and then according to CUsÕ weights, ranks them within the retrieved set.

6.5 Application Examples

Many desktop applications are possible sources of resources that could be managed by the NEPOMUK SSD. By integrating the SDMS services into the NEPOMUK Semantic Middleware we extend the set of possible resources with digital desktop documents, which are first transformed into semantic documents and then stored on the NEPOMUK SSD. Currently, the SDMS supports the transformation of only MS Office documents but in the near future we plan to add support for other common desktop document as well. To provide a user interface to the SDMS services for MS Office users, we have developed two MS Office add-ins: Transformer Add-In

---

[6] Apache Lucene IR Library: http://lucene.apache.org/

and Authoring Recommender Add-In [15]. Transformer Add-In enables users to transform MS Office documents into semantic documents and store them on the NEPOMUK SSD. Authoring Recommender Add-In enables the users to search local and distributed semantic document stores for desired document CUs and incorporate them in their documents. We now briefly describe the main features of these two add-ins from the perspective of the processes in which they participate. Further information, snapshots, and demos can be found on the SDMS Web page [24].

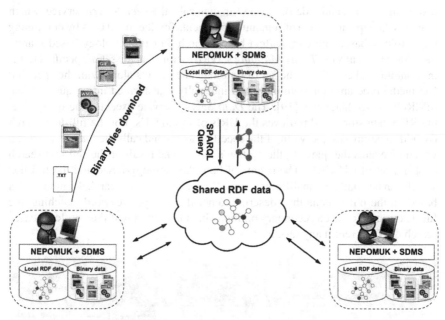

Fig. 6.6 Sharing document CUs between peers in the Social Network using the SDMS

The transformation process is almost fully automated and the user workload is minimized. The GUI of the Transformer Add-In is simple to use and follows the main design principles of the MS Office GUI. Prior to the transformation, the user can select domain ontologies that describe the tentative topic of the document to be transformed. If the ontology repository, which is a part of the NEPOMUK RDF data store, does not contain appropriate domain ontology, the user can add the new ontology to the repository and then select it. After the selection of the ontologies the user starts the transformation. During the transformation, the add-in utilizes four SDMS services: *Transformation*, *Annotation*, *Indexing*, and *Change-Tracing*. At the end of the successful transformation, the MP instance of the document is generated and stored in the local NEPOMUK RDF data store or delegated to the distributed store. The HR instance (i.e., MS Word or MS PowerPoint) is extended with embedded CUs' URIs and document CUs' binary data (e.g. text, images, and audios) is extracted, indexed, and stored in the NEPOMUK binary data store. To store the MP instance as well as binary data the add-in calls the *Data Storage* services.

By integrating semantic documents in the NEPOMUK SSD, semantic documents become part of a collaborative environment, which enables sharing and exchanging of document CUs across social and organizational relationships (see Fig. 6.6). To enable users to search and retrieve document CUs form local or distributed stores while working in MS Office applications we have developed the Authoring Recommender Add-In. Through the GUI of the add-in (see Fig. 6.7), the user can specify following information: (1) a set of ontologies that conceptualize the domain of interest (see Fig. 6.7a), (2) a set of tentative terms, and (3) a CU media type (e.g. text, image, audio, and video). The add-in then calls the *Data Search* service, which searches the repository(ies) of semantic documents for document CUs by combining the ontology-based and content/text-based search. For the ontology-based search, the add-in first calls the *Terms-Mapping* service to translate the set of specified terms into ontological concepts. The set of ontological concepts along with the specified CU media type are then combined and internally transformed into a query in the SPARQL query language [19]. The *Data Search* service executes the query over the RDF data stores and retrieves the URIs of found CUs. For the full-text search the add-in composes query out of the specified terms and calls the *Indexing* service, which delegates the query to the system's index. The result of the full-text search is also a set of CU URIs. The results of both the ontology-based and the full-text search can be combined in different ways. Since, we prefer to search document CUs based on the phenomena they describe rather than simple keyword matching, the full-text search is just a secondary option, which is used only if the ontology-based search does not return any results.

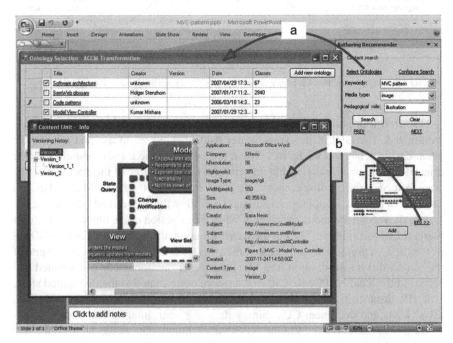

Fig. 6.7 Authoring Recommender add-in: (a) ontology selection (b) content unit preview

Once the search is completed, the add-in calls the *Ranking* service, which ranks the retrieved set of CUs. Finally, based on the CU's URI, the *Data Storage* service determines if the CU's content is stored in the local binary data store or in the binary data store of the other NEPOMUK peers, and retrieves the content to the add-in. The add-in provides a preview of the retrieved CUÕs content as well as the CU's metadata (Fig. 6.7b). In the same preview, the user can find information about the evolution path of the CU. Once the user selects the CU to reuse, the add-in adds the CU to the current cursor position in the active document. Along with the addition of the CU to the document, the add-in also incorporates a hidden-bookmark with the CU's URI.

6.6 Discussion

The existing types of digital desktop documents (e.g., PDF, MS Office, and OpenOffice) offer a plenty of nice features, and many users have become deeply familiar with them. By using the existing types of documents as HR instances of the semantic documents, we do not put any additional burden on users and let them work with documents in the same manner as before. On the other hand, the semantic documents (i.e., the MP instances) bring new services, which can further improve document usability and make users' lives easier. Having the MP instance represented as an RDF graph and by using structured query languages such as SPARQL, RDQL and RQL, we can reach any part (CU) of the document without knowing anything about the document structure, which is not the case with the regular XML-based documents. By linking annotations to RDF nodes in the MP document instance, we solve the problem of insufficiency of appropriate schema elements for different kinds of annotations. Instead of extending schemas with new elements and attributes, which is very difficult because of the strict schema definitions, the new kinds of annotations can be easily added to the RDF nodes by defining the new properties in the annotation ontology. The links between the MP document instance and HR instances allow users to access and modify document data and annotations stored in the MP instance. Moreover, the RDF-based MP instance allows remote search of semantic documents over Semantic Web protocols [19]. The RDF nodes are also envisaged to store binary data, but because of the low performance of currently available RDF stores when RDF nodes store large amount of binary data, we place binary data of document CUs into a binary data store. Storing document binary data outside of the MP instance has some advantages as well. Document binary data can be efficiently indexed and searched by using traditional IR techniques. In the search service that we have developed as a part of the SDMS, we combine structured SPARQL queries with full-text search of binary data.

A critical factor of the introduced SDM is the linkage between the HR and MP document instances. The way of the linkage that we propose in the SDM is possible if document format has the logical structure described via a markup language (e.g., XML). However, the use of existing digital documents as the HR instances was chosen purely for technical reasons since the development of completely new tools for processing the new document format is an expensive investment. However, we believe that over time the HR instances will be rendered from the MP instance at the time when humans want to see the document content and there will be no permanent copy of them. Of course, in this case the MP instance will have to keep some formatting information as well. Believing that the permanent copy of the HR instances in a form of today's documents will disappear, we consider the obvious problem of the linkage between the MP and HR instances to be temporary. The MP instance could serve as the only permanent form of the document, which will be rendered into different human readable forms on demand.

The other possible bottleneck of the SDM, which is a concern of the Semantic Web and Knowledge Representation areas as well, is the existence of many overlapping ontologies that conceptualize the same domain. By using different ontologies to annotate documents whose topics belong to the same domain, there is a lack of shared understanding of knowledge modeled within them. There are two solutions for this problem: (1) all people should use universally recognized, standardized domain ontologies, or (2) apply some ontology alignment techniques [7]. Ontology alignment is the process of determining correspondences between ontological concepts. Both solutions, the standardized ontologies and the ontology alignment, have comparative advantages and drawbacks.

Ontology evolution may also have the influence on the semantic documents modeled by the SDM. The semantics of some concept can change over time and become irrelevant for knowledge modeled within the document. Therefore, the semantic documents will need to be periodically checked in order to determine if some ontological concepts are no longer relevant.

In terms of the development of the SDMS we have faced several problems as well. For example, we apply some content analysis techniques to extract information from textual CUs and then use this information to find appropriate ontological concepts and link them to the CUs. However, for media CUs the existing content analysis techniques are more complicated and they are missing in the current implementation of the SDMS. Media CUs are annotated only with information that comes form context and usage analyses. Moreover, the full-text search, which we use as a secondary (optional) search is only possible for local document stores.

6.7 Related Work

So far, the term "semantic documents" has mainly been used to describe approaches to combining documents and ontologies [6]. The majority of them are focused on document annotation with ontologies by linking ontological concepts to regions of text and graphics in the document. Some examples of annotation frameworks that apply this kind of annotations are (1) PDFTab [6], an extension to the Protg ontology editor that allows developers to annotate PDF documents with OWL-based ontologies; (2) Semantic Word [22], which provides a GUI based tool to help analysts annotate MS Word documents with DAML ontologies; (3) SALT [8], an ontology-based authoring framework that allows authors to semantically annotate LATeX documents; and (4) ActiveDoc [12], which enables annotation of documents at three levels: ontology-based content annotation, free text statements, and on-demand document enrichment. We have identified several general shortcomings that characterize the document annotation approach used in all the above listed frameworks. First, they all try to store annotations and their definitions (i.e., ontological concepts and properties) inside the document's internal representation, so that the annotation is strongly dependent on available schema elements that are designed to store additional information and on provided linkage mechanisms. Second, ontological concepts are related to regions of the document, which are usually delimited by schema-defined structural elements, or by their size and position within the document. These parts of documents are usually not uniquely identified and are hardly addressable. Different schemas have different definitions for the same type of structural elements, so that during the document transformation the links between the annotations and appropriate structural elements are mainly lost. Finally, in order to reach document annotations, knowledge on a document schema is necessary. In spite of these shortcomings, the document annotation with ontologies and the developed frameworks has improved discoverability of document content. However, unlike our approach, these approaches do nothing about document decomposition, CUs versioning, and tracking information about the CUs usage and changing. Their contribution in improving data interoperability across application boundaries is also minor. To access some data from one application-specific document within other applications, it is still necessary to apply export/import functions to transform document data into an appropriate application format.

As our approach does not only consider a problem of semantic annotation, but also document decomposition into reusable and uniquely identified document CUs, we want to compare our approach with some existing Composite Document Models/Frameworks. Accordingly, we found a comparison with OpenDoc [17] to be enlightening. OpenDoc envisages a document as being composed of material contributed from a variety of sources such as MacWrite, Adobe Photoshop and Adobe Illustrator. Each piece of material is rendered by calling on the appropriate application at the appropriate time. The main and crucial difference to our approach is that pieces of materials, which are used in composing the document, exist as parts of diverse application specific documents, while in our approach they are considered as resources that exist independently of the implementation form. In many ways OpenDoc was well ahead of its time, but it floundered because of the need to have a wide variety of authoring applications available.

In terms of applications, we find it interesting to compare our work to the ALOCoM framework [9, 24]. The goal of this framework is sharing and reusing of document CUs of different granularity based on their semantic annotation. The framework decomposes document content into CUs, enriches them with a set of extracted metadata and then stored them into a centralized repository. In this way the extracted document CUs are no longer a part of the document context and their further evolution has no effect on the document. On the contrary, in our approach we transform complete documents into the semantic documents and document CUs remain parts of the document context. Also, ALOCoM CUs are not considered as unique resources, which can be included in different contexts. Instead, they are considered as annotated pieces of the document content, which can be copied and reused many times. Moreover, in our approach we store semantic documents on the local desktop, which is networked over the NEPOMUK SSD platform. This enables users to access and retrieve document CUs directly from the other users, instead of searching the centralized repository as it is the case with the ALOCoM.

6.8 Conclusions

In this paper, we have presented the Semantic Document Model (SDM), which defines semantic documents as composite resources with uniquely identified and semantically annotated CUs, whose data and knowledge can be represented in two forms: human readable (HR) and machine processable (MP). The full potential of the model comes from the MP document instance, which is unique and platform independent and can be accessed from any HR document instances. We have chosen the Semantic Web technologies, in particular ontologies and RDF, as the basis of the proposed MP instance. The proposed MP instance enables: unique CUs identification; flexible semantic annotation of document CUs with different types of annotations; conceptualized representation of document CUs knowledge; and capturing and formal representation of changes made to CUs over time. The user can query the MP instance over Semantic Web protocols and access and retrieve document CUs based on their semantics and conceptualized knowledge. The intelligent software agents can potentially use conceptualized knowledge from the MP instance to answer some domain questions. In accordance with the proposed model and MP instance, we built the SDMS for managing documents represented by the model (i.e., Semantic Documents). The services provided by the SDMS are currently integrated into MS Office (e.g., MS Word and PowerPoint) through the add-ins (i.e., Transformer add-in and Authoring Recommender add-in), which we developed. These add-ins enable office users to transform MS Office documents (i.e., Word and PowerPoint) into semantic documents and search local and distant repositories of semantic documents for document CUs by executing remote SPARQL queries. More importantly, this facilitates a collaboration of users by being able to seamlessly exchange their document CUs. To achieve this, we take advantage of some of the services provided by the NEPOMUK SSD platform.

In the future work, we plan to perform some studies to evaluate the proposed model and to figure out its impact on the document authoring in collaborative environments such as the NEPOMUK SSD. Moreover, we plan to work on capturing different aspects of the interaction between users and document CUs and to apply such observed results to further improve discoverability and retrieval of document CUs. Application support for other common documents, such as PDF and OpenOffice, is also something we plan to work on.

Acknowledgments Research reported in this paper has been partially financed by the European Commission in the NEPOMUK (IST-FP6-027705) project.

References

1. Berger, L.P., Luckmann, T.: The Social Construction of Reality: A Treatise its the Sociology of Knowledge. Anchor Books, pp. 51–55, 59–61 New York (1966)
2. Berners-Lee, T., Hendler, J. and Lassila, O.: The Semantic Web. Scientific Am., 2001, pp. 34–43.
3. Decker, S., Frank, M.: The social semantic desktop. WWW2004 Workshop Application Design, Development and Implementation Issues in the Semantic Web (2004)
4. Dill, S., Eiron, N., Gibson, D., Gruhl, D., Guha, R., Jhingran, A., Kanungo, T., McCurley, K.S., Rajagopalan, S., Tomkins, A., Tomlin, J.A., Zien, J.Y.: A case for automated large-scale semantic annotation. J. Web Semantics 1 (1), (2003)
5. Ecma International: Standard ECMA-376, Office Open XML File Formats, Dec. 2006.
6. Eriksson, H.: The semantic-document approach to combining documents and ontologies. Int'l Journal of Human-Computer Studies, 65(7), pp. 642–639. (2007)
7. Euzenat, J., Shvaiko, P.: Ontology Matching. Springer-Verlag, Berlin (2007)
8. Groza, T., Handschuh, S., Moller, K. and Decker, S. SALT -Semantically Annotated LATEX for Scientific Publications. In: 4th European Semantic Web Conference, (2007)
9. Jovanović, J., Gašević, D., Devedžić, V.: Ontology-based Automatic Annotation of Learning Content. International Journal on Semantic Web and Information Systems. 2(2), pp. 91–119. (2006)
10. Handschuh, S., Groza, T., Moller, M., Grimnes, G., Sauermann L., Jazayeri, M., Mesnage, C., Reif, G., Gudjonsdottir, R.: The Nepomuk Project Ð On the Way to the Social Semantic Desktop. In: I-Semantic 07', pp. 201–211 (2007)
11. Harth, A., Decker, S.: Optimized Index Structures for Querying RDF from the Web. 3rd Latin American Web Congress (2005)
12. Lanfranchi, V., Ciravegna1, F., Petrelli, D.: Semantic Web-based document: editing and browsing in AktiveDoc. In: 2nd European Semantic Web Conference, Heraklion, Greece (2005)
13. Nešić, S., Gašević, D., Jazayeri, M.: An Ontology-Based Framework for Authoring Assisted by Recommendation. In: 7th ICALT Conference, pp. 227–231. (2007)
14. Nešić, S., Jovanović, J., Gašević, D., Jazayeri, M.: Ontology Based Content Model for Scalable Content Reuse. In: 4th ACM K-CAP Conf.2007, pp. 195–196. (2007)
15. Nešić, S., Gašević, D., Jazayeri, M.: Extending MS Office for Sharing Document Content Units Over the Semantic Web. In: 8th International Conference on Web Engineering (2008).
16. OASIS Consortium: Open Document Format for Office Applications, Version 1.1 (2007)
17. OpenDoc Programmers' Guide, Addison Wesley Publishing Company, 1995. ISBN 0-202-47954-0.
18. Priestley, M. DITA XML: a reuse by reference architecturefor technical documentation. In: 19th International Conference on Computer Documentation, pp. 152–156. (2001)
19. PrudÕhommeaux, E., Seaborne, A.: SPARQL Query Language for RDF. http://www.w3.org/TR/rdf-sparql-query/ (2007)
20. Stabb, S., Studer, R.: Handbook on Ontologies, Springer, Berlin, (2004)
21. Sintek, M., Elst, L., Scerri, S., Handschuh, S.: Distributed Knowledge Representation on the Social Semantic Desktop: Named Graphs, Views and Roles in NRL. In: 4th European Semantic Web Conference, pp. 594–608. Innsbruck (2007)
22. Tallis, M. SemanticWord processing for content authors. In: Knowledge Markup and Semantic Annotation Workshop at 2nd K-CAP conf., Sanibel, Florida USA, (2003)

23. Uren, V., Cimiano, P., Iria, J., Handschuh, S., Vargas-Vera, M., Motta, E., Ciravegna, F.: Semantic annotation for knowledge management: Requirements and a survey of the state of the art. J. Web Semantics: Science, Services and Agents on the World Wide Web, 4(1), pp. 14–28 (2006)
24. Verbert, K., Gašević, D., Jovanović, J., Duval, E.: Ontology-based Learning Content Repurposing: The ALOCoM Framework. IntÕl Journal on E-Learning, 5(1), pp. 67–74. (2006)

Section 4: Data Mining, Software Engineering, and Semantic Web

Chapter 7
Ontology-Based Data Mining
in Digital Libraries

Ana Kovačević

7.1 Introduction

Data mining is one of the fastest growing fields in the computer industry and it is an iterative process of searching for new, previously hidden information in large volumes of data [15]. It is very important to preprocess data before continuing with the data mining process [17] because if it is not done properly the results will be misleading. It has been shown that data preparation usually takes up at least 60% of all time and effort needed for the entire data mining process [23].

Ontology is the specification of a conceptualization, and for conceptualization we assume an abstract, simplified view of the world [10]. Ontology is a fundamental part of knowledge and all other knowledge should rely on it and refer to it [7]. Many branches of science and technology have come to realize this fact and have recently begun to develop ontologies to represent their domains [7].

In their essence, data mining and the Semantic Web have the same goal: to find useful knowledge from large databases or the Internet [21]. The way they try to achieve the goal is different. We have joined these two different approaches in order to improve the process of acquiring knowledge about data. We have tried to address the issue of generating ontological knowledge representation such as thesaurus from abbreviated forms and their corresponding longer forms. The simplest relationships between elements of weaker semantic ontological models, such as taxonomies and thesauri, make such models more suitable as candidate targets for the development of automated processes to discover the structural relationships between elements of interest. Ontologies are increasingly used to build applications that utilize domain-specific knowledge [6]. Although thesauri are taken as the weak semantics in the continuum of "semantic strength" [5], the construction of thesauri is also laborious. Automated assistance in the development process is very useful.

Ana Kovačević
Faculty of Security Studies, University of Belgrade, Gospodara Vučića 50, 11040 Beograd, Serbia,
e-mail: fikana1@gmail.com

V. Devedžić and D. Gašević (eds.), *Web 2.0 & Semantic Web*, Annals of Information
Systems 6, DOI 10.1007/978-1-4419-1219-0_7,
© Springer Science+Business Media, LLC 2010

In the real world, data is not perfectly clean and there are various reasons for
that: data entry errors, missing check constraints, lack of standardization in recording data in different sources, etc. In general, data originating from different sources
may vary in value, structure, semantics, and the underlying assumptions [8]. This is
the problem of data heterogeneity. Heterogeneity is further increased in data that are
automatically extracted from Web pages [2]. There are two basic types of data heterogeneity: structural (differently structured data in different databases) and lexical
(diverse representations of the same world entity) [8]. Data heterogeneity may have
a negative impact on the data mining process. In our work, we address the problem of lexical heterogeneity. The task of lexical heterogeneity has been explored
in different research areas: statistics, databases, data mining, digital libraries, and
natural language processing. Researchers in different areas have proposed various
techniques and named the problem differently: record linkage [9], data deduplication [25], database hardening and name matching [2], object identification [26],
approximate matching [11], and entity resolution [1].

The technique for deduplication depends on the particular problem, and there is
no optimal solution for all domains and problems. We used character-based similarity metrics, as well as token-based similarity (TBS) metrics, for deduplication.
Character-based similarity metrics consider distance as the difference between characters and is useful in the case of typographical errors. We used Jaro–Winkler metrics [13, 27] as character-based similarity metrics. TBS metrics, which is based on
statistics for common words, is useful when world order is not important.

The paper is organized as follows. The following section introduces related work.
Section 7.3 presents our approach for matching duplicate records, Sect. 7.4 pro-
vides a detailed account of the performed experiments and the results obtained, and
Sect. 7.5 concludes the paper by outlining our plans for future research.

7.2 Related Work

Fellegi et al. [9] proposed various statistical methods for the deduplication task.
Febrl[1] is a tool which is based on Fellegi's methods and has two boundaries. Those
boundaries serve to define whether records are duplicates, not duplicates, or possible
duplicates (it is necessary to explore further).

WHIRL [3] is a "soft" database management system, which supports general-
purpose similarity metrics for text. Vector space is used to determine the similarity
among text attributes. The weights are calculated by the IDF weighing method.
Cohen et al. [4] achieved the best results with the hybrid model (token-based similarity metrics combined with character-based similarity metrics).

The work of Lawrence et al. [18] is more closely related to our work. They
propose different hand-coded deduplication functions for character-based as well as
token-based similarity metrics as well as subfield extraction for matching citations
from different sources.

---

[1] Febrl, Freely Extensible Biomedical Record Linkage, http://sourceforge.net/projects/febrl

Although the method we propose in this paper also uses character- and token-based similarity metrics, there is an important feature that distinguishes it from the previously mentioned methods. We improve the matching process by extracting knowledge from previously matched data by generating a thesaurus. The thesaurus is then used in further matching and semantically clustering data.

7.3 Duplicate Record Detection

Our goal was to match the abbreviated form of the titles found in the Journal Citation Report (JCR) [14] with the journals (i.e., their full titles) in the digital libraries [16]. The matching problem stems from the fact that in the JCR, the usage of abbreviations is not standardized, and there is usually a range of different abbreviations for one journal title. An additional source of these variations lies in errors made by authors, journal editors, or ISI data entry persons (in the case of references from the Journal Citation Report [14]). For example, there are five different abbreviated titles, for the journal "COMMUNICATIONS OF THE ACM (Association for Computing Machinery)" in the JCR, as shown in Table 7.1. Other identified problems include the change of a journal's name over time and the split of one journal into several new ones. To find out the correct journal, we had to use some journal metadata, such as the volume, the year of publication, and external sources as well (e.g., journal Web page).

Table 7.1 Examples of abbreviated titles (from Journal Citation Report [14]) and potential matches among journal titles in KOBSON digital library [16]

Journal TITLE (KOBSON)	Abbreviated titles
COMMUNICATIONS OF THE ACM (Association for Computing Machinery)	COMM ACM
	COMM ACM JAN
	COMM ACM MAR
	COMMUN ACM
	COMMUNICATION ACM

The following steps are taken in order to identify journal titles from JCR:

- Collect data from various sources, load into the database, and clean.
- Match the short and longer forms:
  - Match according to character-based similarity metrics.
  - Semi-automatically generate a thesaurus out of the correctly matched records.
  - Match the abbreviated forms with their corresponding longer forms using the thesaurus and TBS metrics.
  - Semantic clustering of any unmatched data.
  - Match the data with character-based and token-based similarity metrics using the thesaurus at lower threshold.

- Include new external data (Web resources).
- Incremental matching.

7.3.1 Data Collection and Cleaning

After collecting data from various sources, we created appropriate database tables in Oracle (v 10.2) and loaded the data into them (with SQLLoader). The tables are:

- REFERENCE: the table for data extracted from the Journal Citation Report (178,140 records) [14].
- ACRONYM: the table created after external sources, such as Thomson cite,[2] with correct abbreviations and their corresponding titles (7,513 records).
- KOBSON: the table of titles in digital libraries (42,500 records) [16].

After loading the data into the database it is necessary to clean it. The most efficient way to clean after identifying the problem is by using regular expressions. To avoid any ambiguity, in a few cases, we consulted the domain expert, and made rules for further cleaning. Those rules are incorporated in the cleaning algorithm (e.g., S12 cannot be part of the title `regexp_replace(title,'`
`([S][[:digit:]]+)$', ")`).

Some matching functions are quite sensitive to null values, so if we do not have the abbreviated title, we must investigate further to try to find the missing one from source field (e.g., not properly parsed), or if we do not find that information we will delete that record. If we find abbreviated title it will also be cleaned.

We found out that the success of matching records depends highly on cleaning. Therefore, the following steps were taken in our cleaning algorithm:

- Converted all data to uppercase.
- Removed extraneous words and characters which are not part of the abbreviated title (e.g., JAN in ACM COMM JAN), phrase IN PRESS, also some characters such as - ,&, . , ; , etc.
- Normalize "full" titles in KOBSON for matching: remove extraneous words which are usually in parenthesis (e.g., ACM TRANSACTIONS ON PROGRAMMING LANGUAGES & SYSTEMS (Association for Computing Machinery), remove stop words such as: the, of, in, and, on, etc.
- Remove of extra delimiters (in our case it was space).

7.3.2 Matching Titles

First, we matched the abbreviated titles from the JCR with the correctly abbreviated titles (from external sources, e.g., http://scientific.thomson.com), and 57% of the titles were matched in this way. Second, we applied character-based similarity metrics for further matching. After that, we automatically generated a thesaurus out of the correctly matched data and used it for TBS metrics and semantic clustering of data. After the initial matching, in order to improve the performance, we divided

---

[2] http://www.thomsonscientific.com

the REFERENCE table into three subtables of matched pairs, candidate match, and unmatched pairs.

In the case of ambiguous matching, where we have several candidate titles for one abbreviated title, further research should be carried out in order to find the correct title (e.g., using metadata, such as the author,[3] the year of citation, the context, etc.).

Sometimes for an abbreviated journal a few candidates are obtained (even after using additional metadata) and it is necessary to use additional data from some external sources (e.g., the Web page of corresponding journal) or ask the domain expert for help. After identifying those exceptions we add that rule for further matching.

7.3.2.1 Character-Based Similarity Metrics

We used the function (further referred to as the JWS) which is based on the Jaro–Winkler algorithm [27]. We also tried the function based on the edit-distance algorithm [19], but discovered that it is not as efficient as the JWS. We applied the JWS function on the abbreviated titles found in the references and the correct abbreviations (table ACRONIM), and the result is shown in Table 7.2.

For the JWS, we considered the similarity factor higher than 96. This value was empirically determined by experiments. We set a quite high similarity factor to achieve greater precision. We can set a lower similarity factor, e.g., 90, if we use other fields in matching such as the author and the year of publications, the volume, etc. It was shown that the field of author is the most present and quite reliable data compared with the year of citation and the volume which are usually missing. The matching process is incremental: once we have found a matched title for an abbreviated one, we may consider that title as the correct one in further matching.

Table 7.2 The result of applying JWS in matching

Matched title (from REFERENCE)	Correct title (from ACRONYM)	JWS
ASTROPHYS J SUPPL SE	ASTROPHYS J SUPPL S	99
BONE JOINT SURG A	J BONE JOINT SURG AM	99
J BONE JOINT SURG B	J BONE JOINT SURG Br	99
AM J SPORTS MED	AM J SPORT MED	98
CURR OPIN GENE DEV	CURR OPIN GENET DEV	98
J NON CRYST SOLIDS 1	J NON CRYST SOLIDS	98

7.3.2.2 Thesaurus

A thesaurus may be very useful in matching abbreviated forms with longer ones. The idea is to find the most frequent corresponding terms for each term in the abbreviated titles. The combination of longer terms may be used in further matching for TBS

---

[3] The author is the first author.

(instead of the original abbreviated title from the JCR) and also in the semantic clustering of unmatched records. When we semantically cluster data, we can again use the JWS or TBS records, but with a lower threshold within a cluster.

Our thesaurus was automatically generated by extracting tokens from proper abbreviated titles and their corresponding full titles (identified during the previously described matching process). The process of generating the thesaurus after correctly matched records is automated, but the final checking is performed manually to increase the precision. First, the records where the number of words in the abbreviated title is the same as in their corresponding full title were selected. Subsequently, the abbreviated tokens and their corresponding longer forms were loaded into the thesaurus. Finally, relations between the loaded tokens were created. To improve the performance of the thesaurus usage, the frequency of each token was considered, so that only those tokens which occurred more than ten times were used and the tokens were loaded in the order of decreasing frequency. Scripts for the thesaurus creation are automatically created. Then their correctness is manually checked. For example, several different syntactically corresponding forms were generated for token BIOL (Table 7.3) and we chose to use only BIOLOGY (because of the knowledge base).

For some short terms, the corresponding longer forms may also have a different semantic meaning (Table 7.4) and we do not usually include it in the thesaurus. In that case, in the matching process, the context should be analyzed or further explore the category of journal where the reference came from, etc. We plan to improve that in future to check the existence of semantically different terms.

Table 7.3 The abbreviated form and its corresponding narrow terms from the thesaurus

Short form	Corresponding longer forms
BIOL	BIOLOGICAL
	BIOLOGY
	BIOLOGICA
	BIOLOGIA

Table 7.4 The abbreviated forms and their corresponding narrow terms from the thesaurus with different semantic meanings

Short form	Corresponding narrow form from thesaurus
ASS	ASSOCIATION
	ASSESSMENT
BIO	BIOLOGY
	BIOMEDICINE

7.3.2.3 Clustering

For grouping semantically similar short forms, we employed an unsupervised learning technique – clustering. The data within a cluster is more similar than to that in other clusters. Clustering models are built using optimization criteria that favor high intracluster and low intercluster similarity.

We clustered records according to their semantic meanings using the k-means algorithm. The k-means algorithm is a distance-based clustering algorithm that partitions the data into a predetermined number of clusters [22]. Data points are assigned to the nearest cluster according to the distance metric.

Preprocessing is need, in order to transform a title into a feature vector. In our example, the feature may be a token (abbreviated word) or a theme, which is a concept word including normalized words and phases. In the feature space, each feature represent one dimension. Featues are associated with a numerical value to measure the "impact" of the feature, so that the feature with higher weight can be more representative for the cluster.

In our clustering we used the logTFIDF weighted schema:

$$w_{fd} = \log\left(\text{tf}_{fd} + 0.5\right) \log\left(D/\text{df}_f\right), \tag{7.1}$$

where w_{fd} is the weight of feature f in title d, tf_{fd} the occurrence frequency of feature f in the title d, D the total number of titles in the training set, and df_f is the number of titles containing the feature f.

The k-means algorithm assigns k centers, one for each cluster. Initialy it calculated the distance from the center in the feature space, for each abbreviated title, and assigns the document to the closest cluster. After that it calculates a new cluster's center based on the mean of each title and assigned to it, and repeats the process. Initially, we set 3 for the maximum number of clusters and 10 for maximum number of loops.

We tried to use the default Oracle's knowledge base to cluster semantically similar abbreviated forms. However, the problem was that the abbreviated forms were not mostly recognized. Oracle's knowledge base has 200,000 concepts from very broad domains classified into 2,000 major categories with a total vocabulary of 450,000 [20].

The knowledge base has a hierarchical organization and is designed for its usefulness in information retrieval rather than ontological purity, with a special focus on avoiding problems of semantic ambiguity [20].

It is possible to extend the knowledge base with a specific thesaurus in a ISO-2788 like format [12] or we can first normalize the abbreviated terms to their canonical forms and then use the knowledge base. We decided to choose the second solution. For normalizing abbreviated terms, we used the previously mentioned domain-specific thesaurus.

7.3.2.4 Token-Based Similarity Metrics

Matching only with Jaro–Winkler metrics was not enough, so we decided to try with TBS metrics. We used token-based similarity metrics for phrases that should appear in journal titles. Because we are trying to match abbreviated titles with full ones, we

first need to find an appropriate substitution for each token in the abbreviated title
and then try to match them. We used the previously generated thesaurus with TBS
metrics (Table 7.5).

Table 7.5 Using thesaurus in token-based similarity metrics

Abbreviated title in JCR	By using domain	Found the full journal title as result
IEEE T COMMUN	IEEE T COMMUNICATIONS	IEEE TRANSACTION ON COMMUNICATIONS – correct IEEE TRANSACTIONS ON WIRELESS COMMUNICATIONS wrong

For calculating of scoring algorithm for returned document on TBS metrics, inverse frequency algorithm is used based on Salton's formula [24].

7.3.3 Using External Sources

When we do not have enough information to discover the corresponding journal
for the abbreviated one, we use external sources. For example, we can find the
user's published manuscripts and extract references from them, or search on the
Web, where a large amount of bibliographic information is freely available, such
as the Collection of Computer Science Bibliographies[4] and CiteSeer.[5] If this is not
enough, we must consult a domain expert.

7.3.4 Incremental Matching

As previously mentioned, once the full title for the abbreviated title has been found
and once it has been verified with the metadata (issue, volume, year, author, etc.), it
can be used for further matching or for thesaurus generation. When we have enough
reliable information, we can create database tables of the author's name, abbreviated
titles, and their corresponding mistaken ones.

7.4 Experiment

To test the effectiveness of our method, we chose to check the results against real-
world data. Just for the purpose of our experiment, we extracted the records of the
references in the training table. We chose to create a training table with three sets of

---

[4] http://liinwww.ira.uka.de/bibliography/index

[5] http://citeseer.ist.psu.edu

records according to the significant words (FUZZY, COMMUN, ENDOCRINOL). Later we applied the algorithms on the training table. Finally, we verified the results manually.

We first used the function based on the JWS metric. To increase the precision of the results we used metadata (author and year of publication) and set the similarity factor at 90. In the first iteration, the records from the training table were matched with the "correctly" abbreviated titles. After that in the second iteration, it was assumed that the matched records from the previous step had been correctly matched, and the new records were compared with them. Metadata was used and the similarity threshold was set at 90. The similarity score for the previous correctly matched title is also included in that calculation. The last iteration attempted to match the previously nonmatched records among them. To increase the recall, we used metadata such as author and year of reference and the similarity threshold was set at 90, and without the metadata, similarity score was set to 95. Table 7.6 shows the results of matching with JWS metrics.

Table 7.6 The results among group on JWS metrics

	Number of records	Number of matched records	Found ISSN
TOKEN	676	342	275
COMMUN	318	187	137
ENDOCRINOL	197	99	97
FUZZY	161	56	41

We checked manually the results and found out that all records are correctly discovered as the duplicates by the JWS. The reason for that was the highly set similarity factor 90 (95). We also found out that 28 records, which were duplicates, were detected as well as 14 titles as candidate duplicates.

We tried to match remaining duplicates by using thesaurus with clustering, as well as TBS metrics. We had a rather small set for making a thesaurus, so we also use the ACRONYM table. The inverted index was a set for the test data. The process of creating and uploading the thesaurus was automated, but the final checking was done manually. In the thesaurus, we considered only those tokens which were longer that two letters and tokens which existed at least two times in our training table. In the process of creating the thesaurus, we first created a temporary table with the short form and its corresponding longer forms, and interactively checked which longer forms we would include in the new thesaurus. For each short form, there is only one corresponding longer form. After that, the process of creating the thesaurus, uploading the tokens, and their corresponding relations are automated. This interactive checking is now necessary, and we plan to minimize it in the future. We decided to use nouns to achieve better results with the knowledge base.

Problems arose when the short form had more than one meaning (e.g., COMMUN has COMMUNICATIONS and COMMUNITY). We decided to use COMMUNICATIONS as the longer term, and we did not use COMMUNITY, which rarely occurred (4%) in the ACRONYM table. We decided not to use tokens with diverse meaning and comparable frequency in the thesaurus because of ambiguity. Furthermore, we did not use words without semantic meaning such as ACTA. We may create stop-list after words like ACTA, J (journal), T (transaction) and use it in the clustering process and token-based similarity matching.

First, we clustered data without using domain-specific thesaurus (Table 7.7), and after that with thesaurus (Table 7.8). Abbreviated titles are better clustered with previously normalized terms (Table 7.8), comparing with clustering without using thesaurus. It was shown that the clustering based on theme gave us better results than on tokens. As it is previously mentioned, we set 3 for the maximum number of clusters and 10 for the maximum number of loops.

We compared records with the same score but out of 35 tiles[6] only 14 were correctly matched. For example, the title FUZZY SETS THEORY IT and THEORY FUZZY SETS IT had the same score and they are duplicates (Table 7.9). Records such as PHARMACOL RES COMMUN, CARLSBERG RES COMMUN and RES COMMUN ALCOHOL S also had the same score, but they were not duplicates. We noted that the probability of mismatch is higher with the lower score. In addition, for some titles we could not conclude if they were the same, such as FUZZY SETS THEORY IT and FUZZY SET THEORY BAS. We were unable to conclude whether or not some titles were duplicates since we did not have enough information at our disposal.

Table 7.7 Results of semantically clustering abbreviated forms without normalization

Cluster	Tokens
1	fuzzy sets, COMMUN, systems, MATH, CHEM, mats, fuzz, theories, RES, APPL, POLYM, endocrinology, IEICE, communities, ELECT, HDB, EQ, DIFF, matchableness, uncertainty, COMMUNIC, fuzzy logic, STRUCT
2	ENDOCRINOL, investments, ACTA, copping, cells, mols, EXP, METAB, JAPON, CLIN, Minerva, ADHES, Meta, BIOCH, pars, OXF, HOR
3	COMMUNICATION, COMMUNICATIONS, IEEE – Institute of Electrical and Electronics Engineers, mobile communications, ACM, harts, modernity, SIGNA, purity
0 Misc.	–

Table 7.8 Results of semantically clustering abbreviated forms with using domain thesaurus

Cluster	Tokens
1	ENDOCRINOL, investments, copping, ACTA, cells, mols, CLIN, endocrinology, EXP, METAB, JAPON, Minerva, ADHES, Meta, CONT, BASIC – beginner's all-purpose symbolic instruction code, BIOCH, ECOLO, pars
2	COMMUNICATION, COMMUNICATIONS, IEEE – Institute of Electrical and Electronics Engineers, ACM, modernity, mobile communications, harts, SIGNA, purity
3	fuzzy sets, systems, MATH, CHEM, mats, fuzz, theories, RES, APPL, POLYM, IEICE, ELECT, HDB, DIFF, EQ, matchableness, uncertainty, COMMUNIC, fuzzy logic, CRYST, STRUCT, preferences
0 Misc.	–

---

[6] Note: titles are grouped in clusters.

In the clustering process, abbreviated titles were used. For each token the weight is assigned based on the logTFIDF schema (explained in Sect. 7.3), and then the whole abbreviated title is recalculated and given a score according to how far is it from the center of cluster (Table 7.9). A title that is closer to the center of cluster has higher score.

The most valuable thing about clustering is that the records are segmented into sets, and we may than apply algorithms to smaller sets of data, what is significant especially in the huge amount of data. The data was segmented correctly. Records with the same (or similar) score can be considered as candidate match in the further deduplication process.

Table 7.9 Abbreviated titles with the same clustering score

Abbreviated title	Cluster	Score
FUZZY SETS SYSTEMS	3	55.1895468
FUZZY SETS SYSTEMS T	3	55.1895468
FUZZY SETS SYST	3	55.1895468
FUZZY SETS FUZZY SYS	3	49.1266043
FUZZY SETS	3	44.3366212
FUZZY SETS THEORY IT	3	14.3532547
THEORY FUZZY SETS IT	3	14.3532547
FUZZY SETS THEORY IT	3	32.818519
FUZZY SET THEORY BAS	3	32.818519
PHARMACOL RES COMMUN	3	14.903102
CARLSBERG RES COMMUN	3	14.903102
RES COMMUN ALCOHOL S	3	14.903102

TBS metric is useful for detecting replicas with changed word order (e.g., FUZZY SETS THEORY IT and THEORY FUZZY SETS IT) as it was not our case. We used the TBS with domain thesaurus. As in the case of the JWS, we also used metadata to improve precision. Only eight records were detected as duplicates.

It was shown that the JWS is best for duplicate detection of abbreviated titles, but that may be explained as follows. The JWS does not need as much data as we need for clustering or creating a thesaurus, and also the JWS is useful in the case of typographical errors, what was our case. Clustering is primarily for segmenting records, but also can be useful as the first step in finding replicas. TBS metrics did not give satisfying results, but we will try to improve that, by making thesaurus better suited to TBS metrics.

We were unable to conclude for some titles whether or not they were duplicates, since we did not have enough information at our disposal. As more lexically different titles are found out that are duplicates, we will have more data for matching and have better recall and precision.

7.5 Conclusion

Successful data preparation has major implications for the overall data mining process. This paper has presented an approach in automating the discovery of knowledge from abbreviated short forms by generating a thesaurus that utilizes domain-specific knowledge. With the increasing importance of ontologies in the field of business database application, it is important to extend existing ontologies with domain-specific ones. The automatically generated thesaurus was further used in the token-based and character-based matching (JWS) for record deduplication. Our experience proved that we achieved better results in the duplicate record detection process with a thesaurus. We used the domain-generated thesaurus in semantic clustering. It was shown that semantic clustering may be very useful in partitioning data, what is especially significant in the case of large amount of data, what is usually the case. As well as, semantic clustered records with same or similar score can be considered as candidate records in further deduplication process.

There are a number of directions we will pursue in the immediate future. First, we plan to improve the presented approach for clustering abbreviated titles. More precisely, our goal is to automate the refinement process of the thesaurus as much as possible. We also plan to represent visually results of the clustering and to generate a label for each cluster. Second, the process of deduplication presented in this paper is not constrained only to field of digital libraries and we plan to apply it to other fields as well.

References

1. Benjelloun O, Garcia-Molina H, Su Q, Widom J (2005) Swoosh: A Generic Approach to Entity Resolution. Stanford University technical report, March 2005.
2. Bilenko M, Mooney RJ, Cohen WW, Ravikumar P, Fienber SE (2003) Adaptive name matching in information integration, IEEE Intelligent Systems, 18(5), 16–23.
3. Cohen WW (1998) Integration of Heterogeneous Databases without common domains using query based on textual similarity. In Proceedings of the 1998 ACM SIGMOD International Conference on Management of Data (SIGMOD' 98), 201–212.
4. Cohen WW, Ravikumar P, Feinberg S (2003) A comparison of string metrics for matching names and records. In Proceedings of the KDD2003 (also available at http://www.cs.cmu.edu/~pradeepr/papers/kdd03.pdf).
5. Daconta M, Obst LJ, Smith KT (2003) The Semantic Web, Wiley, New York.
6. Das S, Chong EI, George E, Srinivasan J (2004), Supporting ontology-based semantic matching in RDBMS. In Proceedings of the 30th VLDB Conference, Toronto, Canada.
7. Devedzic V (2006) Semantic Web and Education, Springer, Berlin.
8. Elmagarmid A, Ipeirotis P, Verykios V (2007) Duplicate record detection: a survey, IEEE Transaction on Knowledge and Data Engineering, 19(1), 1–16.
9. Fellegi IP, Sunter AB (1969) A theory for record linkage, Journal of the American Statistical Association, 328(64), 1183–1210.
10. Gruber T (1993) A translation approach to portable ontologies, Knowledge Acquisition, 5(2), 199–220.
11. Guha S, Koudas N, Marathe A, Srivastava D (2004) Merging the results of approximate match operations. In Proceedings of the 30th VLDB Conference 2004, 636–647.

12. International Standard ISO 2788: Documentation – Guidelines for the establishment and development of monolingual thesauri, Second edition – 1986-11-15, International Organization for Standardization.
13. JCR (2005) Journal Citation Report, Institute for Scientific Information, Thomson, http://scientific.thomson.com/products/jcr/
14. Jaro MA (1976) Unimatch: A Record Linkage System: User's Manual,technical report, US Bureau of the Census, Washington, DC.
15. Kantardzic M (2003) Data Mining: Concepts, Models, Methods, and Algorithms, Wiley, New York.
16. KOBSON (2005) Internal data of the project on the evaluation of the Serbian authors publishing productivity.
17. Larose D (2004) Discovering Knowledge in Data, Wiley, New York.
18. Lawrence S, Giles CL, Bollacker K (1999) Digital libraries and autonomous citation indexing, IEEE Computer, 32(6), 67–71.
19. Levenshtein VI (1966), Binary codes capable of correcting deletions, insertions and reversals, Soviet Physics Doklady, 10(8), 707–710.
20. Mahesh K, Kud J, Dixon P (1999) Oracle at Trec8: a lexical approach, NIST Special Publication 500-246. In The Eighth Text REtrieval Conference (TREC 8).
21. Milutinovic V (2007) DataMining Versus Semantic Web (also available at http://galeb.etf.bg. ac.yu/~vm/tutorial/tutorial.html).
22. ODM (2005) Oracle Data Mining Concepts 10g release 2 (also available at http://download. oracle.com/docs/html/B14339_01/4descriptive.htm#i1005741).
23. Pyle D (1999) Data Preparation for Data Mining, Morgan Kaufmann, San Francisco, CA.
24. Salton G, Buckley C (1988) Term weighting approaches in automatic text retrieval, Information and Processing Management, 24(5), 513–523.
25. Sarawagi S, Bhamidipaty A (2002) Interactive deduplication using active learning. In Proceedings of Eight ACM SIGKDD International Conference on Knowledge Discovery and Data Mining (KDD'02), 269–278.
26. Tejada S, Knoblock C, Minton S (2002) Learning domain-independent string transformation for high accuracy object identification. In Proceedings of ACM SIGKDD 2002.
27. Winkler WE (1995) Matching and record linkage. In B. G. Cox (ed.), Business Survey Methods, Wiley, New York, 355–384.

Chapter 8
An Assessment System on the Semantic Web

Sonja Radenković, Nenad Krdžavac, and Vladan Devedžić

8.1 Introduction

Development of current assessment systems is affected by the rapid advance of information technologies. The Semantic Web takes off the burden of data exchange and data processing from the end user. Nowadays, engines are capable of representing semantics of the data they exchange, understanding the meaning of the data, and reasoning about it. This is possible by using the ontologies that describe the metadata.

However, in assessment systems these huge possibilities of the Semantic Web in the data representation and exchange are limited by the fact that the end user still needs to take care of the data. The main problem in creating modern assessment systems on the Semantic Web is how to exchange and enrich the knowledge, as well as to provide the way for knowledge evaluation. Whenever the assessment experts exchange assessments electronically, whatever software and hardware systems they use, interoperability enters the scene. Interoperability is the capability of software systems to use the same formats for storing and retrieving information and to provide the same service on different hardware and software platforms [19]. Once interoperability is achieved, the parts of assessments can be exchanged between experts. They all can edit, store, and reuse them. The key issue here is to create and manage information in such a way that opportunities for exchange and reuse, either within or between institutions, are maximized.

This paper proposes a way to create a flexible, interoperable assessment system that can be easy to maintain and reuse. It is based on the IMS Question and Test Interoperability (QTI) standard [14] and designed using the Model Driven Architecture (MDA) standards [20] that come from software engineering. The core concept here is to change the system's specification rather than implementation using the

Sonja Radenković, Nenad Krdžavac, and Vladan Devedžić

FON – School of Business Administration, University of Belgrade, Serbia, e-mail: sonjam@fon.rs; nenadkr@tesla.rcub.bg.ac.yu; devedzic@etf.rs

V. Devedžić and D. Gašević (eds.), *Web 2.0 & Semantic Web*, Annals of Information Systems 6, DOI 10.1007/978-1-4419-1219-0_8,
© Springer Science+Business Media, LLC 2010

Unified Modeling Language [32] as the standardized modeling language that most tools provide support for.

One of the main ideas the paper proposes is using Description Logic (DL) reasoning techniques for intelligent analysis of students' answers to and solutions of the problems they are working on during assessment sessions with the system. Response processing in the IMS QTI specification is based on matching the student's response to the previously stored correct one. The use of a DL reasoner enables processing of open-ended questions, which is the novelty that can be applied in the IMS QTI standard. Furthermore, this is the way for applying a framework for data sharing and reuse across heterogeneous applications, which is the core of the Semantic Web.

The paper is organized as follows. Section 8.2 describes the system requirements. Section 8.3 presents the IMS QTI standard. Section 8.4 describes basic aspects of the MDA standards. Section 8.5 describes the model of the QTI-based assessment system using the MDA standards. Section 8.6 describes reasoning with QTI models. Section 8.7 presents related work. Section 8.8 shows the conclusions and indicates directions for future work.

8.2 Problem Statement

Each assessment system puts tests, questions, and problems to the users during assessment sessions and the users are supposed to work out the problems, provide solutions, and answer the questions. Note that the system may be quite complex, composed of various subsystems and components. In addition, various authoring tools may have been used to create the learning and assessment materials and the variety of users' approaches in solving the problems and answering the questions during assessment sessions may be huge.

In order to create a flexible assessment system capable of presenting and analyzing the students' solutions and answers, it is necessary to define the system requirements precisely. These requirements are:

- The system should be based on the IMS QTI standard, which is a general specification created to facilitate interoperability between a number of subsystems of a modern assessment system in relation to the actors that use them.
- The system should be designed using the MDA standards in order to be flexible, interoperable, and easy to maintain and reuse, changing the system's specification rather than implementation.
- It has to enable retesting until the student presents a critical amount of knowledge necessary to pass the course.
- It has to provide a well-documented content format for storing items, in a way independent of the authoring tool used to create them.
- It has to support the deployment of item banks across a wide range of learning and assessment delivery systems.

- It has to support the deployment of items and item banks from diverse sources in a single learning or assessment-delivery system.
- It should provide other systems with the capability to report the test results in an intelligent manner, using DL reasoning techniques such as concept classification and consistency checking.

By creating a system to accomplish the above requirements, one obtains:

- A flexible and quickly developed assessment environment
- High-level interoperability between various component systems
- Easy and intuitive testing of the student knowledge, done in an intelligent way
- An easy-to-extend system that can be improved by including new subsystems

8.3 IMS QTI Standard: A Short Overview

To support the exchange of assessment items and test results between systems and components, a specification for interoperability and exchangeability of assessments is required. A specification prescribes, in a complete, precise, and verifiable manner, the requirements, design, behavior, or characteristics of a system [3]. One of the main benefits of a specification is that it offers a shared (controlled) vocabulary in which core concepts and ideas about a specific topic area can be expressed.

The IMS Global Learning Consortium, Inc. (IMS) [13] is defining specifications to allow distributed learning applications and services to work together or *interoperate*. These activities include searching for and using educational content, monitoring the progress and performance of learners, and transferring student records between the systems.

IMS Question and Test Interoperability (QTI) standard (specification) is described in [14]. This is the leading specification for exchange and interoperability of questions and tests between authoring tools, item banks, test construction tools, learning systems, and assessment delivery system, as parts of modern assessment systems. In other words, this specification describes a data model for representation of question and test data and their corresponding results reports [18].

In an attempt to avoid ambiguity, IMS QTI has developed its own terminology. Test is known as *assessmentTest* [29]. It is often necessary to group a series of questions within an assessment. This is done using *sections*. In order to deliver a question, it is necessary to know other things as well, such as the score for getting it correct, layout rendering information, and what feedback should be given. All these things together make the *assessmentItem*. Actually, the questions with their associated data are known as assessmentItems. There are different forms of items, such as multiple-choice questions or fill-in-the-blank tasks. The examples that can be implemented within this specification are described in [17]. At the end of the assessment a *results report* is generated. It describes how the results of a test can be recorded so that other systems can make use of it. There is an exchange of items, assessments, and results between authoring tools, item banks, learning systems, and assessment delivery systems.

8.4 Model Driven Architecture

Model Driven Architecture is defined as a realization of model-driven-engineering principles proposed by Object Management Group (OMG)[1] [20]. This is a software design approach that provides the set of guidelines for structuring specifications expressed as models [4]. MDA defines three view points (levels of abstraction) from which the system can be analyzed. According to [20], there are three models that correspond to these points of view:

- Computation Independent Model – CIM does not show the details of the system structure and it is very similar to the concept of ontology.
- Platform Independent Model – PIM defines the system functionality using an appropriate domain-specific language.
- Platform Specific Model – PSM is a system specification that uses concepts and constructs from concrete domain-specific language, or general-purpose language (like Java) that computers can run.

The central concept of the MDA standards is a four-layer modeling architecture (Fig. 8.1). The topmost layer (M3) is called *meta–meta model* layer and it corresponds to CIM. OMG has defined a standard at this layer – Meta object facility (MOF). According to [21], MOF is the language intended for defining meta-models at M2 layer, which corresponds to PIM. The next layer is the model layer (M1) – the layer where we develop real-world models. It corresponds to PSM.

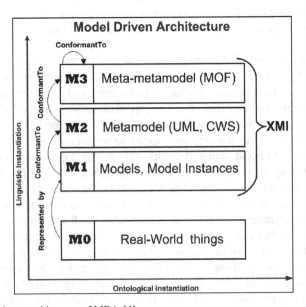

Fig. 8.1 Four-layer architecture of MDA [4]

---

[1] http://www.omg.org

An important, recently defined MOF-based metamodel is the OWL metamodel called the *Ontology Definition Metamodel* (ODM) [22]. It covers common concepts of ontological engineering, such as classes, properties, resources, etc. To an extent, it is similar to RDF Schema and OWL languages, commonly used for ontology development. However, since it is MDA- and MOF-based, it has an important advantage of enabling the use of graphical modeling capabilities of the standardized UML modeling language for ontology development (see [22] for details).

Model transformation is the process of converting one model to another model of the same system [5]. *Model engineering* uses the terms "representedBy" and "conformantTo" [4] to establish relations between the models in the MDA layers. It is possible to define the transformation of one model into another if the metamodels of different models are made in the same language. This language is defined by the XML Meta-Data Interchange (XMI) standard [34] that defines how XML tags are used to represent serialized MOF-compliant models in XML. MOF-based metamodels are translated to XML document type definitions (DTDs) and models are translated into XML documents that are consistent with their corresponding DTDs. Using XMI, it is possible to generate a "middleware" environment automatically, as well as to transform a "middleware" platform into another. Automated tools generally perform these translations, for example tools compliant to the OMG standard named QVT [26].

8.5 Modeling the QTI-Based Assessment System Using MDA Standards

The main reason for applying the MDA standards in development of assessment systems is to make a clear difference between conceptual and concrete modeling, in order to automate transfer and sharing of information and knowledge. The essence of the development of an assessment system based on the IMS QTI (the QTI system, for short) using MDA standards is a transformation from the system's PIM to PSM. The PIM specifies the assessment system's functionality. The PSM is the specification of implementation details in a concrete technical environment. In this case, the PSM is generated using Ecore classes of the Eclipse Modeling Framework (EMF) [9] (see the next paragraph), whereas the transformation from the PIM to the PSM is made using the Atlas Transformation Language (ATL) [1] as the most recent implementation of the QVT standard.

EMF is a Java-based open-source framework and code-generation facility for building tools and other applications based on a structured model. The Eclipse Platform provides a powerful integration framework at the UI and file levels, and EMF enhances this capability to enable fine-grained data sharing among tools and applications. EMF has its own simple metamodel called Ecore. In other words, a MOF-like core metamodel of EMF is called Ecore. Ecore classes can be generated automatically, in the Eclipse Modeling Framework [9], from an Ecore-based metamodel. Ecore classes allow users to create, update, and access instances of metamodels using Java.

ATL is used for model transformation. In case of a QTI system, it means that the assessment items will be transferred from the *Item Bank model* to the *Test Construction Model* (Fig. 8.2), and then the Test Construction Model will be transferred to the DL Reasoning Machine (Fig. 8.14) in the process of evaluating a student's answer. The DL reasoning machine will check the consistency of the answer.

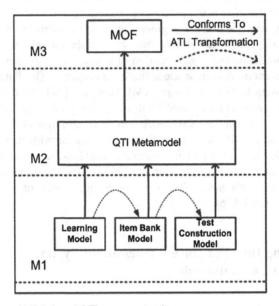

Fig. 8.2 Principles of MDA-based QTI system operation

8.5.1 A QTI Metamodel

The first step in developing a QTI system using the MDA standard is to create a metamodel that captures the main concepts of QTI, i.e., those for creating the models of authoring tools, item banks, test construction tool, and assessment delivery system. The novelty in creating QTI systems here is the improvement of response processing. We propose the applying of DL reasoning techniques in response processing of a QTI system in order to check the semantic consistency of answers to open-ended questions. Because of that, it is necessary to use a DL metamodel as a part of QTI-based assessment system metamodel.

The details of the QTI metamodel are described in [27]. The metamodel is represented in UML, which means that it is understandable and useable for the assessment domain experts knowledgeable in UML. The process of creating the QTI metamodel is shown in Fig. 8.3.

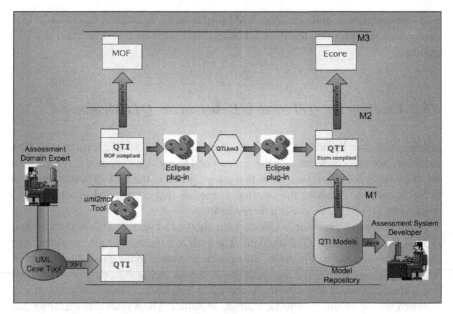

Fig. 8.3 The process of creating the QTI metamodel

The proposed QTI metamodel is designed using the *Poseidon for UML*[2] case tool as a model at the M1 level of the MDA architecture. In order to transfer this model to the M2 level of hierarchy, it is necessary to perform the transformation to MOF representation. First, the QTI metamodel has exported from the tool Poseidon for UML to UML XMI format. The QTI metamodel in XMI format is then adapted to MOF by performing the transformation with the tool *uml2mof*.[3] That tool is designed for the NetBeans Metadata Repository (MDR) where it is possible to store models. That way, the QTI metamodel is fully adapted to MOF, which means that it can be used in the model repositories and is possible to check if the QTI models are compatible with the QTI metamodel.

The next step in generating the QTI metamodel that can be used in EMF is the transformation from MOF-based metamodel into the equivalent Ecore-based metamodel (EMF repository). That transformation is done by Eclipse plug-ins[4] appropriate for the job. The MOF-based QTI metamodel supports the XMI 1.2 standard and the Ecore-based QTI metamodel (EMF repository) supports the XMI 2.0 standard. Because of that, it was necessary to use an intermediate model, in this case a KM3 model. KM3 is a domain-specific language for defining metamodels [5]; its syntax is very similar to that of Java. The MOF-based QTI metamodel is transformed to

[2] http://www.gentleware.com

[3] http://mdr.netbeans.org/uml2mof/

[4] http://www.eclipse.org/gmt

KM3 representation, and then from KM3 further to the equivalent Ecore-based QTI metamodel that presents the PIM for assessment systems based on the IMS QTI standard.

8.5.2 Creating the QTI Models Based on the QTI Metamodel

Having the Ecore-based QTI metamodel that is located at the M2 level of the MDA hierarchy, we can create models that correspond to a given metamodel. There are a lot of examples of *assessmentItems* that are proposed in the IMS QTI standard (see [17]). In order to illustrate the creation of models that correspond to a given QTI metamodel (Fig. 8.3), we present three examples.

The first one is the Simple Choice item shown in Fig. 8.4. This is the simplest type of item in the IMS QTI standard. The system expects a single response from the candidate, because only one of the options presented to the candidate is correct. The Ecore-based model for this example is shown in Fig. 8.5. Response processing in this example is also simple. As shown in Fig. 8.5, the candidate's response is declared on top of the item to be a single identifier. The values this identifier can take are the values of the identifier's attributes corresponding to the individual simpleChoices (ChoiceA, ChoiceB, ChoiceC). The correct answer is included in the *declaration* of the response (Fig. 8.5).

The second example is the text entry interaction, shown in Fig. 8.6. The system here requires from candidates to construct their own response, typically by typing

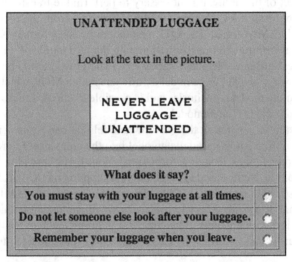

Fig. 8.4 A simple choice item example[5]

---

[5] http://www.imsglobal.org/question/qti_v2p1pd/examples/items/choice.xml

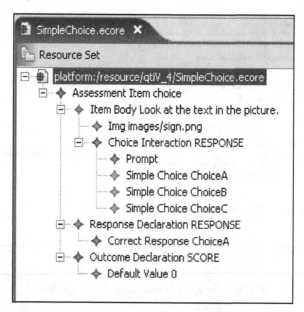

Fig. 8.5 Ecore-based QTI model for the simple choice item

it in. The Ecore-based model for this item that conforms to the QTI metamodel is shown on Fig. 8.7. According to [17], the scoring for this item could have just matched the correct response but actually uses a mapping to enable partial credit for *york* (spelled without a capital letter). When mapping strings, the mapping is always case sensitive. This example also illustrates the mapping in case when the cardinality of the response is 1.

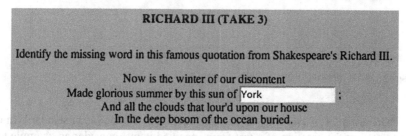

Fig. 8.6 A text entry item example[6]

The third example illustrates an open-ended question in the QTI standard. It is shown in Fig. 8.8. As mentioned above, the response processing for this type of item is "beyond the scope of specification." The Ecore-based model for this type of item is shown in Fig. 8.9.

---

[6] http://www.imsglobal.org/question/qti_v2p1pd/examples/items/text_entry.xml

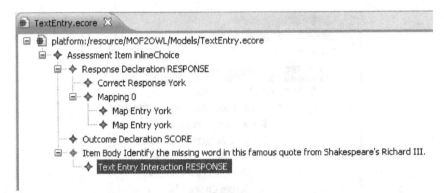

Fig. 8.7 Ecore-based QTI model for the text entry item

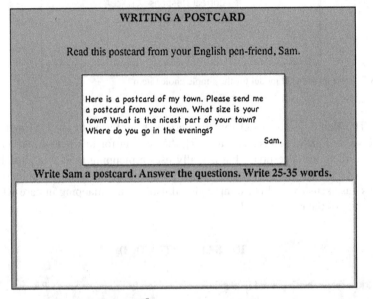

Fig. 8.8 An extended text item example[7]

There are a lot of examples of *assessmentTest*s in the IMS QTI standard. In order to present the creation of a test from specified items, consider an example that includes only one assessment section. This example conforms to the IMS QTI metamodel and is shown in Fig. 8.10. The assessment test example has three assessment items. The navigation mode is *linear*, which means that the candidate is restricted to attempt each item in turn, i.e., once the candidate moves on he is not permitted to return. The *selection* specifies the rules used to select the child elements of a section (in this case two child elements are selected).

---

[7] http://www.imsglobal.org/question/qti_v2p1pd/examples/items/extended_text.xml

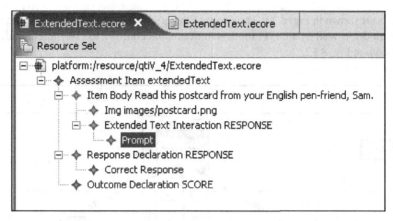

Fig. 8.9 Ecore-based QTI model for the extended text item

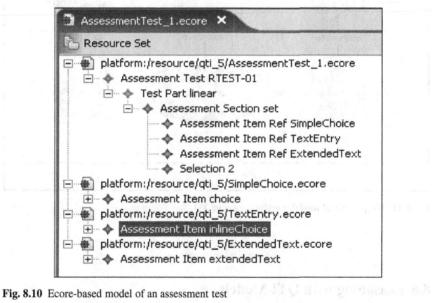

Fig. 8.10 Ecore-based model of an assessment test

8.5.3 Model Transformation in QTI System

In order to use DL reasoning techniques in the process of analyzing students' solutions, it is necessary to transform QTI-based models into the equivalent OWL-based QTI-OWL models. This process is automated by means of ATL. The transformation process is shown in Fig. 8.11. The result of the qti2owl.atl transformation is the QTI metamodel as well as the QTI models in Ecore that conform to OWL metamodel. It is shown in Fig. 8.12.

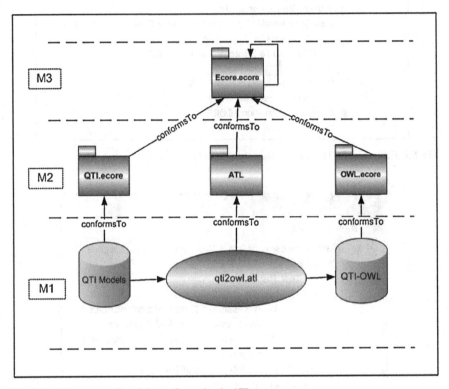

Fig. 8.11 The process of model transformation in ATL

8.6 Reasoning with QTI Models

In this section, we focus on the intelligent analysis of the semantics of students' solutions to the problems they solve during assessment sessions (students' solutions, for short). To this end, we examined using a DL reasoner based on MDA standards. We propose a corresponding architecture for intelligent analysis of students' solutions using a DL reasoner. To explain our idea, we present two simple examples of using a DL reasoner in analyzing a student's answer, in the case of a simple choice item (Fig. 8.4 and 8.5). We do not cover the implementation issues in this section.

The basic notions in description logics (DLs) are concepts (unary predicates) and roles (binary predicates) [2]. One of the most important constructive properties of DLs is their reasoning services, which can be used for reasoning with ontologies.

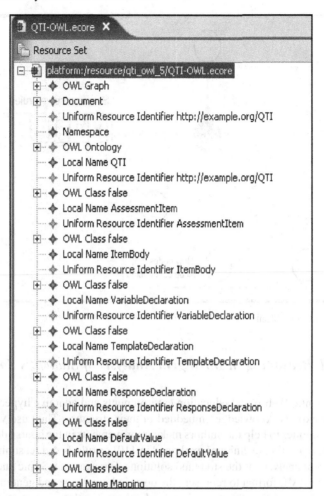

Fig. 8.12 The QTI-OWL.ecore is the result of the qti2owl.atl transformation

Reasoning services in DLs are based on the tableau algorithm [2]. The tableau algorithm tries to prove the satisfiability of concept term C, by demonstrating a model in which C can be satisfied [12]. A tableau is a graph that represents such a model (Fig. 8.13), with nodes corresponding to individuals and edges corresponding to relationships between individuals. New nodes are created according to expansion rules [2]. These rules are different in different description logics.

Some DL reasoners like PELLET [31] and FACT [12] are of YES/NO kind of software – their reasoning algorithm generates only Yes or No answers when checking the consistency of ontology. It is difficult to use them that way in, e.g., intelligent analysis of the semantics of students' solutions in Intelligent Semantic Web-Based Education Systems (ISWBESs). We use tableau model [15] to analyze the semantics of students' answers.

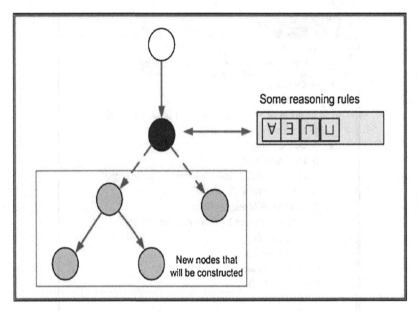

Fig. 8.13 A tree of tableau

8.6.1 DL Reasoning in Intelligent Analysis of Student's Solutions

Many Semantic Web-based education environments and adaptive hypermedia systems have experts' knowledge embedded in their structure. They use various reasoning techniques to help the authors make improvements in the course design (e.g., case-based reasoning techniques explained in [10] or rule-based reasoning [30]) or for intelligent analysis of the students' solutions. For example, Simic and Devedzic [30] used an XML format to represent the domain knowledge and generate a CLIPS file (*.clp) before using the reasoning mechanism. The Jess expert system shell's inference engine was used as the reasoning mechanism. However, some problems are difficult for Jess to solve:

1. Reasoning about the course material subsumed by another one (i.e., classification of the learning material)
2. Reasoning about a student's answer that is a model of domain knowledge (in the sense the term "model" is used in DLs)
3. Intelligent analysis of the semantics of students' solutions

Intelligent analysis of students' solutions using a DL reasoner may fulfill the following requirements:

1. Check whether the student's answer is satisfiable w.r.t. the question
2. Find the student's mistakes (semantic inconsistencies) in the answer
3. Find if the student's answer can be described with an uncertainty, rather than just as a true answer

4. Use various pedagogical strategies in the analysis of students' solutions, according to a hierarchy of answers

These requirements may be satisfied using DL reasoning services like classification (subsumption) and consistency. Using some DLs reasoning techniques in this paper, we focus on the above stated problem number 1.

According to [12, 2], consistency and subsumption can be calculated with satisfiability of concept terms. Classification is useful in cases of checking the hierarchy of students' answers or teaching courses. A question submitted to the student may imply a few different answers, and all of the answers may be true. In this paper, we present an example in which our reasoner solves this problem (see Sect. 8.6.2). In case of a few true answers, the reasoner may find the most common answer and give positive (but different) marks to the student. The answer hierarchy can be calculated using the DL subsumption reasoning technique. This classification cannot be applied in cases when there is only one answer for the question.

The benefit of applying consistency checking is finding (by means of the DL reasoner) logical mistakes in the students' answers. Some existing DL reasoners [12, 31] may fulfill the above requirements, but there are few problems in using these reasoners in such software environment. The problems are related to their architectures. For example, the FACT reasoner [12], implemented in LISP, is difficult to integrate with ISWBESs. FACT may check the consistency of some students' answers (if they are submitted as an ontology), but cannot discover inconsistencies precisely.

For intelligent analysis of the semantics of the students' solutions to fulfill the above-mentioned requirements, we propose a DL reasoner (Fig. 8.14) that uses MDA model transformations. We assume that the students' answers are submitted to the reasoning machine as OWL models (Fig. 8.14), transformed from a QTI model (Fig. 8.11). Ontology model conforms to OWL metamodel, which is defined in Ontology Definition Metamodel (ODM) [22].

The tableau model can be described using XMI. XMI has a tree structure – every tableau model is a tree (graph) [12]. Using the interfaces generated for the tableau metamodel (JMI interfaces [7] and Ecore classes), we can analyze such a tableau model, i.e., the reasoner can find the student's mistakes and return them to the Assessment Delivery System [14].

To transform OWL models of students' solutions to the corresponding tableau models, we used ATL. It satisfies *OMG's QVT RFP* standard [21].

8.6.2 Examples of Applying DLs Reasoning in Intelligent Analysis of Student's Solutions

How to use DLs reasoning when a student answers multiple-choice questions (Fig. 8.5) specified according to the QTI standard? In the example presented here, we explain advantages of using an MDA-based DL reasoner w.r.t existing ones.

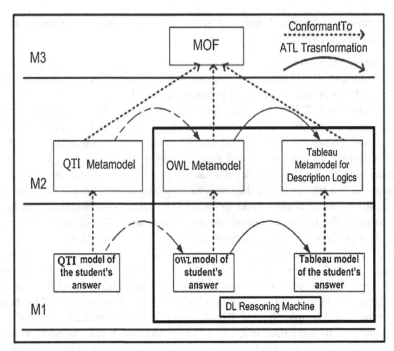

Fig. 8.14 Analysis of students' solution in MDA using a DL reasoner

Among a few possible answers, a student may choose one or more. Using DLs terms, the items corresponding to TBox (Rbox) axioms are described using description logic (Table 8.1), where questions are presented as concepts using a description logic language. These choice items (Fig. 8.5) are parts of the QTI model (Fig. 8.5). We transformed the model into its OWL equivalent, which conforms to the OWL metamodel (Fig. 8.14).

At the M2 level, the "SimpleChoice" metaclass corresponds to the "OWL meta-class" in the OWL metamodel [22]. In this example, at the M1 level there are three instances of this metaclass (three choices), i.e. we have three possible answers represented in the model. The QTI model of this example shown in Fig. 8.5, and the corresponding OWL model is presented in Fig. 8.15.

There are at least two ways to apply our DLs reasoning machine in this example (Fig. 8.5), i.e., to choice items:

1. Instance checking (Abox query)
2. Checking the satisfiability of the student's answer

Instance checking is applicable in cases when one or more OWL classes have a few instances. As a very concrete and specific example, suppose that the class STUDENT has the following instances (individuals): John, Mary, and Philip. Mahesh is also a person, not a student. A multiple-choice question can ask "Pick a student from the list" and offer these four names. Intuitively, the student's answer is an instance of the class STUDENT and can be checked using an instance checking reasoning

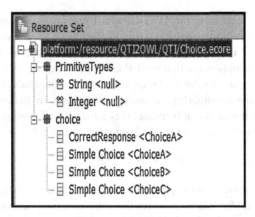

Fig. 8.15 A part of the OWL model transformed form the QTI model (Fig. 8.5)

technique. This is the simplest case, and some cases can include more complex Abox formulas. In this case, the assessment system can ask the student:

$$\text{Student}(\text{Mary}) \sqcup \text{Student}(\text{John}) \sqcup \text{Student}(\text{Philip}) \qquad (8.1)$$

In this multiple-choice question, the student must choose one name from the list of four. This is a good example of the case when two different students may submit syntactically different but semantically equivalent answers. For example, student A may answer "MARY," but student B may answer "JOHN." Both answers are true, but are syntactically different.

Application of the satisfiability technique is presented here in more details, returning to the more general example from the QTI standard (Fig. 8.5). This reasoning technique is explained through transformations from the OWL model to the tableau model (Fig. 8.16). This example also shows the main advantage of our MDA-based reasoner over those that are more widely known in the DLs world [12].

In this example, the questions are saved in the knowledge base (i.e., in the OWL model) as instances of the "SimpleChoice" class (Fig. 8.5). If student chooses one among a few answers, the reasoner can check if this answer is satisfiable w.r.t the knowledge base (the OWL model). Assume that the correct answer in our case is "Choice A." The QTI standard proposes the possibility of saving answers as instances of the "ReponseDeclaration" class (Figs. 8.5 and 8.15), but in some cases answers may not be saved as instances of this class, because the reasoner can check the satisfiability of the answer with respect to the axioms (Tbox/Rbox) in the knowledge base.

Table 8.1 DLs expressions corresponding to the OWL model shown in Fig.8.7

DLs expressions	Formula number
(Choice B ⊓ Choice C) ⊑ Choice A	(1)
Choice A ⊔ (¬ Choice B ⊔¬ Choice C)	(2)

Table 8.1 represents how the OWL model from Fig. 8.15 can be described in Tbox axioms (1) (only the question, without the answers). It means that the OWL model is satisfiable if and only if (iff) formula (1) is satisfiable. Formula (1) is an example of a subsumption relation (called concept inclusion) in Tbox.

The satisfiability of this concept inclusion (without the student's answer) can be transformed into the satisfiability of concept expression. In this case, it is the union of three concepts. It means that formula (1) is satisfiable iff formula (2) is satisfiable. The consequence of formulas (1) and (2) equality is a tautology:

$$(P => Q) \Leftrightarrow (\neg P \vee Q)^8$$

Our reasoner tries to satisfy the definition of the concept satisfiability, i.e., it tries to construct a model for this formula (in the sense of model definition in description logic formalisms), i.e., for the given OWL model plus the student's answer as OWL model, too.

Using the same simple choice item (Fig. 8.5), the first example is an unsatisfiable case, but the second one is a satisfiable student's answer. As a solution, the reasoner generates the corresponding tableau models conformant to the tableau metamodel [15] for both cases. The reasoning process is done during the model transformations, and it is the main differences between our reasoner and the existing ones, like FACT [12]. The advantage of this methodology is that the generated tableau model can be analyzed later using Ecore classes or JMI interfaces, as we mentioned in Sect. 7.1. It means that the tableau model saves implicit knowledge of the reasoning process. Using the tableau model we may find out useful information about the student's semantic mistakes, such as what is logically wrong in the student's answers and, more generally, what are the flaws in their process of learning. We can also use the reasoner to test how some pedagogical strategies can help students to progress in their learning effectively.

There are some disadvantages of using, for example, the FACT reasoner [12], in this situation. First, from the pragmatic perspective it should be noted that FACT cannot be used as a plug-in. FACT can be called from our framework only using the 8080 port. It is very difficult to adapt that reasoner in case of extension of the functionality of the assessment system. Second, FACT answers only YES/NO to questions when reasoning about satisfiability/unsatisfiability, respectively. Contrary to FACT, our reasoner can find out where the student's mistake is, and even why the student has made the mistake in this question, i.e., it can analyze the student's answer step-by-step. Our reasoner will include such an analysis using a special graphical user interface, which allows the teacher to analyze the progress of the student's study. In contrast, FACT answers only YES/NO. A recent version of FACT can be integrated with the eProtégé ontology tool (http://protege.stanford.edu/), but it is still not flexible in terms of solving problems of the kind we discussed here.

---

[8] In this example, the correspondence between the OWL models and DLs formulas means that the reasoner can be used to test the satisfiability of the questions w.r.t the OWL models too. However, this issue is beyond the scope of this paper.

8.6.2.1 Example of an Unsatisfiable Student's Answer

Suppose that a student has submitted "**ChoiceA**" as the answer to the question presented in Fig. 8.5. The reasoner takes this answer as an OWL class (model), calculates (un)satisfiability of the class with respect to the OWL model (Fig. 8.15), and generates the tableau model shown in Fig. 8.16. It is important to say that, before starting the reasoning process, the models are saved in the negation normal form. To explain the reasoning mechanisms applied to OWL models, we used the DLs notation.

Checking subsumption can be reduced to the satisfiability of concepts [12]. In this case, it means: "*Does the question subsume the answer*"? as written in formula (8.2).

$$ChoiceA \sqsubseteq ChoiceA \sqcup (\neg ChoiceB \sqcup \neg ChoiceC) \tag{8.2}$$

The question in formula (8.2) subsumes the answer (Choice) iff formula (8.3) is not satisfiable.

$$(ChoiceA \sqcap \neg ChoiceA) \sqcap (ChoiceB \sqcap ChoiceC) \tag{8.3}$$

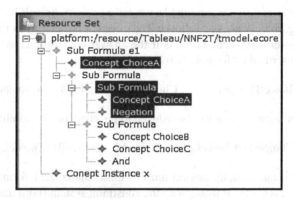

Fig. 8.16 Tableau model of the unsatisfiable student's answer

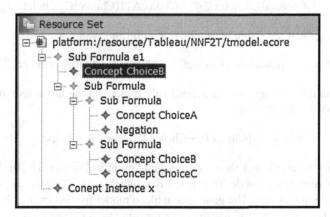

Fig. 8.17 Tableau model of the satisfiable student's answer

A system of constraints is the starting point in the reasoning process. This system can be presented as a finite set of classes (models) as follows:

$$L(x) = \{\text{ChoiceA} \sqcap \neg\text{ChoiceA} \sqcap (\text{ChoiceB} \sqcap \text{ChoiceC})\} \qquad (8.4)$$

The individual "x" (see Fig. 8.16) is an instance of all subconcepts in this set. Using the reasoning rules (in this case, it is the intersection rule of the ALC logic [12]), this constraint system, described by formula (8.4), can be extended to new ones:

$$L(x) = \{\text{ChoiceA}, \neg\text{ChoiceA}\} \sqcup L(x) \qquad (8.5)$$

This constraint system leads to a contradiction and formula (8.3) is not satisfiable, which implies that the question subsumes the answer and the student has given a true answer. Unsatisfiable points of the starting model are shaded in Fig. 8.16.

8.6.2.2 Example of a Satisfiable Student's Answer

Suppose that the student has submitted a wrong answer ("**ChoiceB**" or "**ChoiceC**"). The reasoning process goes as follows: The question (similar as in the case of the satisfiable answer discussed above) is if the answer is subsumed by the question. This can be described by formula (8.6).

$$(\text{ChoiceB} \sqcup \text{ChoiceC}) \sqsubseteq \text{ChoiceA} \sqcup (\neg\text{ChoiceB} \sqcup \neg\text{ChoiceC}) \qquad (8.6)$$

The subsumption relation can be reduced to the concept satisfiability as follows:

$$(\text{ChoiceB} \sqcup \text{ChoiceC}) \sqcap \neg\text{ChoiceA} \sqcap (\text{ChoiceB} \sqcap \text{ChoiceC}) \qquad (8.7)$$

To fulfill this question, the answer must be unsatisfiable w.r.t. formula (8.7). The reasoning process starts, as usual, with the constraint system (Formula 8.8):

$$L(x) = \{(\text{ChoiceB} \sqcup \text{ChoiceC}) \sqcap \neg\text{ChoiceA} \sqcap (\text{ChoiceB} \sqcap \text{ChoiceC})\} \qquad (8.8)$$

Applying the intersection reasoning rule to formula (8.8), we obtain:

$$L(x) = \{(\text{ChoiceB} \sqcup \text{ChoiceC}), \neg\text{ChoiceA}, \text{ChoiceB}, \text{ChoiceC}\} \qquad (8.9)$$

Now the reasoner applies the second rule (union) to the last constraint system (Formula (8.9)), resulting in:

$$L(x,y) = \{\text{ChoiceB}, \neg\text{ChoiceA}, \text{ChoiceB}, \text{ChoiceC}\} \qquad (8.10)$$

It is easy to check that there is no contradiction in Formula (8.10). It implies that the starting OWL model (Fig. 8.15) is satisfiable, i.e., that the question does not subsume the answer. The generated tableau model for this answer is shown in Fig. 8.17. The individual "x" has the same meaning as in the previous example.

8.7 Related Work

There were efforts to develop a specific methodology in order to improve reusability of assessment systems [8]. They developed an extensible educational model of assessment to provide a broader basis for interoperability specifications for the assessment process from construction to evaluation. The model was cast in the Unified Modeling Language (UML). It allows a tight embedding of assessments in educational practice and caters for new types of observation and interpretation giving priority to the completeness, interoperability, flexibility, reproducibility, reusability, and formalization. The model has been validated in a number of validation studies where the team of experts and UML modelers analyzed assessments and tried to express the identified assessments and concepts in the model. This educational model has been constructed to match the new approach to assessment and to be used to describe new assessment types.

This model, however, cannot provide interoperability of assessment systems at all. It can be used to create Java classes and method bodies, for example, using Java UML profile [33], and then to transform this UML model into Java code and complete the Java program using a Java IDE such as Eclipse J2EE IDE [9]. However, it cannot be used to create a heterogeneous assessment system that interoperates at the level of standard component interfaces.

On the other hand, there is a lot of virtual learning environments [23,6], commercial assessment systems [28,25], as well as research assessment tools [16] with QTI import and/or export facilities. All of them support exchange of items that are stored in item banks. A test developer who wants to use these items has to make sure that they match, based on learning objectives, their wording and format. By using a specification such as QTI to code the items, it is possible to exchange these items between different platforms and present them to the students in various formats. The structure of the items must be comprehensive with regard to the domain to make them useful for domain specialists. Unfortunately, in most of cases that is just a good theory.

Full implementation of the QTI specification has proven to be difficult. In a review of software applications that claim to support QTI, Gorissen has found that in almost all cases the support was restricted to the item layer, leaving the Assessment and Section layer aside [11].

By applying the MDA standard to a QTI-based assessment system development results in creating a flexible, robust, and interoperable assessment system.

First, it is possible to provide interoperability in both homogeneous and heterogeneous QTI assessment systems. According to [24] the reasons are as follows:

- The interoperability in heterogeneous environments could be achieved via shared metadata of subsystems that create the assessment system.
- The overall strategy for sharing and understanding metadata automates development, publishing, management, and interpretation of models.

Second, the use of metamodels and ontologies in an assessment system development influences the system behavior and the decision making. As shown in this paper, it is possible to enhance the storage and exchange of the assessment items, as well as entire tests by using the reflections of programming language implementations, repository and middleware services, and most importantly, generalized metadata management.

8.8 Conclusions and Future Work

The main idea proposed in this paper is the use of DL reasoning techniques in intelligent analysis of the students' solutions. Analysis of the semantics of the student's answer is the key for providing the response processing of open-ended questions in the IMS QTI standard.

The core problem of assessment software development is to reconcile increased productivity with flexibility and standardization. Until the introduction of MDA, existing languages met one or two of these requirements, but never all three. With the advent of MDA, it becomes realistic to expect high productivity within a standard environment, while retaining full flexibility. MDA strikes a compromise between power, flexibility, and standardization. It allows development to move smoothly between levels of abstraction, with much of the work being automated. Application quality is likely to improve too, as less code is written by hand, and the use of patterns help to incorporate best practices. By making a clear difference between conceptual and concrete modeling, developers can successfully select mechanisms to automate transfer and sharing of information and knowledge. Assessment systems resulting from applying MDA development standards and practices are knowledge based. The "knowledge" is supported by an advanced and highly evolved concept of ubiquitous metadata, in which the ability to act upon, as well as revise, knowledge at run time is provided through adaptive object models.

Our future work will be focused on integration of the IMS QTI standard and other logic-based reasoning techniques. The ultimate idea is to develop a UML Profile for E-Learning and a UML Profile for Theorem Provers.

References

1. ATL (2006) *Atlas Tansformation Language - User Manual*, verzion 0.7, ATLAS group, Nant. [Online]. Available: http://www.eclipse.org/gmt/atl/doc/ATL_User_Manual[v0.7].pdf
2. Baader, F., Calvanese, D., McGuinness, D., Nardi, D., and Patel-Schneider, P. (2003) *The Description Logic Handbook-Theory, Implementation and Application*, Cambridge University Press, Cambridge.
3. Beshears, F.M. (2004) *Open Standards and Open Source Development Strategies for e-Learning.*Presentation for IS224 Strategic Computing and Communications Technology 10/2/2003. Retrieved October 11, 2004 from http://istsocrates.berkeley.edu/$\sim$fmb/events/sakai-2004-01-12/IS224-2003-10-02.ppt. Educational Technology Services, University of California, Berkeley, CA.
4. Bezivin, J. (2004) In Search of Basic Principles for Model Driven Architecture, *The European Journal for The Informatics Professional*, 5(2), 21–24.

5. Bezivin, J., Jouault, F., and Paliès, J. (2005) Towards Model Transformation Design Patterns. In: *Proceedings of the First European Workshop on Model Transformation (EWMT 2005)*, Rennes, France.
6. Blackboard (2007) Blackboard. [Online]. Available: http://www.blackboard.com
7. Dirckze, R. (spec. leader) (2002) *Java Metadata Interface (JMI) Specification Version 1.0.* [Online]. Available: http://jcp.org/aboutJava/communityprocess/final/jsr040/index.html
8. Desirée J B., van Bruggen, J., Hermans, H., Latour, I., Burgers, J., Giesbers B., and Koper, R. (2006) *Modeling Assessment for Re-use of Traditional and New Types of Assessment* [Online]. Available: http://dspace.ou.nl/bitstream/1820/355/4/modelling-assessment.pdf
9. EMF (2007) *Discover the Eclipse Modeling Framework (EMF) and Its Dynamic Capabilities.* [Online]. Available: http://www.devx.com/Java/Article/29093
10. Ferrario, M. and Smyth, B. (2001) Collaborative Knowledge Management and Maintenance. In: *Proceedings of German Workshop of Case Based Reasoning*, pp. 14–15, Germany.
11. Gorissen, P. (2003). *Quickscan QTI.* Retrieved November 15, 2005 from http://www.digiuni.nl/digiuni//download/35303.DEL.306.pdf. De Digitale Universiteit, Utrecht.
12. Horrocks, I. (1997). *Optimizing Tableaux Decision Procedures for Description Logics*, PhD Thesis, University of Manchester.
13. IMS Global Learning Consortium, Inc. (IMS) (2007) Official Site. [Online]. http://www.imsglobal.org
14. IMS QTI (2006) *IMS Question & Test Interoperability.* Version 2.1. Public Draft Specification. IMS Global Learning Consortium, Inc. Retrieved May 2, 2006 from http://www.imsglobal.org/question/index.cfm
15. Krdzavac, N. and Devedžić, V. (2006) A Tableau Metamodel for Description Logics. In: *Proceedings of 13th Workshop on Automated Reasoning (ARW 2006)*, pp. 7–9, Bristol, UK.
16. Lalos, P., Retalis, S., and Psaromiligkos, Y. (2005) Creating Personalised Quizzes Both to the Learner and to the Access Device Characteristics: The Case of CosyQTI. In: Third International Workshop on Authoring of Adaptive and Adaptable Educational Hypermedia (A3EH), Amsterdam.
17. Lay, S., Pierre, G., IMS Global Learning Consortium (2006b) *IMS Question and Test Interoperability Implementation Guide, Version 2.1 Public draft.* [Online]. http://www.imsglobal.org/question/qti_v2p1pd/imsqti_implv2p1pd.html
18. Lay, S., Pierre, G., IMS Global Learning Consortium (2006c) *IMS Question and Test Interoperability Overview, Version 2.1 Public draft.* [Online]. http://www.imsglobal.org/question/qti_v2p1pd/imsqti_oviewv2p1pd.html
19. Miller, P. (2004) *Interoperability. What Is It and Why Should I Want It? Ariadne*, 24. Retrieved March 10, 2004 from http://www.ariadne.ac.uk/issue24/interoperability
20. Miller, J. and Mukerji, J. (eds.) (2006), *MDA Guide Version 1.0.1*, OMG, 2003, Retrieved November 25, 2006, from http://www.omg.org/docs/omg/03-06-01.pdf
21. MOF (2002) *Meta Object Facility (MOF) Specification, v1.4*, [Online]. Available: http://www.omg.org/docs/formal/02-04-03.pdf
22. ODM (2003) *Ontology Definition Metamodel*, Preliminary Revised Submission to OMG RFP ad/2003-03-40 1, 2004. [Online]. Available: http://codip.grci.com/odm/draft
23. Oracle iLearning (2007) *Oracle iLearning.* [Online]. Available: http://www.oracle.com/ilearning
24. Poole, J. D. (2001) Model-Driven Architecture: Vision, Standards and Emerging Technologies. In: *Workshop on Metamodeling and Adaptive Object Models ECOOP*
25. QMP (2007) *Question Mark Perception.* [Online]. Available: http://www.questionmark.com
26. QVT (2002) *Request for Proposal: MOF 2.0 Query/Views/Transformations RFP*, OMG Document: ad/2002-04-10 2002. [Online]. Available: http://www.omg.org/docs/ad/02-04-10.pdf
27. Radenković, S., Krdžavac, N., and Devedžić V. (2007) A QTI Metamodel. In: *Proceedings of International Multiconference on Computer Science and Information Technology*, ISSN 1896-7094, pp. 1123–1132.
28. RIVA Technologies, Inc. (2007) e-Test 3. [Online]. Available: http://www.riva.com

29. Sclater, N. and Low, B. (2002) *IMS Question and Test Interoperability: An Idiot's Guide*, CETIS Assessment Special Interest Group Version 0.5, March 2002. [Online]. http://www.assessment.cetis.ac.uk
30. Simic, G. (2004) The Multi-Courses Tutoring System Design, *ComSIS*, 1(1), pp. 141–155. [Online]. Available: http://www.comsis.org/ComSIS/Volume01/Papers/GoranSimic.htm.
31. Sirin, E. and Parsia, B. (2004) An OWL DL Reasoner. In: *Proceedings on International Workshop on Description Logics (DL2004)*, British Columbia, Canada.
32. UML (2007) *UML 2.0 Infrastructure Overview*. [Online]. Available: http://www.omg.org/issues/UMLSpec.pdf
33. UML_Profile (2007) Catalog of UML Profile. [Online]. Available: http://www.omg.org/technology/documents/profile_catalog.htm
34. XMI (2002) *OMG XMI Specification, ver. 1.2*, OMG Document Formal/02-01-01, 2002. [Online]. Available: http://www.omg.org/cgi-bin/doc?formal/2002-01-01.pdf

Author Index